Reader's Digest

Treasury of Wit & Wisdom

Wit, by itself, is of little account.
It becomes of moment only when
grounded on wisdom.

— MARK TWAIN

Reader's
Digest

Treasury of
Wit
& Wisdom

4,000 of the funniest, cleverest, most insightful *things ever said*

Compiled by Jeff Bredenberg

The Reader's Digest Association, Inc.
Pleasantville, NY • Montreal

Project Staff

Quote Editor Jeff Bredenberg
Editor Don Earnest
Designers Michele Laseau
& Elizabeth Tunnicliffe
Copy Editor Jeanette Gingold
Indexer Denise Getz
Illustration © Zach Trenholm

Reader's Digest Books

Editor in Chief
Neil Wertheimer

Managing Editor
Suzanne G. Beason

Creative Director
Michele Laseau

Production Technology Director
Douglas A. Croll

Manufacturing Manager
John L. Cassidy

President, North American Books & Home Entertainment
Tom Gardner

Reader's Digest Association, Inc.

President and Chief Executive Officer
Mary G. Berner

Library of Congress Cataloging-in-Publication Data
Treasury of wit & wisdom : 4,000 of the funniest, cleverest, most insightful things ever said. / The Reader's Digest Association, Inc. ; [editor, Jeff Bredenberg].
    p. cm.
  Includes index.
  ISBN 0-7621-0733-2 (hardcover)
  1. Quotations, English. I. Title: Treasury of wit and wisdom. II. Reader's Digest Association.
PN6081T74 2006
082—dc22
        2006001070

Address any comments about *Reader's Digest Treasury of Wit and Wisdom* to:
The Reader's Digest Association (Canada) Ltd.
Book Editor
1100 René-Lévesque Blvd. West
Montreal, QC H3B 5H5

To order copies of *Reader's Digest Treasury of Wit and Wisdom*, call 1-800-465-0780.

Visit our website at **rd.ca**

Printed in the United States of America
1 3 5 7 9 10 8 6 4 2

Note to Readers
The editors of Reader's Digest Books and the contributors working for Reader's Digest have taken reasonable measures to confirm the authenticity, accuracy, and correct attribution of the quotations in this book. But quotations that were first spoken are only as reliable as the listener who reports them. And it is not uncommon for even the most original writers and speakers to paraphrase—or even repeat exactly—ideas or phrases first created by others. When the same or a similar quotation is attributed to more than one source, we have selected the earliest known citation. Some unusual and nonstandard spellings have been modernized.

Words for the Heart

When you encounter a piece of art—be it a painting, a novel, a song, or just a piece of pottery—there are several ways to enjoy it. We're no experts on this subject, but four main approaches come to mind:

First is to consider the art as a reflection of the artist. The mere fact that a painting is by Pablo Picasso or a symphony is by Ludwig van Beethoven, for example, colors many people's thinking about it. What period of the artist's life did the piece come from? What effect did his state of mind, his health, or his relationships have on it? How does it fit into his fuller body of work? Particularly for fans of a particular artist, it is often hard to separate the work from the person.

Second is to consider the art as a reflection of the times in which it was created. How can one separate a Charles Dickens novel from the harsh world of nineteenth-century Britain? The works of F. Scott Fitzgerald from the Roaring Twenties? The music of Frank Sinatra or Count Basie from the giddy, swinging years of the '40s and '50s? This explains why most art museums are organized like history museums.

Third is the academic approach—to take the piece apart and study its technical mastery, its intellectual riches. There's no better example than the works of Johann Sebastian Bach. His genius was to use mathematical patterns and forms to create music. For centuries, music students have studied how he constructed his fugues and cantatas. The same could be said of Shakespeare—that there is more riches to be had dissecting his sentences than sitting back and absorbing the full play. Even for casual observers, the first reaction to an amazing piece of art is often "How did he do that?"

Last there is the fourth way: just you and your emotions. Does the art stir you, make you smile, make you sad? Does it stop time for you? Does it speak to your life, your fears, pleasures, or challenges? In this approach, the artist fades away, and so does all the context, history, and technique in which the piece was made. All that is left is the art itself, and your own immediate responses to it.

There is validity to all four approaches to enjoying art, but for those of us who aren't students or professors, the last way is the most important. Sure, the story behind the art and the artist is intriguing and fun to learn. But those are pleasures of the mind. Great art touches your heart. It speaks uniquely to you. It influences you, makes you better.

We would be hard-pressed to call the more than 4,000 quotations in this book "art." In fact, many are quite the opposite—in the pages ahead you'll find punch lines from comedy routines, wickedly amusing insults, humorous responses to absurd questions, silly tombstone inscriptions, and plenty of off-the-cuff remarks from people one would hardly call artists. But each quote shares one thing with great art—a kernel of truth or insight that instantly speaks to both the mind and the heart.

As it turns out, it's easy to apply any of the above four approaches to art to a great quotation. You could focus on the person who said it, or the time and context in which it was said, or on the elegance and brevity of the language. We say, don't. Our goal in compiling the quotations in *The Reader's Digest Treasury of Wit and Wisdom* wasn't to create a history book, or to honor smart people, or to create an ode to the English language. Our goal, clear and simple, was to touch your heart.

Most books of quotations are pretty intellectual. They dwell extensively on the writers and history, and they provide many quotes from centuries-old philosophers that are lengthy, arduous, and filled with "thees," "thous," and "henceforths." These books often avoid citing "non-intellectuals" and instead focus on "great thinkers." There's no better example than the grandfather of all quotation books, *Bartlett's Familiar Quotations*. Filled with kings, philosophers, poets, and playwrights, it is organized chronologically by date of the person's birth; in the 2002 edition, you don't get a quote from someone born in the 20th century until page 757!

This book is different. Our quest was for quotations that cut through the fogginess of life today and open our eyes wide, simply and entertainingly. Certainly there are plenty of remarks by Benjamin Franklin, Albert Einstein, President Kennedy, and modern luminaries known for their keen insight and eloquence—people you would find in any scholarly collection of great quotations. But you'll also find Hollywood starlets, great comedians, a few criminals, and many beloved celebrities like Groucho Marx and Fred Astaire.

We focus on what was spoken, rather than who spoke it. We searched far and wide, through every conceivable media form, to find simple quotations that spoke with wit and cleverness to the issues of our times. We then gathered them into logical groupings. The result is in your hands. You will discover that as you read the quotations, they tend to gain momentum. Each quotation magnifies the one that came before, and makes you want to read the next all the more. You'll find this book highly addictive for that very reason.

There's another reason it's addictive. Even when dealing with hard subjects like war and death, the quotations on the pages ahead mostly radiate optimism and hope. If humor books are supposed to make you laugh, then we hope *The Reader's Digest Treasury of Wit and Wisdom* will make you smile, over and over again. This is in good part reflective of who we are at Reader's Digest. For more than 80 years, we've been a compelling voice for positive values and goodness throughout the world. Not coincidentally, the Quotable

Quotes page in each month's edition of *Reader's Digest* magazine speaks with similar humor and optimism.

This is a conscious choice. It is easy to find quotations that are filled with despair and criticism and anger. And we don't deny the world is filled with things to despair about, to be critical of, or to be angry about. But to make the world a better place, isn't it wiser to focus on our potential, to motivate rather than denigrate? Cynics often mistake optimism for naiveté, hopeful thinking for simplistic thinking. We say cynical thinking, like insults, rarely contributes to a better world.

A wise man once said, let your heart be your guide. Our hope is that the pages ahead will speak to your heart as much as to your mind. Yes, you might discover some interesting people and learn some interesting things as you read on. In fact, we decided to provide special presentations on eighteen people who speak particularly eloquently to these modern times. But if we did our job right, your sense of humor and rightness will be as engaged by this book as your brain will be. That would make us very pleased—and the world a better place.

Neil Wertheimer

EDITOR IN CHIEF
READER'S DIGEST BOOKS

$\mathcal{T}$able of Contents

The Path Through **Life**

Babies don't speak. Neither do the dearly departed. But many of those laboring to make sense of life in between those two mileposts have a lot of wisdom—and a little foolishness, too— to share about the path through life.

Childhood

A baby is God's opinion that the world should go on. — *Carl Sandburg*

People who say they sleep like a baby usually don't have one. — *Leo J. Burke*

When I was born I was so surprised I didn't talk for a year and a half. — *Gracie Allen*

A two-year-old is kind of like having a blender, but you don't have a top for it. — *Jerry Seinfeld*

The young do not know enough to be prudent, and therefore they attempt the impossible—and achieve it, generation after generation. — *Pearl S. Buck*

The hardest job kids face today is learning good manners without seeing any. — *Fred Astaire*

Nothing separates the generations more than music. By the time a child is eight or nine, he has developed a passion for his own music that is even stronger than his passions for procrastination and weird clothes. — *Bill Cosby*

We think boys are rude, unsensitive animals but it is not so in all cases. Each boy has one or two sensitive spots, and if you can find out where they are located you have only to touch them and you can scorch him as with fire. — *Mark Twain*

The trouble with children is that they're not returnable. — *Quentin Crisp*

A child of five would understand this. Send someone to fetch a child of five. — *Groucho Marx*

Every time a child says "I don't believe in fairies" there is a little fairy somewhere that falls down dead. — *James M. Barrie*

There are three terrible ages of childhood— 1 to 10, 10 to 20, and 20 to 30. — *Cleveland Amory*

I have the heart of a child. I keep it in a jar on my shelf. — *Robert Bloch*

Youth is that period when a young boy knows everything but how to make a living. — *Carey Williams*

If you want to see what children can do, you must stop giving them things. — *Norman Douglas*

Youth would be an ideal state if it came a little later in life. — *Herbert Henry Asquith*

The deepest definition of youth is life as yet untouched by tragedy. — *Alfred North Whitehead*

The surest way to corrupt a youth is to instruct him to hold in higher esteem those who think alike than those who think differently. — *Friedrich Nietzsche*

Children need love, especially when they do not deserve it. — *Harold S. Hulbert*

Children are not things to be molded, but are people to be unfolded. — *Jess Lair*

We cannot always build the future for our youth, but we can build our youth for the future. — *Franklin D. Roosevelt*

Every child is an artist. The problem is how to remain an artist once he grows up. — *Pablo Picasso*

Any system named Dewey was all right with us. We looked forward to hearing about the Huey and Louie decimal systems too. — *Chris Van Allsburg*

Many ideas grow better when transplanted into another mind than in the one where they sprung up. — *Oliver Wendell Holmes*

Kids are great. That's one of the best things about our business, all the kids you get to meet. It's a shame they have to grow up to be regular people and come to the games and call you names. — *Charles Barkley*

It's important for survival that children have their own experiences, the kind they learn from. The kind their parents arrange for them are not as useful. Good parents are the hardest to get rid of. — *Garrison Keillor*

Your children need your presence more than your presents. — *Jesse Jackson*

One of the most obvious facts about grownups to a child is that they have forgotten what it is like to be a child. — *Randall Jarrell*

You know that children are growing up when they start asking questions that have answers. — *John J. Plomp*

I've never understood why people consider youth a time of freedom and joy. It's probably because they have forgotten their own. — *Margaret Atwood*

 Level with your child by being honest. Nobody spots a phony quicker than a child.

— MARY MACCRACKEN

In case you're worried about what's going to become of the younger generation, it's going to grow up and start worrying about the younger generation. — *Roger Allen*

A happy childhood has spoiled many a promising life. — *Robertson Davies*

Home computers are being called upon to perform many new functions, including the consumption of homework formerly eaten by the dog. — *Doug Larson*

Beware of him who hates the laugh of a child. — *Henry Ward Beecher*

If you want children to keep their feet on the ground, put some responsibility on their shoulders. — *Abigail Van Buren*

You should never do anything wicked and lay it on your brother, when it is just as convenient to lay it on some other boy. — *Mark Twain*

Another possible source of guidance for teenagers is television, but television's message has always been that the need for truth, wisdom and world peace pales by comparison with the need for a toothpaste that offers whiter teeth and fresher breath.

— DAVE BARRY

Never help a child with a task at which he feels he can succeed.   *— Maria Montessori*

The young are generally full of revolt, and are often pretty revolting about it.
— Mignon McLaughlin

It goes without saying that you should never have more children than you have car windows.   *— Erma Bombeck*

I'm gonna put a curse on you and all your kids will be born completely naked.
— Jimi Hendrix

A torn jacket is soon mended; but hard words bruise the heart of a child.
— Henry Wadsworth Longfellow

To nourish children and raise them against odds is in any time, any place, more valuable than to fix bolts in cars or design nuclear weapons.   *— Marilyn French*

Nobody understands anyone 18, including those who are 18.   *—Jim Bishop*

Lucky are the children who know there is a jolly fat man in a red suit who pilots a flying sleigh. We should envy them. And we should envy the people who are so certain Martians will land in their backyard that they keep a loaded Polaroid camera by the back door.
— Chris Van Allsburg

What music is more enchanting than the voices of young people, when you can't hear what they say?   *— Logan Pearsall Smith*

You don't have to suffer to be a poet; adolescence is enough suffering for anyone.
—John Ciardi

Adolescence is just one big walking pimple.
— Carol Burnett

Education

Education is not the filling of a pail, but the lighting of a fire. — *William Butler Yeats*

If you think education is expensive— try ignorance. — *Derek Bok*

Most of what you learn in the first four years of elementary school will be valid all your life. Most of what you learn in four years of college won't be. This is another reason some people contend grade school teachers should be paid more than university professors. — *L. M. Boyd*

What we become depends on what we read after all of the professors have finished with us. The greatest university of all is a collection of books. — *Thomas Carlyle*

Our progress as a nation can be no swifter than our progress in education. Our requirements for world leadership, our hopes for economic growth, and the demands of citizenship itself in an era such as this all require the maximum development of every young American's capacity. The human mind is our fundamental resource. — *John F. Kennedy*

The fool wonders, the wise man asks. — *Benjamin Disraeli*

Education is like a double-edged sword. It may be turned to dangerous uses if it is not properly handled. — *Wu Ting-Fang*

Some people drink from the fountain of knowledge, others just gargle. — *Robert Anthony*

It is a miracle that curiosity survives formal education. — *Albert Einstein*

The cure for boredom is curiosity. There is no cure for curiosity. — *Dorothy Parker*

No other job in the world could possibly dispossess one so completely as this job of teaching. You could stand all day in a laundry, for instance, still in possession of your mind. But this teaching utterly obliterates you. It cuts right into your being: essentially, it takes over your spirit. It drags it out from where it would hide. — *Sylvia Ashton-Warner*

Human history becomes more and more a race between education and catastrophe. — *H. G. Wells*

Nothing in education is so astonishing as the amount of ignorance it accumulates in the form of inert facts. — *Henry B. Adams*

It is possible to store the mind with a million facts and still be entirely uneducated. — *Alec Bourne*

Highly educated bores are by far the worst; they know so much, in such fiendish detail, to be boring about.   — *Louis Kronenberger*

Good teaching is one-fourth preparation and three-fourths theater.   — *Gail Godwin*

Let the teachers teach English and I will teach baseball. There is a lot of people in the United States who say "isn't," and they ain't eating.   — *Dizzy Dean*

The immature mind hops from one thing to another; the mature mind seeks to follow through.   — *Harry A. Overstreet*

Men are born ignorant, not stupid. They are made stupid by education.   — *Bertrand Russell*

Education is when you read the fine print. Experience is what you get if you don't.   — *Pete Seeger*

Education is the period during which you are being instructed by somebody you do not know, about something you do not want to know.   — *G. K. Chesterton*

Those people who think they know everything are a great annoyance to those of us who do.   — *Isaac Asimov*

The trouble with learning from experience is that you never graduate.   — *Doug Larson*

The average Ph.D. thesis is nothing but a transference of bones from one graveyard to another.   — *J. Frank Dobie*

What sculpture is to a block of marble, education is to the soul.   — *Joseph Addison*

You can never learn less, you can only learn more.   — *R. Buckminster Fuller*

Education is what remains after one has forgotten everything he learned in school.   — *Albert Einstein*

If little else, the brain is an educational toy.   — *Tom Robbins*

A college degree is not a sign that one is a finished product but an indication a person is prepared for life.   — *Edward A. Malloy*

Growth demands a temporary surrender of security.   — *Gail Sheehy*

Growth is an erratic forward movement: two steps forward, one step back. Remember that and be very gentle with yourself.   — *Julia Cameron*

Everybody wants to be somebody; nobody wants to grow.   — *Johann von Goethe*

All growth is a leap in the dark, a spontaneous unpremeditated act without the benefit of experience.   — *Henry Miller*

Learning is not compulsory ... neither is survival.   — *W. Edwards Deming*

Education is not preparation for life; education is life itself.   — *John Dewey*

Experience is a good teacher, but she sends in terrific bills.   — *Minna Antrim*

Everywhere I go, I'm asked if I think the universities stifle writers. My opinion is that they don't stifle enough of them. There's many a best seller that could have been prevented by a good teacher.   — *Flannery O'Connor*

A sense of curiosity is nature's original school of education.   — *Smiley Blanton*

Education's purpose is to replace an empty mind with an open one.   — *Malcolm Forbes*

A teacher affects eternity; he can never tell where his influence stops.   — *Henry Adams*

The illiterate of the 21st century will not be those who cannot read and write, but those who cannot learn, unlearn, and relearn.
— *Alvin Toffler*

Just think of the tragedy of teaching children not to doubt.   — *Clarence Darrow*

The freethinking of one age is the common sense of the next.   — *Matthew Arnold*

Skepticism: the mark and even the pose of the educated mind.   — *John Dewey*

Sex education may be a good idea in the schools, but I don't believe the kids should be given homework.   — *Bill Cosby*

America believes in education: The average professor earns more money in a year than a professional athlete earns in a whole week.
— *Evan Esar*

I think sleeping was my problem in school. If school had started at four in the afternoon, I'd be a college graduate today.
— *George Foreman*

You ain't learnin' nothin' when you're talkin'.   — *Lyndon B. Johnson*

Students achieving Oneness will move on to Twoness.   — *Woody Allen*

A lot of fellows nowadays have a B.A., M.D., or Ph.D. Unfortunately, they don't have a J.O.B.

— FATS DOMINO

It is the mark of an educated mind to be able to entertain a thought without accepting it.   — *Aristotle*

The fireworks begin today. Each diploma is a lighted match. Each one of you is a fuse.
— *Ed Koch*

We now accept the fact that learning is a lifelong process of keeping abreast of change. And the most pressing task is to teach people how to learn.
— *Peter F. Drucker*

A moment's insight is sometimes worth a life's experience.   — *Oliver Wendell Holmes*

In the beginner's mind there are many possibilities. In the expert's mind there are few.
— *Shunryu Suzuki*

Learn as much by writing as by reading.
— *Lord Acton*

Education is learning what you didn't even know you didn't know.   — *Daniel J. Boorstin*

I read Shakespeare and the Bible, and
I can shoot dice. That's what I call a
liberal education. — *Tallulah Bankhead*

I was a modest, good-humored boy. It is
Oxford that has made me insufferable.
— *Max Beerbohm*

Try to learn something about everything
and everything about something.
— *Thomas H. Huxley*

I find that a great part of the information I
have was acquired by looking up something
and finding something else on the way.
— *Franklin P. Adams*

It is important that students bring a certain
ragamuffin, barefoot, irreverence to their
studies; they are not here to worship what
is known, but to question it.
— *Jacob Chanowski*

Education is the ability to listen to almost
anything without losing your temper or
your self-confidence. — *Robert Frost*

I won't say ours was a tough school, but we
had our own coroner. We used to write essays
like: What I'm going to be if I grow up.
— *Lenny Bruce*

A university is what a college becomes
when the faculty loses interest in students.
— *John Ciardi*

College isn't the place to go for ideas.
— *Helen Keller*

Education is the movement from darkness
to light. — *Allan Bloom*

In the first place God made idiots. This was
for practice. Then he made School Boards.
— *Mark Twain*

I was asked why I did not give a rod
with which to fish, in the hands of the poor,
rather than give the fish itself as this
makes them remain poor.
So I told them:
The people whom we pick up
are not able to stand with a rod.
So today I will give them fish
and when they are able to stand,
then I shall send them to you
and you can give them the rod.
That is your job. Let me do my work today.

— MOTHER TERESA

Give a man a fish
and you feed him for a day.
Teach him how to fish
and you feed him for a lifetime.   — *Lao-tzu*

It is necessary for us to learn from others'
mistakes. You will not live long enough to
make them all yourself.

— *Hyman G. Rickover*

The wisest mind has something yet to learn.

— *George Santayana*

Education: that which reveals to the wise,
and conceals from the stupid, the vast limits
of their knowledge.   — *Mark Twain*

The highest result of education is tolerance.

— *Helen Keller*

Colleges hate geniuses, just as convents
hate saints.   — *Ralph Waldo Emerson*

It is the province of knowledge to speak and
it is the privilege of wisdom to listen.

— *Oliver Wendell Holmes*

To the uneducated, an A is just three sticks.

— *A. A. Milne*

College ain't so much where you been as
how you talk when you get back.

— *Ossie Davis*

What is important is to keep learning, to
enjoy challenge, and to tolerate ambiguity.
In the end there are no certain answers.

— *Martina Horner*

I was born not knowing and have had only a
little time to change that here and there.

— *Richard P. Feynman*

Some people talk in their sleep.
Lecturers talk while other people sleep.

— *Albert Camus*

I have tried to know absolutely nothing
about a great many things, and I have
succeeded fairly well.   — *Robert Benchley*

Whatever career you may choose for yourself—doctor, lawyer, teacher—let me propose
an avocation to be pursued along with it.
Become a dedicated fighter for civil rights.
Make it a central part of your life. It will
make you a better doctor, a better lawyer, a
better teacher. It will enrich your spirit as
nothing else possibly can. It will give you
that rare sense of nobility that can only
spring from love and selflessly helping your
fellow man. Make a career of humanity.
Commit yourself to the noble struggle for
human rights. You will make a greater person
of yourself, a greater nation of your country,
and a finer world to live in.

— *Martin Luther King, Jr.*

Erma Bombeck

Endless Wit

Any writer who titles a book *The Grass Is Always Greener Over the Septic Tank* is a shoo-in for a "most quotable" award.

Erma Bombeck began her column-writing career in junior high school in Dayton, Ohio, providing her biting wit to the school newspaper. In the 1950s, she plunged into her housewife role, which she found lonely and unsatisfying. When she returned to newspaper work, she combined her penchant for humor with the frustrations of keeping house. Finding an appreciative audience among post-World War II women, her column in the *Dayton Journal-Herald* was quickly syndicated, and within a few years "At Wit's End" was appearing in 500 newspapers.

Books followed, too, volumes with such memorable titles as *I Lost Everything in the Post-Natal Depression; If Life Is a Bowl of Cherries—What Am I Doing in the Pits?;* and *When You Look Like Your Passport Photo, It's Time to Go Home.* She was a regular for 11 years on ABC's *Good Morning America* and also wrote and produced the short-lived TV sitcom *Maggie.*

She died in 1996 at age 69, following a failed kidney transplant.

*

Housework, if you do it right, will kill you.

*

Seize the moment.
Remember all those women on the Titanic who waved off the dessert cart.

*

Kids have little computer bodies with disks that store information.
They remember who had to do the dishes the last time you had spaghetti,
who lost the knob off the TV set six years ago, who got punished
for teasing the dog when he wasn't teasing the dog
and who had to wear girls' boots the last time it snowed.

*

When your mother asks, "Do you want a piece of advice?"
it's a mere formality. It doesn't matter if you answer yes or no.
You're going to get it anyway.

*

Have you any idea
how many kids it takes to turn off one light in the kitchen?
Three. It takes one to say, "What light?"
and two more to say, "I didn't turn it on."

*

My theory on housework is, if the item doesn't multiply,
smell, catch on fire or block the refrigerator door, let it be.
No one cares. Why should you?

Adulthood

All appears to change when we change.
— *Henri-Frédéric Amiel*

I'm 30 years old, but I read at the 34-year-old level.
— *Dana Carvey*

The really frightening thing about middle age is that you know you'll grow out of it.
— *Doris Day*

He not busy being born is busy dying.
— *Bob Dylan*

The reward for conformity was that everyone liked you except yourself.
— *Rita Mae Brown*

I'm just a person trapped inside a woman's body.
— *Elayne Boosler*

Being in the army is like being in the Boy Scouts, except that the Boy Scouts have adult supervision.
— *Blake Clark*

Boys will be boys, and so will a lot of middle-aged men.
— *Kin Hubbard*

Don't accept rides from strange men, and remember that all men are strange.
— *Robin Morgan*

The male is a domestic animal which, if treated with firmness, can be trained to do most things.
— *Jilly Cooper*

Men who never get carried away should be.
— *Malcolm Forbes*

Men are like a deck of cards. You'll find the occasional king, but most are jacks.
— *Laura Swenson*

A man's brain has a more difficult time shifting from thinking to feeling than a woman's brain does.
— *Barbara De Angelis*

Life's a tough proposition, and the first hundred years are the hardest.
— *Wilson Mizner*

Better be wise by the misfortunes of others than by your own.
— *Aesop*

Middle age is when your broad mind and narrow waist begin to change places.
— *E. Joseph Crossman*

After 30, a body has a mind of its own.
— *Bette Midler*

It's the friends you can call up at 4 a.m. that matter.
— *Marlene Dietrich*

Health consists of having the same diseases as one's neighbors.
— *Quentin Crisp*

Call it a clan, call it a network, call it a tribe, call it a family. Whatever you call it, whoever you are, you need one.
— *Jane Howard*

Even as the cell is the unit of the organic body, so the family is the unit of society.
— *Ruth Nanda Anshen*

Every man's life is a fairy tale written by God's fingers.
— *Hans Christian Andersen*

When you dance, your purpose is not to get to a certain place on the floor. It's to enjoy each step along the way.
— *Wayne Dyer*

You grow up the day you have the first real laugh at yourself.
— *Ethel Barrymore*

THE PATH THROUGH LIFE

The creative adult is the child who
has survived. — *Ursula K. Le Guin*

When you grow up your mother says,
"Wear rubbers or you'll catch cold." When
you become an adult you discover that you
have the right not to wear rubbers and to
see if you catch cold or not. It's something
like that. — *Diane Arbus*

If the world were a logical place, men would
ride sidesaddle. — *Rita Mae Brown*

True maturity is only reached when a man
realizes he has become a father figure to his
girlfriends' boyfriends—and he accepts it.
— *Larry McMurtry*

The willingness to accept responsibility for
one's own life is the source from which self-
respect springs. — *Joan Didion*

Women now have choices. They can be
married, not married, have a job, not have a
job, be married with children, unmarried
with children. Men have the same choice
we've always had: work or prison.
— *Tim Allen*

If you surveyed a hundred typical middle-
aged Americans, I bet you'd find that only
two of them could tell you their blood
types, but every last one of them would
know the theme song from *The Beverly
Hillbillies.* — *Dave Barry*

If you ever start feeling like you have the goofiest,
craziest, most dysfunctional family in the world, all
you have to do is go to a state fair. Because five
minutes at the fair, you'll be going, "You know,
we're all right. We are dang near royalty."

— JEFF FOXWORTHY

A good home must be made, not bought.
— *Joyce Maynard*

Middle age is that perplexing time of life
when we hear two voices calling us, one
saying, "Why not?" and the other, "Why
bother?" — *Sydney J. Harris*

Everything has been figured out, except
how to live. — *Jean-Paul Sartre*

When childhood dies, its corpses are
called adults. — *Brian Aldiss*

Middle age occurs when you are too
young to take up golf and too old to rush
up to the net. — *Franklin P. Adams*

Habits are safer than rules; you don't have to
watch them. And you don't have to keep
them either. They keep you. — *Frank Crane*

The future is like heaven—everyone exalts
it, but no one wants to go there now.
— *James A. Baldwin*

Life is what happens to you while you're
busy making other plans. — *John Lennon*

It's too bad I'm not as wonderful a person as people say I am, because the world could use a few people like that. — *Alan Alda*

Every generation imagines itself to be more intelligent than the one that went before it, and wiser than the one that comes after it. — *George Orwell*

Middle age is when you've met so many people that every new person you meet reminds you of someone else. — *Ogden Nash*

A safe but sometimes chilly way of recalling the past is to force open a crammed drawer. If you are searching for anything in particular you don't find it, but something falls out at the back that is often more interesting. — *James M. Barrie*

Philosophers are adults who persist in asking childish questions. — *Isaiah Berlin*

The youth of the present day are quite monstrous. They have absolutely no respect for dyed hair. — *Oscar Wilde*

Back in the 1960s, birthday parties were major fun. The Grateful Dead was on the hi-fi and you danced and took powerful drugs and swam naked in the lake and lay on the sand talking about what you were feeling. But I can't do that anymore for fear of embarrassing my children. — *Garrison Keillor*

The man who views the world at 50 the same as he did at 20 has wasted 30 years of his life. — *Muhammad Ali*

Maturity begins to grow when you can sense your concern for others outweighing your concern for yourself. — *John MacNaughton*

Imagination grows by exercise, and contrary to common belief, is more powerful in the mature than in the young. — *W. Somerset Maugham*

Acting is a masochistic form of exhibitionism. It is not quite the occupation of an adult. — *Laurence Olivier*

THE PATH THROUGH LIFE

ove

When you love a man, he becomes more than a body. His physical limbs expand, and his outline recedes, vanishes. He is rich and sweet and right. He is part of the world, the atmosphere, the blue sky and the blue water. — *Gwendolyn Brooks*

The only time a woman really succeeds in changing a man is when he's a baby.
— *Natalie Wood*

Most women set out to try to change a man, and when they have changed him they do not like him. — *Marlene Dietrich*

The only thing worse than a man you can't control is a man you can. — *Margo Kaufman*

Love is an irresistible desire to be irresistibly desired. — *Robert Frost*

We are most alive when we're in love.
— *John Updike*

Love is an act of endless forgiveness, a tender look which becomes a habit.
— *Peter Ustinov*

I love Mickey Mouse more than any woman I have ever known. — *Walt Disney*

If you aren't good at loving yourself, you will have a difficult time loving anyone, since you'll resent the time and energy you give another person that you aren't even giving to yourself. — *Barbara De Angelis*

You will find as you look back upon your life that the moments when you have truly lived are the moments when you have done things in the spirit of love.
— *Henry Drummond*

Love is staying up all night with a sick child—or a healthy adult. — *David Frost*

Love does not begin and end the way we seem to think it does. Love is a battle, love is a war; love is a growing up.
— *James Baldwin*

There is a rule in sailing where the more maneuverable ship should give way to the less maneuverable craft. I think this is some-times a good rule to follow in human relationships as well. — *Joyce Brothers*

Nobody will ever win the battle of the sexes. There's too much fraternizing with the enemy. — *Henry Kissinger*

Love him and let him love you. Do you think anything else under heaven really matters?
— *James Baldwin*

Among those whom I like or admire, I can find no common denominator, but among those whom I love, I can: All of them make me laugh. — *W. H. Auden*

Love means not ever having to say you're sorry. — *Erich Segal*

The first duty of love is to listen.
— *Paul Tillich*

The moment we choose to love we begin to move towards freedom. — *Bell Hooks*

Sex is a momentary itch; love never lets you go. — *Kingsley Amis*

If grass can grow through cement, love can find you at every time in your life. — *Cher*

Friendship is certainly the finest balm for the pangs of disappointed love.

— *Jane Austen*

Looking back, I have this to regret, that too often when I loved, I did not say so.

— *David Grayson*

It is probably not love that makes the world go around, but rather those mutually supportive alliances through which partners recognize their dependence on each other for the achievement of shared and private goals.

— *Fred Allen*

Love doesn't just sit there, like a stone; it has to be made, like bread, remade all the time, made new.

— *Ursula K. Le Guin*

To love is to receive a glimpse of heaven.

— *Karen Sunde*

To love and be loved is to feel the sun from both sides.

— *David Viscott*

'Tis better to have loved and lost
Than never to have loved at all.

— *Alfred, Lord Tennyson*

To fall in love is to create a religion that has a fallible god.

— *Jorge Luis Borges*

Love is the triumph of imagination over intelligence.

— *H. L. Mencken*

Intimate relationships cannot substitute for a life plan. But to have any meaning or viability at all, a life plan must include intimate relationships.

— *Harriet Lerner*

Oh, life is a glorious cycle of song,
A medley of extemporanea;
And love is a thing that can never go wrong;
And I am Marie of Romania.

— *Dorothy Parker*

In love, one and one are one.

— *Jean-Paul Sartre*

A man is already halfway in love with any woman who listens to him.

— *Brendan Francis*

Every instance of heartbreak can teach us powerful lessons about creating the kind of love we really want.

— *Martha Beck*

The best proof of love is trust.

— *Joyce Brothers*

We love because it's the only true adventure.

— *Nikki Giovanni*

Don't brood. Get on with living and loving. You don't have forever.

— *Leo Buscaglia*

Love is said to be blind, but I know some fellows in love who can see twice as much in their sweethearts as I do.

— *Josh Billings*

I was born when you kissed me. I died when you left me. I lived a few weeks while you loved me.

— HUMPHREY BOGART

THE PATH THROUGH LIFE

I am certainly not an authority on love because there are no authorities on love, just those who've had luck with it and those who haven't. — *Bill Cosby*

Love is metaphysical gravity.
— *R. Buckminster Fuller*

The great question that has never been answered, and which I have not yet been able to answer, despite my 30 years of research into the feminine soul, is "What does a woman want?" — *Sigmund Freud*

Love is a perky elf dancing a merry little jig and then suddenly he turns on you with a miniature machine gun. — *Matt Groening*

Men are not the enemy, but the fellow victims. The real enemy is women's denigration of themselves. — *Betty Friedan*

The mark of a true crush . . . is that you fall in love first and grope for reasons afterward.
— *Shana Alexander*

Men and women belong to different species and communications between them is still in its infancy. — *Bill Cosby*

There is love of course. And then there's life, its enemy. — *Jean Anouilh*

A man never knows how to say good-bye; a woman never knows when to say it.
— *Helen Rowland*

When you realize you want to spend the rest of your life with somebody, you want the rest of your life to start as soon as possible.
— *Billy Crystal*

Women want mediocre men, and men are working hard to become as mediocre as possible. — *Margaret Mead*

There are three things men can do with women: love them, suffer for them, or turn them into literature.
— *Stephen Stills*

Can you imagine a world without men? No crime and lots of happy fat women.
— *Nicole Hollander*

One is very crazy when in love.
— *Sigmund Freud*

There is one thing I would break up over and that is if she caught me with another woman. I wouldn't stand for that.
— *Steve Martin*

There is no reciprocity. Men love women, women love children, children love hamsters.
— *Alice Thomas Ellis*

The formula for achieving a successful relationship is simple: you should treat all disasters as if they were trivialities but never treat a triviality as if it were a disaster.
— *Quentin Crisp*

Nature gives you the face you have at 20; it is up to you to merit the face you have at 50. — *Coco Chanel*

I don't believe man is a woman's natural enemy. Perhaps his lawyer is.
— *Shana Alexander*

The only creatures that are evolved enough to convey pure love are dogs and infants.
— *Johnny Depp*

The entire sum of existence is the magic of being needed by just one other person.
— *Vi Putnam*

We cannot really love anybody with whom we never laugh. — *Agnes Repplier*

It is a curious thought, but it is only when you see people looking ridiculous that you realize just how much you love them.
— *Agatha Christie*

Passion is the quickest to develop, and the quickest to fade. Intimacy develops more slowly, and commitment more gradually still.
— *Robert Sternberg*

Love is a fire. But whether it is going to warm your hearth or burn down your house, you can never tell. — *Joan Crawford*

Love builds bridges where there are none.
— *R. H. Delaney*

Intimacy is being seen and known as the person you truly are. — *Amy Bloom*

Men want the same thing from their underwear that they want from women: a little bit of support, and a little bit of freedom.
— *Jerry Seinfeld*

It is not love that is blind, but jealousy.
— *Lawrence Durrell*

I don't want to live. I want to love first, and live incidentally. — *Zelda Fitzgerald*

You never lose by loving. You always lose by holding back. — *Barbara De Angelis*

The heart of another is a dark forest, always, no matter how close it has been to one's own. — *Willa Cather*

***

Marriage

My wife and I were happy for 20 years. Then we met. — *Rodney Dangerfield*

'Tis more blessed to give than receive; for example, wedding presents. — *H. L. Mencken*

The best way to get husbands to do something is to suggest that perhaps they are too old to do it. — *Shirley MacLaine*

The value of marriage is not that adults produce children but that children produce adults. — *Peter De Vries*

He taught me housekeeping; when I divorce I keep the house. — *Zsa Zsa Gabor*

A happy marriage is the world's best bargain.
— *O. A. Battista*

I know you've been married to the same woman for 69 years. That is marvelous. It must be very inexpensive. — *Johnny Carson*

There is more to marriage than four bare legs under a blanket. — *Robertson Davies*

The majority of husbands remind me of an orangutan trying to play the violin.
— *Honoré de Balzac*

It's not a good idea to put your wife into a novel; not your latest wife anyway.
— *Norman Mailer*

What do I know about sex? I'm a
married man.
— *Tom Clancy*

Intimacy is what makes a marriage, not
a ceremony, not a piece of paper from
the state.
— *Kathleen Norris*

Always get married early in the morning.
That way, if it doesn't work out, you haven't
wasted a whole day.
— *Mickey Rooney*

My advice to you is get married: if you find
a good wife you'll be happy; if not, you'll
become a philosopher.
— *Socrates*

One has to be able to count if only so that
at 50 one doesn't marry a girl of 20.
— *Maxim Gorky*

I believe in the institution of marriage, and I
intend to keep trying till I get it right.
— *Richard Pryor*

I'd marry again if I found a man who had
fifteen million dollars, would sign over half to me,
and guarantee that he'd be dead within a year.

— BETTE DAVIS

Marriage is about the most expensive way
for the average man to get laundry done.
— *Burt Reynolds*

The married are those who have taken the
terrible risk of intimacy and, having taken it,
know life without intimacy to be impossible.
— *Carolyn Heilbrun*

Marriage is not a noun; it's a verb. It isn't
something you get. It's something you do.
It's the way you love your partner every day.
— *Barbara De Angelis*

A successful marriage requires falling in love
many times, always with the same person.
— *Mignon McLaughlin*

"I am" is reportedly the shortest sentence in
the English language. Could it be that "I do"
is the longest sentence?
— *George Carlin*

A great marriage is not when the
"perfect couple" comes together. It is
when an imperfect couple learns to enjoy
their differences.
— *Dave Meurer*

Nobody wants to be married to a doctor
who works weekends and makes house calls
at 2 a.m. But every patient would like to
find one.
— *Ellen Goodman*

In every marriage more than a week old,
there are grounds for divorce. The trick
is to find, and continue to find, grounds
for marriage.
— *Robert Anderson*

I used to believe that marriage would
diminish me, reduce my options. That you
had to be someone less to live with someone
else when, of course, you have to be someone more.
— *Candice Bergen*

Most wives think of their husbands as bumbling braggarts with whom they happen to be in love. — *Jackie Gleason*

For marriage to be a success, every woman and every man should have her and his own bathroom. The end. — *Catherine Zeta-Jones*

Keep your eyes wide open before marriage, half shut afterwards. — *Benjamin Franklin*

Almost no one is foolish enough to imagine that he automatically deserves great success in any field of activity; yet almost everyone believes that he automatically deserves success in marriage.
— *Sydney J. Harris*

A good marriage would be between a blind wife and a deaf husband.
— *Honoré de Balzac*

If variety is the spice of life, marriage is the big can of leftover Spam. — *Johnny Carson*

Marriage has no guarantees. If that's what you're looking for, go live with a car battery.
— *Erma Bombeck*

If men knew how women pass the time when they are alone, they'd never marry.
— *O. Henry*

It seemed to me that the desire to get married—which, I regret to say, I believe is basic and primal in women—is followed almost immediately by an equally basic and primal urge—which is to be single again.
— *Nora Ephron*

I married beneath me, all women do.
— *Nancy Astor*

My toughest fight was with my first wife.
— *Muhammad Ali*

All men make mistakes, but married men find out about them sooner. — *Red Skelton*

Half a loafer is better than no husband at all.
— *Louis Safian*

An archaeologist is the best husband a woman can have; the older she gets the more interested he is in her.
— *Agatha Christie*

Husbands are like fires—they go out when unattended. — *Zsa Zsa Gabor*

I don't think I'll get married again. I'll just find a woman I don't like and give her a house. — *Lewis Grizzard*

For a while we pondered whether to take a vacation or get a divorce. We decided that a trip to Bermuda is over in two weeks, but a divorce is something you always have. — *Woody Allen*

In Hollywood, an equitable divorce settlement means each party getting 50 percent of publicity. — *Lauren Bacall*

Don't forget Mother's Day. Or as they call it in Beverly Hills, Dad's Third Wife Day.
— *Jay Leno*

I have often wanted to drown my troubles, but I can't get my wife to go swimming.
— *Jimmy Carter*

Parenthood

We spend the first 12 months of our children's lives teaching them to walk and talk, and the next 12 years telling them to sit down and shut up. — *Phyllis Diller*

Giving birth is like taking your lower lip and forcing it over your head. — *Carol Burnett*

There are two things in life for which we are never truly prepared: twins. — *Josh Billings*

Children have never been very good at listening to their elders, but they have never failed to imitate them. — *James Baldwin*

Onion rings in the car cushions do not improve with time. — *Erma Bombeck*

Outings are so much more fun when we can savor them through the children's eyes. — *Lawana Blackwell*

I want my children to have all the things I couldn't afford. Then I want to move in with them. — *Phyllis Diller*

Ask your child what he wants for dinner only if he's buying. — *Fran Lebowitz*

Motherhood is a wonderful thing—what a pity to waste it on children. — *Judith Pugh*

Grown-ups never understand anything for themselves, and it is tiresome for children to be always and forever explaining things to them. — *Antoine de Saint-Exupéry*

A king, realizing his incompetence, can either delegate or abdicate his duties. A father can do neither. If only sons could see the paradox, they would understand the dilemma. — *Marlene Dietrich*

Nothing you do for children is ever wasted. They seem not to notice us, hovering, averting our eyes, and they seldom offer thanks, but what we do for them is never wasted. — *Garrison Keillor*

Tired mothers find that spanking takes less time than reasoning and penetrates sooner to the seat of the memory. — *Will Durant*

If evolution really works, how come mothers only have two hands? — *Milton Berle*

Never raise your hand to your kids. It leaves your groin unprotected. — *Red Buttons*

Always end the name of your child with a vowel, so that when you yell the name will carry. — *Bill Cosby*

Live so that when your children think of fairness and integrity, they think of you. — *H. Jackson Brown, Jr.*

It is very important that children learn from their fathers and mothers how to love one another—not in the school, not from the teacher, but from you. It is very important that you share with your children the joy of that smile. There will be misunderstandings; every family has its cross, its suffering. Always be the first to forgive with a smile. Be cheerful, be happy. — *Mother Teresa*

If you bungle raising your children, I don't think whatever else you do matters very much. — *Jackie Kennedy Onassis*

Douglas Adams

Universal Humor

Not many people get to blow up Earth and then enjoy a fabulous literary career. But that's how it started for Douglas Adams, the British creator of *The Hitchhiker's Guide to the Galaxy.*

When he was just 26, the BBC began broadcasting his tale about a young man who roves among the stars after his planet has been destroyed to make way for an intergalactic highway. *Hitchhiker* took on many forms over the years, including a book series, a television series, stage adaptations, a computer game, and a movie. Adams's non–*Hitchhiker* books included *Dirk Gently's Holistic Detective Agency* and *The Long Dark Tea-Time of the Soul.*

Adams showed a particular fondness for wildlife in both his fiction and nonfiction. He also relished skewering the planet's most peculiar species, *Homo sapiens,* with his unique brand of absurdist wit.

Adams himself unexpectedly departed this world in 2001, dying of a heart attack at age 49.

*

All it takes to fly is to hurl yourself at the ground ... and miss.

*

People complain that there's a lot of rubbish online, or that it's dominated by Americans, or that you can't necessarily trust what you read on the Web. Imagine trying to apply any of those criticisms to what you hear on the telephone. Of course you can't "trust" what people tell you on the Web any more than you can "trust" what people tell you on megaphones, postcards or in restaurants.

*

My absolute favorite piece of information is the fact that young sloths are so inept that they frequently grab their own arms and legs instead of tree limbs, and fall out of trees.

*

I love deadlines. I like the whooshing sound they make as they fly by.

*

There is a theory which states that if ever anybody discovers exactly what the Universe is for and why it is here, it will instantly disappear and be replaced by something even more bizarre and inexplicable. There is another theory which states that this has already happened.

*

Human beings, who are almost unique in having the ability to learn from the experience of others, are also remarkable for their apparent disinclination to do so.

*

Anything that is in the world when you're born is normal and ordinary and is just part of the way the world works. Anything that's invented between when you're 15 and 35 is new and exciting and revolutionary and you can probably get a career in it. Anything invented after you're 35 is against the natural order of things.

*

I really didn't foresee the Internet. But then, neither did the computer industry. Not that that tells us very much, of course—the computer industry didn't even foresee that the century was going to end.

If you have never been hated by your child, you have never been a parent.   — *Bette Davis*

There was a time when we expected nothing of our children but obedience, as opposed to the present, when we expect everything of them but obedience.

    — *Anatole Broyard*

A child who is allowed to be disrespectful to his parents will not have true respect for anyone.   — *Billy Graham*

When I was a kid my parents moved a lot, but I always found them.

    — *Rodney Dangerfield*

I take my children everywhere, but they always find their way back home.

    — *Robert Orben*

There is no such thing as "fun for the whole family."   — *Jerry Seinfeld*

I have found the best way to give advice to your children is to find out what they want and then advise them to do it.

    — *Harry S. Truman*

The best way to keep children at home is to make the home atmosphere pleasant— and let the air out of the tires.

    — *Dorothy Parker*

If your parents never had children, chances are you won't either.   — *Dick Cavett*

Always be nice to those younger than you, because they are the ones who will be writing about you.   — *Cyril Connolly*

Always be nice to your children because they are the ones who will choose your rest home.   — *Phyllis Diller*

No matter how many communes anybody invents, the family always creeps back.

    — *Margaret Mead*

If a woman has to choose between catching a fly ball and saving an infant's life, she will choose to save the infant's life without even considering if there is a man on base.

    — *Dave Barry*

We should never permit ourselves to do anything that we are not willing to see our children do.   — *Brigham Young*

The emotional, sexual, and psychological stereotyping of females begins when the doctor says, "It's a girl."

    — *Shirley Chisholm*

Human beings are the only creatures on earth that allow their children to come back home.   — *Bill Cosby*

A baseball manager has learned a lot about his job from having played the game, but a parent has not learned a thing from having once been a child.   — *Bill Cosby*

Because I am a mother, I am capable of being shocked: as I never was when I was not one.   — *Margaret Atwood*

Watching your daughter being collected by her date feels like handing over a million-dollar Stradivarius to a gorilla.

    — *Jim Bishop*

Setting a good example for children takes all the fun out of middle age.

    — *William Feather*

Having children makes you no more a parent than having a piano makes you a pianist.   — *Michael Levine*

THE PATH THROUGH LIFE

Aging

My parents didn't want to move to Florida, but they turned 60 and that's the law.

— *Jerry Seinfeld*

Age is a question of mind over matter. If you don't mind, it doesn't matter.

— *Satchel Paige*

All would live long, but none would be old.

— *Benjamin Franklin*

Age is a high price to pay for maturity.

— *Tom Stoppard*

Each has his past shut in him like the leaves of a book known to him by heart and his friends can only read the title.

— *Virginia Woolf*

Beautiful young people are accidents of nature, but beautiful old people are works of art.

— *Eleanor Roosevelt*

The secret of staying young is to live honestly, eat slowly, and lie about your age.

— *Lucille Ball*

Men do not quit playing because they grow old; they grow old because they quit playing.

— *Oliver Wendell Holmes*

While there's snow on the roof, it doesn't mean the fire has gone out in the furnace.

— *John G. Diefenbaker*

Men become much more attractive when they start looking older. But it doesn't do much for women, though we do have an advantage: makeup.

— *Bette Davis*

And in the end, it's not the years in your life that count. It's the life in your years.

— *Abraham Lincoln*

You're only as young as the last time you changed your mind.

— *Timothy Leary*

I wasted time, and now doth time waste me.

— *William Shakespeare*

There's nothing worse than being an aging young person.

— *Richard Pryor*

There is still no cure for the common birthday.

— *John Glenn*

My doctor recently told me that jogging could add years to my life. I think he was right. I feel ten years older already.

— *Milton Berle*

Time goes by: Reputation increases, ability declines.

— *Dag Hammarskjöld*

First you forget names, then you forget faces. Next you forget to pull your zipper up and finally, you forget to pull it down.

— *George Burns*

Age is no guarantee of maturity.

— LAWANA BLACKWELL

Old age is like everything else. To make a success of it, you've got to start young.

— *Fred Astaire*

I think it would be interesting if old people got anti-Alzheimer's disease where they slowly began to recover other people's lost memories.

— *George Carlin*

If wrinkles must be written upon our brows, let them not be written upon the heart. The spirit should never grow old.

— *John Kenneth Galbraith*

I'll see a beautiful girl walking up to me and I'll think, Oh, my God, I can't believe my good luck. But then she'll say, "Where's your son?" or "My mother loves you."

— *James Caan*

Cherish all your happy moments: they make a fine cushion for old age.

— *Christopher Morley*

It's no longer a question of staying healthy. It's a question of finding a sickness you like.

— *Jackie Mason*

I refuse to admit that I am more than 52, even if that does make my sons illegitimate.

— *Nancy Astor*

A legend is an old man with a cane known for what he used to do. I'm still doing it.

— *Miles Davis*

To me, old age is always 15 years older than I am.

— *Bernard M. Baruch*

When I was young I was called a rugged individualist. When I was in my 50s I was considered eccentric. Here I am doing and saying the same things I did then and I'm labeled senile.

— GEORGE BURNS

You know you're getting old when all the names in your black book have M.D. after them.

— *Arnold Palmer*

It is not all bad, this getting old, ripening. After the fruit has got its growth it should juice up and mellow. God forbid I should live long enough to ferment and rot and fall to the ground in a squash.

— *Josh Billings*

Age is not important unless you're a cheese.

— *Helen Hayes*

I don't have false teeth. Do you think I'd buy teeth like these?

— *Carol Burnett*

One of the good things about getting older is you find you're more interesting than most of the people you meet.

— *Lee Marvin*

Another belief of mine: that everyone else
my age is an adult, whereas I am merely
in disguise.   — *Margaret Atwood*

It is very strange that the years teach us
patience—that the shorter our time, the
greater our capacity for waiting.
                — *Elizabeth Taylor*

Forty is the old age of youth;
50 is the youth of old age.   — *Victor Hugo*

Beware of the young doctor
and the old barber.   — *Benjamin Franklin*

You can't reach old age by another man's
road. My habits protect my life but they
would assassinate you.   — *Mark Twain*

Time sneaks up on you like a windshield
on a bug.   — *John Lithgow*

You can judge your age by the amount of
pain you feel when you come in contact
with a new idea.   — *Pearl S. Buck*

I look better, feel better, make love better
and I'll tell you something else…
I never lied better.   — *George Burns*

The dead might as well try to speak to the
living as the old to the young.
                — *Willa Cather*

To keep the heart unwrinkled, to be
hopeful, kindly, cheerful, reverent—that is to
triumph over old age.
                — *Thomas Bailey Aldrich*

Gray hair is God's graffiti.   — *Bill Cosby*

Life is a moderately good play with a badly
written third act.   — *Truman Capote*

You know you're getting old when you get
that one candle on the cake. It's like, "See if
you can blow this out."   — *Jerry Seinfeld*

You know you're getting old when you've
got money to burn, but the fire's gone out.
                — *Hy Gardner*

I have a problem about being nearly 60:
I keep waking up in the morning and
thinking I'm 31.   — *Elizabeth Janeway*

My grandmother started walking five
miles a day when she was sixty. She's
ninety-seven now, and we don't know
where the hell she is.   — *Ellen DeGeneres*

How old would you be if you didn't know
how old you are?   — *Satchel Paige*

I used to dread getting older because I
thought I would not be able to do all the
things I wanted to do, but now that I am
older I find that I don't want to do them.
                — *Nancy Astor*

If you live long enough, the venerability
factor creeps in; first, you get accused of
things you never did, and later, credited for
virtues you never had.   — *I. F. Stone*

Men should think twice before making
widowhood women's only path to power.
                — *Gloria Steinem*

A man who correctly guesses a woman's age
may be smart, but he's not very bright.
                — *Lucille Ball*

A man is not old until regrets take the place
of dreams.   — *John Barrymore*

At my age flowers scare me.   — *George Burns*

Of all the self-fulfilling prophecies in our culture, the assumption that aging means decline and poor health is probably the deadliest.
— *Marilyn Ferguson*

You must have been warned against letting the golden hours slip by; but some of them are golden only because we let them slip by.
—*James M. Barrie*

When doctors and undertakers meet, they always wink at each other.   — *W. C. Fields*

Health nuts are going to feel stupid someday, lying in hospitals dying of nothing.
— *Redd Foxx*

***

Death

Like everyone else who makes the mistake of getting older, I begin each day with coffee and obituaries.   — *Bill Cosby*

On the plus side, death is one of the few things that can be done as easily lying down.
— *Woody Allen*

He's so old that when he orders a three-minute egg, they ask for the money up front.   — *Milton Berle*

My doctor gave me six months to live, but when I couldn't pay the bill he gave me six months more.   — *Walter Matthau*

I look upon life as a gift from God. I did nothing to earn it. Now that the time is coming to give it back, I have no right to complain.   —*Joyce Cary*

It is a sobering thought that when Mozart was my age, he had been dead for two years.
— *Tom Lehrer*

Frisbeetarianism is the belief that when you die, your soul goes up on the roof and gets stuck.   — *George Carlin*

Desire is half of life; indifference is half of death.   — *Kahlil Gibran*

Nothing dies harder than a bad idea.
—*Julia Cameron*

Once you're dead you're made for life.
—*Jimi Hendrix*

When I stand before God at the end of my life, I would hope that I would not have a single bit of talent left, and could say, "I used everything you gave me."
— *Erma Bombeck*

I submit to you that if a man hasn't discovered something he will die for, he isn't fit to live.   — *Martin Luther King, Jr.*

THE PATH THROUGH LIFE

Do not fear death so much, but rather the inadequate life.
— *Bertolt Brecht*

If life was fair, Elvis would be alive and all the impersonators would be dead.
— *Johnny Carson*

They say such nice things about people at their funerals that it makes me sad that I'm going to miss mine by just a few days.
— *Garrison Keillor*

Death is caused by swallowing small amounts of saliva over a long period of time.
— *George Carlin*

Our brains are seventy-year clocks. The Angel of Life winds them up once for all, then closes the case, and gives the key into the hand of the Angel of the Resurrection.
— *Oliver Wendell Holmes*

I detest life-insurance agents; they always argue that I shall some day die, which is not so.
— *Stephen Leacock*

I am dying from the treatment of too many physicians.
— *Alexander the Great*

Death is the sound of distant thunder at a picnic.
— *W. H. Auden*

If the doctor told me I had only six minutes to live, I'd type a little faster.
— *Isaac Asimov*

His death was the first time that Ed Wynn ever made anyone sad.
— *Red Skelton*

That would be a good thing for them to cut on my tombstone: Wherever she went, including here, it was against her better judgment.
— *Dorothy Parker*

That's all a man can hope for during his lifetime—to set an example—and when he is dead, to be an inspiration for history.
— *William McKinley*

Immortality is a long shot, I admit. But somebody has to be first.
— *Bill Cosby*

Death ends a life, not a relationship.

— JACK LEMMON

Why are our days numbered and not, say, lettered?
— *Woody Allen*

In the city a funeral is just an interruption of traffic; in the country it is a form of popular entertainment.
— *George Ade*

I'm always relieved when someone is delivering a eulogy and I realize I'm listening to it.
— *George Carlin*

If you live to be one hundred, you've got it made. Very few people die past that age.
— *George Burns*

If I could drop dead right now, I'd be the happiest man alive.
— *Samuel Goldwyn*

Dying is a very dull, dreary affair. And my advice to you is to have nothing whatever to do with it.
— *W. Somerset Maugham*

Last Words

When the Grim Reaper signals you to make your final exit from the world stage, how well will you perform? Will you have the presence of mind to summon up an inspired line or two? Here's a collection of several famous people's last words—some touching, some ironic, and a few downright funny.

The ladies have to go first. Get in the lifeboat, to please me. Good-bye, dearie. I'll see you later.
 ⌁ JOHN JACOB ASTOR IV, aboard the *Titanic*

Codeine ... bourbon.
 ⌁ TALLULAH BANKHEAD

How were the receipts today at Madison Square Garden?
 ⌁ P. T. BARNUM

Friends applaud, the comedy is finished.
 ⌁ LUDWIG VAN BEETHOVEN

I should never have switched from Scotch to martinis.
 ⌁ HUMPHREY BOGART

That was the best ice-cream soda I ever tasted.
 ⌁ LOU COSTELLO

That was a great game of golf, fellers.
 ⌁ BING CROSBY

I am not the least afraid to die.
 ⌁ CHARLES DARWIN

The fog is rising.
 ⌁ EMILY DICKINSON

KHAQQ calling Itasca. We must be on you,
but cannot see you. Gas is running low.

⤳ AMELIA EARHART

I've never felt better.

⤳ DOUGLAS FAIRBANKS, SR.

I've had a hell of a lot of fun and I've enjoyed every minute of it.

⤳ ERROL FLYNN

Turn up the lights. I don't want to go home in the dark.

⤳ O. HENRY

Leave the shower curtain on the inside of the tub.

⤳ CONRAD N. HILTON

Go on, get out—last words are for fools who haven't said enough.

⤳ KARL MARX

I am just going outside and may be some time.

⤳ LAWRENCE OATES, Antarctic expedition, 1912

You can keep the things of bronze and stone and give me
one man to remember me just once a year.

⤳ DAMON RUNYON

Drink to me.

⤳ PABLO PICASSO

Everybody has got to die, but I have always believed an
exception would be made in my case. Now what?

⤳ WILLIAM SAROYAN

They couldn't hit an elephant at this dist—.

⤳ JOHN SEDGWICK, Union Civil War general

I have offended God and mankind because my work did
not reach the quality it should have.

⤳ LEONARDO DA VINCI

Either that wallpaper goes, or I do.

⤳ OSCAR WILDE

41

A cynic is a man who, when he smells flowers, looks around for a coffin.

— *H. L. Mencken*

He is one of those people who would be enormously improved by death.   — *Saki*

There is no such thing as bad publicity except your own obituary.

— *Brendan Behan*

Death is nothing, but to live defeated and inglorious is to die daily.

— *Napoleon Bonaparte*

If physical death is the price that I must pay to free my white brothers and sisters from a permanent death of the spirit, then nothing can be more redemptive.

— *Martin Luther King, Jr.*

What I look forward to is continued immaturity followed by death.   — *Dave Barry*

I do not believe that any man fears to be dead, but only the stroke of death.

— *Francis Bacon*

When I die, if the word *thong* appears in the first or second sentence of my obituary, I've screwed up.   — *Albert Brooks*

I'm the one that has to die when it's time for me to die, so let me live my life, the way I want to.   — *Jimi Hendrix*

There are some days when I think I'm going to die from an overdose of satisfaction.

— *Salvador Dalí*

Let us endeavor so to live that when we come to die even the undertaker will be sorry.   — *Mark Twain*

Suicide is a permanent solution to a temporary problem.   — *Phil Donahue*

The bitterest tears shed over graves are for words left unsaid and deeds left undone.

— *Harriet Beecher Stowe*

An autobiography is an obituary in serial form with the last installment missing.

— *Quentin Crisp*

My friends are my estate.   — *Emily Dickinson*

Any man who has $10,000 left when he dies is a failure.   — *Errol Flynn*

Death is a challenge. It tells us not to waste time. ... It tells us to tell each other right now that we love each other.

— *Leo Buscaglia*

You don't die in the United States, you underachieve.   — *Jerzy Kosinski*

I have never killed a man, but I have read many obituaries with a lot of pleasure.

— *Clarence Darrow*

Truth sits upon the lips of dying men.

— *Matthew Arnold*

Do not go gentle into that good night
Old age should burn and rave at close of day;
Rage, rage against the dying of the light.

— *Dylan Thomas*

Life is pleasant. Death is peaceful.
It's the transition that's troublesome.

— *Isaac Asimov*

Death is not the end. There remains the litigation over the estate.

— *Ambrose Bierce*

Life is tragic simply because the earth turns and the sun inexorably rises and sets, and one day, for each of us, the sun will go down for the last, last time. — *James Baldwin*

The thinker dies, but his thoughts are beyond the reach of destruction. Men are mortal; but ideas are immortal. — *Richard Adams*

Life is hardly more than a fraction of a second. Such a little time to prepare oneself for eternity! — *Paul Gauguin*

To die will be an awfully big adventure. — *James M. Barrie*

I don't believe in dying. It's been done. I'm working on a new exit. Besides, I can't die now—I'm booked. — *George Burns*

Death will be a great relief. No more interviews. — *Katharine Hepburn*

When you are about to die, a wombat is better than no company at all. — *Roger Zelazny*

Always go to other people's funerals; otherwise they won't come to yours.

—YOGI BERRA

The Human **Spirit**

Okay, let's go deeper now. The subject for the quotations in this part is nothing less profound than religion, the meaning of life, and our own particular places within humanity and the world.

Faith

We trust, sir, that God is on our side. It is more important to know that we are on God's side.
— *Abraham Lincoln*

One, on God's side, is a majority.
— *Wendell Phillips*

I do not feel obliged to believe that the same God who has endowed us with sense, reason, and intellect has intended us to forgo their use.
— *Galileo*

Science without religion is lame, religion without science is blind.
— *Albert Einstein*

Beware when the great God lets loose a thinker on this planet.
— *Ralph Waldo Emerson*

There is no question that there is an unseen world. The problem is, how far is it from midtown and how late is it open?
— *Woody Allen*

Treat the other man's faith gently; it is all he has to believe with. His mind was created for his own thoughts, not yours or mine.
— *Henry S. Haskins*

We must respect the other fellow's religion, but only in the sense and to the extent that we respect his theory that his wife is beautiful and his children smart.
— *H. L. Mencken*

This only is denied to God: the power to undo the past.
— *Agathon*

I have an everyday religion that works for me. Love yourself first, and everything else falls into line. You really have to love yourself to get anything done in this world.
— *Lucille Ball*

Can you see the holiness in those things you take for granted—a paved road or a washing machine? If you concentrate on finding what is good in every situation, you will discover that your life will suddenly be filled with gratitude, a feeling that nurtures the soul.
— *Harold S. Kushner*

You ask: What is the meaning or purpose of life? I can only answer with another question: Do you think we are wise enough to read God's mind?
— *Freeman Dyson*

God grant me the serenity to accept the things I cannot change, the courage to change the things I can, and the wisdom to know the difference.
— *Reinhold Niebuhr*

Faith is taking the first step even when you don't see the whole staircase.
— *Martin Luther King, Jr.*

There's nothing written in the Bible, Old or New Testament, that says, "If you believe in Me, you ain't going to have no troubles."
— *Ray Charles*

Holiness is not the luxury of a few. It is everyone's duty, yours and mine.
— *Mother Teresa*

Every charitable act is a stepping stone toward heaven.
— *Henry Ward Beecher*

What is faith worth if it is not translated into action?
— *Mahatma Gandhi*

The gods help them that help themselves.
— *Aesop*

If God can work through me, he can work through anyone. — *Saint Francis of Assisi*

We're here for a reason. I believe a bit of the reason is to throw little torches out to lead people through the dark.
— *Whoopi Goldberg*

As far as we can discern, the sole purpose of human existence is to kindle a light in the darkness of mere being. — *Carl Jung*

The fact that I can plant a seed and it becomes a flower, share a bit of knowledge and it becomes another's, smile at someone and receive a smile in return, are to me continual spiritual exercises. — *Leo Buscaglia*

God is not a cosmic bellboy for whom we can press a button to get things done.
— *Harry Emerson Fosdick*

There is no need to go to India or anywhere else to find peace. You will find that deep place of silence right in your room, your garden or even your bathtub.
— *Elisabeth Kubler-Ross*

I conceive the essential task of religion to be "to develop the consciences, the ideals, and the aspirations of mankind."
— *Robert Millikan*

I think vital religion has always suffered when orthodoxy is more regarded than virtue. The scriptures assure me that at the last day we shall not be examined on what we thought but what we did.
— *Benjamin Franklin*

The belief in a supernatural source of evil is not necessary; men alone are quite capable of every wickedness. — *Joseph Conrad*

Religion is what keeps the poor from murdering the rich.

— NAPOLEON BONAPARTE

God made Truth with many doors to welcome every believer who knocks on them.
— *Kahlil Gibran*

In the name of God, stop a moment, cease your work, look around you. — *Leo Tolstoy*

It's faith in something and enthusiasm for something that makes life worth living.
— *Oliver Wendell Holmes*

The devil can cite Scripture for his purpose.
— *William Shakespeare*

Believe those who are seeking the truth; doubt those who find it. — *André Gide*

Say not, "I have found the truth," but rather, "I have found a truth." — *Kahlil Gibran*

Say nothing of my religion. It is known to God and myself alone. Its evidence before the world is to be sought in my life: if it has been honest and dutiful to society the religion which has regulated it cannot be a bad one. — *Thomas Jefferson*

Faith moves mountains, but you have to keep pushing while you are praying.

— *Mason Cooley*

Pray as if everything depended upon God and work as if everything depended upon man.

— *Francis Cardinal Spellman*

Earth's crammed with heaven,
And every common bush afire with God;
But only he who sees, takes off his shoes;
The rest sit round it and pluck blackberries.

— *Elizabeth Barrett Browning*

Character is what God and the angels know of us; reputation is what men and women think of us.

— *Horace Mann*

An honest man is the noblest work of God.

— *Alexander Pope*

The wish to pray is a prayer in itself. God can ask no more than that of us.

— *Georges Bernanos*

The time to pray is not when we are in a tight spot but just as soon as we get out of it.

— *Josh Billings*

God moves in a mysterious way His wonders to perform.

— *William Cowper*

The Lord had the wonderful advantage of being able to work alone.

— *Kofi Annan*

Sooner or later ... you are going to be looking at God saying, "We're going to be lucky if we get out of here." Your life is going to be in front of you and then you are going to realize that you'd rather be grocery shopping.

— *Ed Barry*

Yesterday is history, tomorrow is a mystery, today is God's gift, that's why we call it the present.

— *Joan Rivers*

My religion is very simple. My religion is kindness.

— *The Dalai Lama*

We are always on the anvil; by trials God is shaping us for higher things.

— *Henry Ward Beecher*

It is difficult to make a man miserable while he feels worthy of himself and claims kindred to the great God who made him.

— *Abraham Lincoln*

We have just enough religion to make us hate, but not enough to make us love one another.

— *Jonathan Swift*

Sometimes you struggle so hard to feed your family one way, you forget to feed them the other way, with spiritual nourishment. Everybody needs that.

— *James Brown*

Every religion is true one way or another. It is true when understood metaphorically. But when it gets stuck in its own metaphors, interpreting them as facts, then you are in trouble.

— *Joseph Campbell*

Practically speaking, your religion is the story you tell about your life.

— *Andrew Greeley*

Coincidences are spiritual puns.

— *G. K. Chesterton*

I personally believe that each of us was put here for a purpose—to build, not to destroy. If I can make people smile, then I have served my purpose for God.

— *Red Skelton*

There are two ways to live: you can live as if nothing is a miracle; you can live as if everything is a miracle.

— *Albert Einstein*

I don't believe in astrology; I'm a Sagittarius and we're skeptical.

— *Arthur C. Clarke*

THE HUMAN SPIRIT

If only God would give me some clear sign!
Like making a large deposit in my name
at a Swiss bank.

— WOODY ALLEN

A belief is not merely an idea the mind possesses; it is an idea that possesses the mind.
— *Robert Bolton*

Preaching is to much avail, but practice is far more effective. A godly life is the strongest argument you can offer the skeptic.
— *Hosea Ballou*

Churchgoers are like coals in a fire. When they cling together, they keep the flame aglow; when they separate, they die out.
— *Billy Graham*

We have grasped the mystery of the atom and rejected the Sermon on the Mount.
— *Omar N. Bradley*

It is the final proof of God's omnipotence that he need not exist in order to save us.
— *Peter De Vries*

I would rather live my life as if there is a God and die to find out there isn't, than live my life as if there isn't and die to find out there is.
— *Albert Camus*

We have to pray on behalf of those who do not pray.
— *Mother Teresa*

If there were no God, there would be no atheists.
— *G. K. Chesterton*

I respect faith, but doubt is what gets you an education.
— *Wilson Mizner*

I'm still an atheist, thank God.
— *Luis Buñuel*

Gods are fragile things; they may be killed by a whiff of science or a dose of common sense.
— *Chapman Cohen*

You don't have to be religious to have a soul; everybody has one. You don't have to be religious to perfect your soul; I have found saintliness in avowed atheists.
— *Harold S. Kushner*

It is the test of a good religion whether you can joke about it.
— *G. K. Chesterton*

The secret of a good sermon is to have a good beginning and a good ending, then having the two as close together as possible.
— *George Burns*

The lion and the calf shall lie down together but the calf won't get much sleep.
— *Woody Allen*

I finally found out how priests get holy water. They boil the hell out of it.
— *Joan Rivers*

If there is no God, who pops up the next Kleenex?
— *Art Hoppe*

God is a comedian playing to an audience too afraid to laugh.
— *Voltaire*

The gods, too, are fond of a joke.
— *Aristotle*

Imagine the Creator as a stand-up comedian—and at once the world becomes explicable.
— *H. L. Mencken*

Mahatma Gandhi

Selfless Peacemaker

When the thin little man dressed only in a loincloth spoke, the world listened.

Mohandas K. Gandhi was born in British-ruled India in 1869, earned a law degree in London, and then spent 20 years immersed in opposing social injustice in South Africa. It was there that he developed his concept of nonviolent resistance. He returned to India in 1915 and earned renown as a social reformer—resisting oppression, trying to end British domination, and making peace between Hindus and Muslims. He was given the title Mahatma, meaning Great Soul.

Gandhi had ideas for improving virtually every aspect of life—work, education, nutrition, and more. He was able to deliver his ideas to the Indian people through the many newspapers that he founded, and he is still remembered today, among his many social accomplishments, as a major force in Indian journalism.

*

I hate privilege and monopoly.
Whatever cannot be shared with the masses is taboo to me.

*

The best way of losing a cause is to abuse your opponent
and to trade upon his weakness.

*

Whenever I see an erring man, I say to myself I have also erred;
when I see a lustful man, I say to myself so was I once; and in this way,
I feel kinship with everyone in the world and feel that I cannot be happy without the
humblest of us being happy.

*

To forget how to dig the earth and tend the soil is to forget ourselves.

*

Blaming the wolf would not help the sheep much.
The sheep must learn not to fall into the clutches of the wolf.

*

I cannot intentionally hurt anything that lives, much less fellow human beings, even
though they may do the greatest wrong to me and mine.

*

I shall have to answer my God and my Maker if I give anyone less
than his due, but I am sure that He will bless me if He knows
that I gave someone more than his due.

*

What I have done will endure, not what I have said or written.

The creator of the universe works in mysterious ways. But he uses a base ten counting system and likes round numbers.

— *Scott Adams*

There is hope for the future because God has a sense of humor and we are funny to God.

— *Bill Cosby*

I still say a church steeple with a lightning rod on top shows a lack of confidence.

— *Doug McLeod*

God gives us relatives; thank God we can choose our friends.

— *Ethel Mumford*

I am determined that my children shall be brought up in their father's religion, if they can find out what it is.

— *Charles Lamb*

In the beginning there was nothing. God said, "Let there be light!" And there was light. There was still nothing, but you could see it a whole lot better.

— *Ellen DeGeneres*

I have as much authority as the Pope—I just don't have as many people who believe it.

— *George Carlin*

See everything; overlook a great deal; correct a little.

— *Pope John XXIII*

***

Making Sense of It All

Realize deeply that the present moment is all you ever have.

— *Eckhart Tolle*

Hope is only the love of life.

— *Henri-Frédéric Amiel*

Hope begins in the dark, the stubborn hope that if you just show up and try to do the right thing, the dawn will come. You wait and watch and work: You don't give up.

— *Anne Lamott*

Few people even scratch the surface, much less exhaust the contemplation of their own experience.

— *Randolph Bourne*

I happen to feel that the degree of a person's intelligence is directly reflected by the number of conflicting attitudes she can bring to bear on the same topic. — *Lisa Alther*

The way I see it, if you want the rainbow you gotta put up with the rain.

— *Dolly Parton*

Life is like an ever-shifting kaleidoscope— a slight change, and all patterns alter.

— *Susan Salzberg*

If you are going to ask yourself life-changing questions, be sure to do something with the answers.

— *Bo Bennett*

Those who dream by day are cognizant of many things which escape those who dream only by night.

— *Edgar Allan Poe*

It is said an eastern monarch once charged his wise men to invent a sentence, to be ever in view, and which should be true and appropriate in all times and situations. They presented him with the words, "And this, too, shall pass away." How much it expresses! How chastening in the hour of pride! How consoling in the depths of affliction!

— *Abraham Lincoln*

Most things get better by themselves. Most things, in fact, are better by morning.

— *Lewis Thomas*

Things in life will not always run smoothly. Sometimes we will be rising toward the heights—then all will seem to reverse itself and start downward. The great fact to remember is that the trend of civilization itself is forever upward, that a line drawn through the middle of the peaks and the valleys of the centuries always has an upward trend.

— *Endicott Peabody*

Life's a voyage that's homeward bound.

— *Herman Melville*

Learning to live what you're born with is the process, the involvement, the making of a life.

— *Diane Wakoski*

We are here to add what we can to life, not to get what we can from it.

— *William Osler*

Life isn't fair. It's just fairer than death, that's all.

— *William Goldman*

We would often be sorry if our wishes were gratified.

— *Aesop*

Wisdom consists of the anticipation of consequences.

— *Norman Cousins*

In order to be walked on, you have to be lying down.

— *Brian Weir*

Experience is a hard teacher because she gives the test first, the lesson afterwards.

— *Vernon Sanders Law*

It is our choices ... that show what we truly are, far more than our abilities.

— *J. K. Rowling*

Everything you can imagine is real.

— *Pablo Picasso*

We grow great by dreams. All big men are dreamers.

— *Woodrow Wilson*

All that counts in life is intention.

— *Andrea Bocelli*

You and I are essentially infinite choice-makers. In every moment of our existence, we are in that field of all possibilities where we have access to an infinity of choices.

— *Deepak Chopra*

We don't see things as they are, we see them as *we* are.

— *Anaïs Nin*

Self-esteem is the reputation we acquire with ourselves.

— *Nathaniel Branden*

No one can make you feel inferior without your consent.

— *Eleanor Roosevelt*

Vanity and pride are different things, though the words are often used synonymously. A person may be proud without being vain. Pride relates more to our opinion of ourselves, vanity to what we would have others think of us.

— *Jane Austen*

Every problem has a gift for you in its hands.

— *Richard Bach*

If a problem has no solution, it may not be a problem, but a fact—not to be solved, but to be coped with over time.

— *Shimon Peres*

All generalizations are dangerous, even
this one. — *Alexandre Dumas*

The minute one utters a certainty, the
opposite comes to mind. — *May Sarton*

Human beings have an inalienable right to
invent themselves. — *Germaine Greer*

It's a poor sort of memory that only
works backward. — *Lewis Carroll*

When I discover who I am, I'll be free.
— *Ralph Ellison*

He will always be a slave who does not
know how to live upon a little. — *Horace*

There are really only three types of people: those
who make things happen, those who watch things
happen, and those who say, "What happened?"

— ANN LANDERS

Life can only be understood backwards; but
it must be lived forwards.
— *Soren Kierkegaard*

The past is a foreign country; they do things
differently there. — *L. P. Hartley*

To be able to look back upon one's past
life with satisfaction is to live twice.
— *Lord Acton*

I look to the future because that's where I'm
going to spend the rest of my life.
— *George Burns*

Never regret. If it's good, it's wonderful.
If it's bad, it's experience. — *Victoria Holt*

Live out of your imagination,
not your history. — *Stephen Covey*

You only live once—but if you work it
right, once is enough. — *Joe E. Lewis*

A thousand words will not leave so deep an
impression as one deed. — *Henrik Ibsen*

That which does not kill us makes
us stronger. — *Friedrich Nietzsche*

Prudence and compromise are necessary
means, but every man should have an impu-
dent end which he will not compromise.
— *Charles Horton Cooley*

It is not easy to find happiness in ourselves,
and it is not possible to find it elsewhere.
— *Agnes Repplier*

The grand essentials of happiness are:
something to do, something to love, and
something to hope for. — *Allan K. Chalmers*

Why do you have to be a nonconformist
like everybody else? — *James Thurber*

The more refined one is, the more unhappy.
— *Anton Chekhov*

THE HUMAN SPIRIT

Wisdom is the quality that keeps you from getting into situations where you need it.
— *Doug Larson*

When I hear somebody sigh, "Life is hard," I am always tempted to ask, "Compared to what?"
— *Sydney J. Harris*

The main things which seem to me important on their own account, and not merely as means to other things, are knowledge, art, instinctive happiness, and relations of friendship or affection.
— *Bertrand Russell*

There are three constants in life ... change, choice and principles.
— *Stephen Covey*

It's easier to go down a hill than up it but the view is much better at the top.
— *Henry Ward Beecher*

Every exit is an entry somewhere.
— *Tom Stoppard*

Tradition is a guide and not a jailer.
— *W. Somerset Maugham*

Here is the test to find whether your mission on earth is finished: if you're alive, it isn't.
— *Richard Bach*

Normal is nothing more than a cycle on a washing machine.
— *Whoopi Goldberg*

Failure is unimportant. It takes courage to make a fool of yourself.
— *Charlie Chaplin*

We are all special cases.
— *Albert Camus*

We have been taught to believe that negative equals realistic and positive equals unrealistic.
— *Susan Jeffers*

If egotism means a terrific interest in one's self, egotism is absolutely essential to efficient living.
— *Arnold Bennett*

A person is only as good as what they love.
— *Saul Bellow*

An inexhaustible good nature is one of the most precious gifts of heaven, spreading itself like oil over the troubled sea of thought, and keeping the mind smooth and equable in the roughest weather.
— *Washington Irving*

A hunch is creativity trying to tell you something.
— *Frank Capra*

The trouble with so many of us is that we underestimate the power of simplicity. We have a tendency, it seems, to overcomplicate our lives and forget what's important and what's not. We tend to mistake movement for achievement. We tend to focus on activities instead of results. And as the pace of life continues to race along in the outside world, we forget that we have the power to control our lives regardless of what's going on outside.
— *Robert Stuberg*

Women who seek to be equal with men lack ambition.
— *Timothy Leary*

Science is organized knowledge. Wisdom is organized life.
— *Immanuel Kant*

Peace is when time doesn't matter as it passes by.
— *Maria Schell*

Any philosophy that can be put in a nutshell belongs there.
— *Sydney J. Harris*

Where is here?
— *Northrop Frye*

Mother Teresa

Saint of the Gutters

By her own choosing, she lived and worked in service of the poorest of the poor.

Agnes Gonxha Bojaxhiu, later to be known as Mother Teresa, was born to an Albanian family in Macedonia in 1910. Determined to be a missionary, at age 18 she joined an order of Roman Catholic nuns that sent her to India, where she taught high school for 17 years. Deeply affected by the poverty in Calcutta, the diminutive nun founded a school for the poorest of slum children, and in 1950 she started her own order, the Missionaries of Charity, to care for people that no one else would help. The order now has hundreds of centers—in more than 100 countries—that tend to the dying, drug addicts, AIDS patients, natural disaster victims, and social castoffs. Mother Teresa, often called the Saint of the Gutters, received the Nobel Peace Prize in 1979.

Small and frail late in her life, Mother Teresa was still an inveterate campaigner for her causes. "I have said to Jesus that if I don't go to heaven for anything else, I will be going to heaven for all the traveling with all the publicity, because it has purified me and sacrificed me and made me really ready to go to heaven."

She declined to speculate on whether she would be canonized, commenting, "Let me die first." She died in 1997. Her beatification, a step on the path toward formal sainthood, took place in 2003.

*

Yesterday is gone. Tomorrow has not yet come. We have only today. Let us begin.

*

*When a poor person dies of hunger, it has not happened because
God did not take care of him or her. It has happened because neither you
nor I wanted to give that person what he or she needed.*

*

*It isn't how much we do, but how much love we put into
what we do that really counts.*

*

*Everybody today seems to be in such a terrible rush, anxious for greater
developments and greater riches and so on, so that children have very little time
for their parents. Parents have very little time for each other, and in the home
begins the disruption of peace of the world.*

*

*The other day I dreamed that I was at the gates of heaven. . . .
And Saint Peter said, "Go back to Earth. There are no slums up here."*

*

Let no one ever come to you without leaving better and happier.

*

*Love is a fruit, in season at all times and within the reach of every hand.
Anyone may gather it and no limit is set. Everyone can reach this love
through meditation, the spirit of prayer, and sacrifice.*

*

God doesn't require us to succeed; he only requires that you try.

Choosing Your Path

He who laughs, lasts! — *Mary Pettibone Poole*

I live to laugh, and I laugh to live.
— *Milton Berle*

Enjoy life. There's plenty of time to be dead.
— *Hans Christian Andersen*

Live as though it were your last day on earth. Someday you will be right.
— *Robert Anthony*

Time is the coin of your life. It is the only coin you have, and only you can determine how it will be spent. Be careful lest you let other people spend it for you.
— *Carl Sandburg*

Suspect each moment, for it is a thief, tip-toeing away with more than it brings.
— *John Updike*

Regret for the things we did can be tempered by time; it is regret for the things we did not do that is inconsolable.
— *Sydney J. Harris*

Avoiding the phrase "I don't have time" will soon help you to realize that you do have the time needed for just about anything you choose to accomplish in life. — *Bo Bennett*

Life is without meaning. You bring the meaning to it. The meaning of life is whatever you ascribe it to be. Being alive is the meaning. — *Joseph Campbell*

If I had to live my life again, I'd make the same mistakes, only sooner.
— *Tallulah Bankhead*

It takes little talent to see what lies under one's nose, a good deal to know in what direction to point that organ.
— *W. H. Auden*

Some men see things as they are and ask, "Why?" I dream things that never were and ask, "Why not?" — *Robert F. Kennedy*

Life loves to be taken by the lapel and told, "I'm with you, kid. Let's go."
— *Maya Angelou*

You've got to keep fighting—you've got to risk your life every six months to stay alive.
— *Elia Kazan*

A wise man will make more opportunities than he finds. — *Francis Bacon*

Stop acting as if life is a rehearsal. Live this day as if it were your last. The past is over and gone. The future is not guaranteed.
— *Wayne Dyer*

Live as if you were living a second time, and as though you had acted wrongly the first time. — *Viktor E. Frankl*

Love the moment, and the energy of that moment will spread beyond all boundaries.
— *Corita Kent*

If we take care of the moments, the years will take care of themselves.
— *Maria Edgeworth*

Life lived for tomorrow will always be just a day away from being realized.
— *Leo Buscaglia*

I have found that if you love life, life will love you back. — *Arthur Rubinstein*

The words printed here are concepts. You must go through the experiences. — *Saint Augustine*

Mix a little foolishness with your prudence: It's good to be silly at the right moment. — *Horace*

Laugh at yourself first, before anyone else can. — *Elsa Maxwell*

We could never learn to be brave and patient, if there were only joy in the world. — *Helen Keller*

When you're through changing, you're through. — *Bruce Barton*

Everyone thinks of changing the world, but no one thinks of changing himself. — *Leo Tolstoy*

The third-rate mind is only happy when it is thinking with the majority. The second-rate mind is only happy when it is thinking with the minority. The first-rate mind is only happy when it is thinking. — *A. A. Milne*

You are today where your thoughts have brought you; you will be tomorrow where your thoughts take you. — *James Lane Allen*

There are things I can't force. I must adjust. There are times when the greatest change needed is a change of my viewpoint. — *Denis Diderot*

Courage is saying, "Maybe what I'm doing isn't working; maybe I should try something else." — *Anna Lappe*

He who loses wealth loses much; he who loses a friend loses more; but he that loses his courage loses all. — *Miguel de Cervantes*

A life spent making mistakes is not only more honorable but more useful than a life spent in doing nothing. — *George Bernard Shaw*

Eliminate something superfluous from your life. Break a habit. Do something that makes you feel insecure. — *Piero Ferrucci*

The great pleasure in life is doing what people say you cannot do. — *Walter Bagehot*

Even though you may want to move forward in your life, you may have one foot on the brakes. In order to be free, we must learn how to let go. Release the hurt. Release the fear. Refuse to entertain your old pain. The energy it takes to hang onto the past is holding you back from a new life. What is it you would let go of today? — *Mary Manin Morrissey*

You've got to make a conscious choice every day to shed the old—whatever *the old* means for you. — *Sarah Ban Breathnach*

Without change, something sleeps inside us, and seldom awakens. The sleeper must awaken. — *Frank Herbert*

Change your thoughts and you change your world. — *Norman Vincent Peale*

I would rather regret the things that I have done than the things that I have not. — *Lucille Ball*

Never feel self-pity, the most destructive emotion there is. How awful to be caught up in the terrible squirrel cage of self. — *Millicent Fenwick*

There are lots of ways of being miserable,
but there's only one way of being comfortable,
and that is to stop running round after happiness.
If you make up your mind not to be happy
there's no reason why you shouldn't have
a fairly good time.

— EDITH WHARTON

One of the most adventurous things left us is
to go to bed. For no one can lay a hand on
our dreams.   — *E. V. Lucas*

Life is a great big canvas. Throw all the paint
you can at it.   — *Danny Kaye*

The most pathetic person in the world is
someone who has sight, but has no vision.
            — *Helen Keller*

Use your imagination not to scare yourself
to death but to inspire yourself to life.
            — *Adele Brookman*

There's only one corner of the universe you
can be certain of improving, and that's your
own self.   — *Aldous Huxley*

The thing that is really hard, and really
amazing, is giving up on being perfect and
beginning the work of becoming yourself.
            — *Anna Quindlen*

The easiest thing to be in the world is you.
The most difficult thing to be is what other
people want you to be. Don't let them put
you in that position.   — *Leo Buscaglia*

To try to be better is to be better.
            — *Charlotte Cushman*

The creative is the place where no one
else has ever been. You have to leave the city
of your comfort and go into the wilderness
of your intuition. What you'll discover will
be wonderful. What you'll discover will
be yourself.   — *Alan Alda*

Follow the grain in your own wood.
            — *Howard Thurman*

In business or in life, don't follow the wagon
tracks too closely.   — *H. Jackson Brown, Jr.*

Read, every day, something no one else is
reading. Think, every day, something no
one else is thinking. Do, every day, something no one else would be silly enough to
do. It is bad for the mind to be always part
of unanimity.   — *Christopher Morley*

The main thing is to keep the main thing
the main thing.   — *Stephen Covey*

I still find each day too short for all the
thoughts I want to think, all the walks I
want to take, all the books I want to read,
and all the friends I want to see.
            — *John Burroughs*

Think like a man of action, act like a man
of thought.   — *Henri Bergson*

The smart ones ask when they don't know. And, sometimes when they do.

— *Malcolm Forbes*

Trust yourself. Think for yourself. Act for yourself. Speak for yourself. Be yourself. Imitation is suicide.

— *Marva Collins*

How can you come to know yourself? Never by thinking, always by doing. Try to do your duty, and you'll know right away what you amount to.

— *Johann von Goethe*

All I want is a little more than I'll ever get.

— *Ashleigh Brilliant*

My candle burns at both ends
It will not last the night;
But ah, my foes, and oh, my friends—
It gives a lovely light.

— *Edna St. Vincent Millay*

The master in the art of living makes little distinction between his work and his play, his labor and his leisure, his mind and his body, his information and his recreation, his love and his religion. He hardly knows which is which. He simply pursues his vision of excellence at whatever he does, leaving others to decide whether he is working or playing. To him he's always doing both.

— *James A. Michener*

A smile is a curve that sets everything straight.

— *Phyllis Diller*

Act the way you'd like to be and soon you'll be the way you act.

— *Leonard Cohen*

Sometimes when I consider what tremendous consequences come from little things, I am tempted to think there are no little things.

— *Bruce Barton*

Pick battles big enough to matter, small enough to win.

— *Jonathan Kozol*

To pretend, I actually do the thing: I have therefore only pretended to pretend.

— *Jacques Derrida*

I define comfort as self-acceptance. When we finally learn that self-care begins and ends with ourselves, we no longer demand sustenance and happiness from others.

— *Jennifer Louden*

Happiness is different from pleasure. Happiness has something to do with struggling and enduring and accomplishing.

— *George Sheehan*

Happiness is neither virtue nor pleasure nor this thing nor that but simply growth. We are happy when we are growing.

— *William Butler Yeats*

No one is in control of your happiness but you; therefore, you have the power to change anything about yourself or your life that you want to change.

— *Barbara De Angelis*

The Constitution only gives people the right to pursue happiness. You have to catch it yourself.

— *Benjamin Franklin*

It is the paradox of life that the way to miss pleasure is to seek it first. The very first condition of lasting happiness is that a life should be full of purpose, aiming at something outside self.

— *Hugo Black*

You must try to generate happiness within yourself. If you aren't happy in one place, chances are you won't be happy anyplace.

— *Ernie Banks*

Nobody really cares if you're miserable,
so you might as well be happy.

— *Cynthia Nelms*

It's a helluva start, being able to recognize
what makes you happy. — *Lucille Ball*

I have no money, no resources, no hopes.
I am the happiest man alive. — *Henry Miller*

Our subconscious minds have no sense
of humor, play no jokes and cannot tell
the difference between reality and an
imagined thought or image. What we
continually think about eventually will
manifest in our lives. — *Robert Collier*

The art of being wise is the art of knowing
what to overlook. — *William James*

The remarkable thing is we have a
choice every day regarding the attitude
we will embrace for that day. We cannot
change our past . . . we cannot change
the fact that people will act in a certain
way. We cannot change the inevitable.
The only thing we can do is play on
the one string we have, and that is our
attitude. . . . I am convinced that life is
10 percent what happens to me and
90 percent how I react to it. And so it
is with you. . . . We are in charge of
our attitudes. — *Charles Swindoll*

A positive attitude may not solve all your
problems, but it will annoy enough people
to make it worth the effort. — *Herm Albright*

A proverb is no proverb to you till life has
illustrated it. — *John Keats*

When one man, for whatever reason, has the
opportunity to lead an extraordinary life, he
has no right to keep it to himself.

— *Jacques Yves Cousteau*

You desire to know the art of living, my
friend? It is contained in one phrase: Make
use of suffering. — *Henri-Frédéric Amiel*

The truth that many people never understand, until it is too late, is that the more you
try to avoid suffering the more you suffer
because smaller and more insignificant
things begin to torture you in proportion to
your fear of being hurt. — *Thomas Merton*

Don't judge each day by the harvest you
reap but by the seeds that you plant.

— *Robert Louis Stevenson*

Our lives improve only when we take
chances—and the first and most difficult risk
we can take is to be honest with ourselves.

— *Walter Anderson*

Go confidently in the direction of your
dreams! Live the life you've imagined. As
you simplify your life, the laws of the universe will be simpler. — *Henry David Thoreau*

An adventure is only an inconvenience
rightly considered. An inconvenience is only
an adventure wrongly considered.

— *G. K. Chesterton*

As a well-spent day brings happy sleep, so a
life well spent brings happy death.

— *Leonardo da Vinci*

Things turn out best for the people who
make the best of the way things turn out.

— *Art Linkletter*

If you can't get rid of the skeleton in your
closet, you'd best teach it to dance.

— *George Bernard Shaw*

The minute you settle for less than you
deserve, you get even less than you settled for.

— *Maureen Dowd*

THE HUMAN SPIRIT

To avoid criticism, do nothing, say nothing, and be nothing.
— *Elbert Hubbard*

Blessed is he who expects nothing, for he shall never be disappointed.
— *Alexander Pope*

I don't want to get to the end of my life and find that I lived just the length of it. I want to have lived the width of it as well.
— *Diane Ackerman*

The tragedy of life is not that it ends so soon, but that we wait so long to begin it.
— *W. M. Lewis*

Doing your best at this moment puts you in the best place for the next moment.
— *Oprah Winfrey*

A woman who is convinced that she deserves to accept only the best challenges herself to give the best. Then she is living phenomenally.
— *Maya Angelou*

One of the keys to happiness is a bad memory.
— *Rita Mae Brown*

A pessimist is one who makes difficulties of his opportunities and an optimist is one who makes opportunities of his difficulties.
— *Harry S. Truman*

I am an optimist. It does not seem too much use being anything else.
— *Winston Churchill*

Stick with the optimists. It's going to be tough enough even if they're right.
— *James Reston*

Hope is the thing with feathers that perches in the soul.
— *Emily Dickinson*

Every tomorrow has two handles. We can take hold of it with the handle of anxiety or the handle of faith.
— *Henry Ward Beecher*

If you see ten troubles coming down the road, you can be sure that nine will run into the ditch before they reach you.
— *Calvin Coolidge*

We are confronted with insurmountable opportunities.
— *Walt Kelly*

No pessimist ever discovered the secret of the stars, or sailed to an uncharted land, or opened a new doorway for the human spirit.
— *Helen Keller*

Hitch your wagon to a star.
— *Ralph Waldo Emerson*

Aim at the sun, and you may not reach it; but your arrow will fly far higher than if aimed at an object on a level with yourself.
— *Joel Hawes*

The optimist proclaims that we live in the best of all possible worlds; and the pessimist fears this is true.
— *James Branch Cabell*

Sometimes people call me an idealist. Well, that is the way I know am an American. America is the only idealistic nation in the world.
— *Woodrow Wilson*

Never leave that till tomorrow which you can do today. — *Benjamin Franklin*

Never do today what you can put off till tomorrow. Delay may give clearer light as to what is best to be done. — *Aaron Burr*

Remember, today is the tomorrow you worried about yesterday. — *Dale Carnegie*

Forever is composed of nows. — *Emily Dickinson*

Learning to ignore things is one of the great paths to inner peace. — *Robert J. Sawyer*

Courage is the art of being the only one who knows you're scared to death. — *Harold Wilson*

Courage is doing what you're afraid to do. There can be no courage unless you're scared. — *Eddie Rickenbacker*

Whatever you do will be insignificant, but it is very important that you do it. — *Mahatma Gandhi*

The greatest glory in living lies not in never falling, but in rising every time we fall. — *Nelson Mandela*

Blessed are they who heal you of self-despisings. Of all services which can be done to man, I know of none more precious. — *William Hale White*

The true test of character is not how much we know how to do, but how we behave when we don't know what to do. — *John Holt*

Experience is not what happens to a man. It is what a man does with what happens to him. — *Aldous Huxley*

What you do speaks so loud that I cannot hear what you say. — *Ralph Waldo Emerson*

Experience is that marvelous thing that enables you to recognize a mistake when you make it again. — *Franklin P. Jones*

Every action of our lives touches on some chord that will vibrate in eternity. — *Sean O'Casey*

Action is eloquence. — *William Shakespeare*

Mere brave speech without action is letting off useless steam. — *Mahatma Gandhi*

Knowledge is of no value unless you put it into practice. — *Anton Chekhov*

The man who insists on seeing with perfect clearness before he decides, never decides. — *Henri-Frédéric Amiel*

Surely there comes a time when counting the cost and paying the price aren't things to think about anymore. All that matters is value—the ultimate value of what one does. — *James Hilton*

He who joyfully marches in rank and file has already earned my contempt. He has been given a large brain by mistake, since for him the spinal cord would suffice. — *Albert Einstein*

I must create a system, or be enslaved by another man's. — *William Blake*

I have a simple philosophy. Fill what's empty. Empty what's full. And scratch where it itches. — *Alice Roosevelt Longworth*

A strong positive mental attitude will create more miracles than any wonder drug. — *Patricia Neal*

THE HUMAN SPIRIT

Look to your health; and if you have it, praise God and value it next to conscience; for health is the second blessing that we mortals are capable of, a blessing money can't buy.

— *Izaak Walton*

The human body experiences a powerful gravitational pull in the direction of hope. That is why the patient's hopes are the physician's secret weapon. They are the hidden ingredients in any prescription.

— *Norman Cousins*

When you can't remember why you're hurt, that's when you're healed.

— *Jane Fonda*

All sanity depends on this: that it should be a delight to feel heat strike the skin, a delight to stand upright, knowing the bones are moving easily under the flesh.

— *Doris Lessing*

How poor are they who have not patience! What wound did ever heal but by degrees?

— *William Shakespeare*

Water, air, and cleanness are the chief articles in my pharmacy.

— *Napoleon Bonaparte*

My doctor is wonderful. Once, in 1955, when I couldn't afford an operation, he touched up the X-rays.

— *Joey Bishop*

I think that age as a number is not nearly as important as health. You can be in poor health and be pretty miserable at 40 or 50. If you're in good health, you can enjoy things into your 80s.

— *Bob Barker*

Your heaviest artillery will be your will to live. Keep that big gun going.

— *Norman Cousins*

***

Giving

In charity there is no excess. — *Francis Bacon*

After the verb "to love," "to help" is the most beautiful verb in the world.

— *Bertha von Suttner*

I don't think there's any richer reward in life than helping someone. You can't measure it in money or fame or anything else. But if we're not put here for anything else but to help each other get through life, I think that's a very honorable existence.

— *Tom Brokaw*

What we have done for ourselves alone dies with us; what we have done for others and the world remains and is immortal.

— *Albert Pike*

Givers have to set limits because takers rarely do.

— *Irma Kurtz*

The service we render to others is really the rent we pay for our room on this earth.

— *Wilfred Grenfell*

If you want others to be happy, practice compassion. If you want to be happy, practice compassion.

— *The Dalai Lama*

Never look down on anybody unless you're helping him up.

— *Jesse Jackson*

William Shakespeare

The World Is His Stage

For William Shakespeare, yes, the play was the thing.

Shakespeare was born in Stratford-on-Avon in 1564. He was not overly educated—his formal schooling ended at age 15. He plunged into London's theater scene as an actor and writer in the late 1580s, and by 1611 he had written the most highly regarded collection of plays in history, including *A Comedy of Errors, As You Like It, Hamlet, Othello,* and *A Midsummer Night's Dream.* While one critic skewered Shakespeare as "an upstart crow," he was a great success in his own time—writing for London's foremost acting troupe and having his works published as popular literature.

While plenty is known about the structure of Shakespeare's life—his works, where he lived, and such—little is known about the man as a person. He was known to be a practical man, multitalented and good at business.

Despite his limited education, Shakespeare had a heroic command of the language. Our modern tongue is lavishly dappled with words and phrases that are traced directly back to the Bard's pen, including "To be or not to be—that is the question," "Out, damned spot!," "All the world's a stage," "Friends, Romans, countrymen," "Beware the ides of March," and "Something is rotten in the state of Denmark."

Shakespeare died in 1616 at age 52.

*

The first thing we do, let's kill all the lawyers.

*

The play's the thing
Wherein I'll catch the conscience of the king.

*

All the world's a stage,
And all the men and women merely players.
They have their exits and their entrances;
And one man in his time plays many parts.

*

Brevity is the soul of wit.

*

What a piece of work is man!

*

Cowards die many times before their deaths;
The valiant never taste of death but once.
Of all the wonders that I yet have heard,
It seems to me most strange that men should fear;
Seeing that death, a necessary end,
Will come when it will come.

*

Neither a borrower nor a lender be.

*

What's in a name? That which we call a rose
By any other name would smell as sweet.

*

Out, out, brief candle!
Life's but a walking shadow, a poor player
That struts and frets his hour upon the stage
And then is heard no more; it is a tale
Told by an idiot, full of sound and fury,
Signifying nothing.

Those who bring sunshine into the lives of others cannot keep it from themselves.

— *James M. Barrie*

How wonderful it is that nobody need wait a single moment before starting to improve the world.

— *Anne Frank*

You must give some time to your fellow men. Even if it's a little thing, do something for others—something for which you get no pay but the privilege of doing it.

— *Albert Schweitzer*

From what we get, we can make a living; what we give, however, makes a life.

— *Arthur Ashe*

It's easy to make a buck. It's a lot tougher to make a difference.

— *Tom Brokaw*

The smallest deed is better than the greatest intention.

— *John Burroughs*

If I can stop one heart from breaking, I shall not live in vain.

— *Emily Dickinson*

***

 A friend is a second self.

— ARISTOTLE

*R*elationships

At the end of your life, you will never regret not having passed one more test, not winning one more verdict or not closing one more deal. You will regret time not spent with a husband, a friend, a child, or a parent.

— *Barbara Bush*

The meeting of two personalities is like the contact of two chemical substances: if there is any reaction, both are transformed.

— *Carl Jung*

The true measure of a man is how he treats someone who can do him absolutely no good.

— *Ann Landers*

Isn't everyone a part of everyone else?

— *Budd Schulberg*

Good humor is one of the best articles of dress one can wear in society.

— *William Makepeace Thackeray*

Don't criticize what you don't understand, son. You never walked in that man's shoes.

— *Elvis Presley*

Until you walk a mile in another man's moccasins you can't imagine the smell.

— *Robert Byrne*

If a man be gracious and courteous to strangers, it shows he is a citizen of the world, and that his heart is no island cut off from other lands, but a continent that joins to them.
— *Francis Bacon*

The best time to make friends is before you need them.
— *Ethel Barrymore*

Friendship is the hardest thing in the world to explain. It's not something you learn in school. But if you haven't learned the meaning of friendship, you really haven't learned anything.
— *Muhammad Ali*

If you find it in your heart to care for somebody else, you will have succeeded.
— *Maya Angelou*

A true friend knows your weaknesses but shows you your strengths; feels your fears but fortifies your faith; sees your anxieties but frees your spirit; recognizes your disabilities but emphasizes your possibilities.
— *William Arthur Ward*

It is one of the blessings of old friends that you can afford to be stupid with them.
— *Ralph Waldo Emerson*

When you find the right people, you never let go. The people who count are the ones who are your friends in lean times. You have all the friends you want when things are going well.
— *James Lee Burke*

Every man should keep a fair-sized cemetery in which to bury the faults of his friends.
— *Henry Ward Beecher*

Treat your friends as you do your pictures, and place them in their best light.
— *Jennie Jerome Churchill*

Remember that the most valuable antiques are dear old friends.
— *H. Jackson Brown, Jr.*

The real test of friendship is: can you literally do nothing with the other person? Can you enjoy those moments of life that are utterly simple?
— *Eugene Kennedy*

Until you've lost your reputation, you never realize what a burden it was.
— *Margaret Mitchell*

One thing you will probably remember well is any time you forgive and forget.
— *Franklin P. Jones*

Whenever anyone has offended me, I try to raise my soul so high that the offense cannot reach it.
— *René Descartes*

Forgiveness is a virtue of the brave.
— *Indira Gandhi*

Life appears to me too short to be spent in nursing animosity or registering wrongs.
— *Charlotte Brontë*

Forget injuries; never forget kindnesses.
— *Confucius*

Forgiveness does not change the past, but it does enlarge the future.
— *Paul Boese*

You cannot go around and keep score. If you keep score on the good things and the bad things, you'll find out that you're a very miserable person. God gave man the ability to forget, which is one of the greatest attributes you have. Because if you remember everything that's happened to you, you generally remember that which is the most unfortunate.
— *Hubert H. Humphrey*

Holding on to anger, resentment and hurt only gives you tense muscles, a headache and a sore jaw from clenching your teeth. Forgiveness gives you back the laughter and the lightness in your life. — *Joan Lunden*

Contrary to general belief, I do not believe that friends are necessarily the people you like best, they are merely the people who got there first. — *Peter Ustinov*

I always like to know everything about my new friends, and nothing about my old ones. — *Oscar Wilde*

If we listened to our intellect, we'd never have a love affair. We'd never have a friendship. We'd never go into business, because we'd be cynical. Well, that's nonsense. You've got to jump off cliffs all the time and build your wings on the way down. — *Ray Bradbury*

You can make more friends in two months by becoming interested in other people than you can in two years by trying to get other people interested in you. — *Dale Carnegie*

An ounce of loyalty is worth a pound of cleverness. — *Elbert Hubbard*

When a friend is in trouble, don't annoy him by asking if there is anything you can do. Think up something appropriate and do it. — *Edgar Watson Howe*

The real art of conversation is not only to say the right thing at the right place but to leave unsaid the wrong thing at the tempting moment. — *Dorothy Nevill*

They may forget what you said, but they will never forget how you made them feel. — *Carl W. Buechner*

Sometimes being a friend means mastering the art of timing. There is a time for silence. A time to let go. ...And a time to prepare to pick up the pieces when it's all over. — *Gloria Naylor*

If you're afraid to let someone else see your weakness, take heart: Nobody's perfect. Besides, your attempts to hide your flaws don't work as well as you think they do. — *Julie Morgenstern*

Never apologize for showing feeling. When you do so, you apologize for the truth. — *Benjamin Disraeli*

The joy that isn't shared dies young. — *Anne Sexton*

Better to remain silent and be thought a fool than to speak out and remove all doubt. — *Abraham Lincoln*

The most important thing in communication is to hear what isn't being said. — *Peter F. Drucker*

Never miss a chance to keep your mouth shut. — *Robert Newton Peck*

Be a good listener. Your ears will never get you in trouble. — *Frank Tyger*

When people talk, listen completely. Most people never listen. — *Ernest Hemingway*

The habit of common and continuous speech is a symptom of mental deficiency. — *Walter Bagehot*

Men of few words are the best men. — *William Shakespeare*

I have never been hurt by anything I didn't say. — *Calvin Coolidge*

THE HUMAN SPIRIT

Laugh and the world laughs with you,
snore and you sleep alone.

— ANTHONY BURGESS

Don't talk unless you can improve the silence.
— *Jorge Luis Borges*

It's good to shut up sometimes.
— *Marcel Marceau*

No one has a finer command of language
than the person who keeps his mouth shut.
— *Sam Rayburn*

Lord, give us the wisdom to utter words that
are gentle and tender, for tomorrow we may
have to eat them.   — *Morris K. Udall*

A loud voice cannot compete with a clear
voice, even if it's a whisper.
— *Barry Neil Kaufman*

One voice can enter ten ears, but ten voices
cannot enter one ear.   — *Leone Levi*

We have two ears and one tongue so that we
would listen more and talk less.   — *Diogenes*

When you talk, you repeat what you
already know; when you listen, you often
learn something.   — *Jared Sparks*

When you say yes, say it quickly. But always
take a half hour to say no, so you can understand the other fellow's side.
— *Francis Cardinal Spellman*

The only reward of virtue is virtue; the only
way to have a friend is to be one.
— *Ralph Waldo Emerson*

No man has the right to dictate what other
men should perceive, create or produce, but
all should be encouraged to reveal themselves, their perceptions and emotions, and
to build confidence in the creative spirit.
— *Ansel Adams*

Seek first to understand, then to
be understood.   — *Stephen Covey*

A slip of the foot you may soon recover, but
a slip of the tongue you may never get over.
— *Benjamin Franklin*

People will accept your ideas much more
readily if you tell them Benjamin Franklin
said it first.   — *David H. Comins*

Everything that irritates us about others can
lead us to an understanding of ourselves.
— *Carl Jung*

You can tell whether a man is clever by his
answers. You can tell whether a man is wise
by his questions.   — *Naguib Mahfouz*

Just when you think that a person is just
a backdrop for the rest of the universe,
watch them and see that they laugh, they
cry, they tell jokes . . . they're just friends
waiting to be made.   — *Jeffrey Borenstein*

A chief event of life is the day in which we
have encountered a mind that startled us.
— *Ralph Waldo Emerson*

We are here on earth to do good to others. What the others are here for, I don't know.

— *W. H. Auden*

Good manners will open doors that the best education cannot. — *Clarence Thomas*

Personality can open doors, but only character can keep them open.

— *Elmer G. Letterman*

Our character is what we do when we think no one is looking. — *H. Jackson Brown, Jr.*

Public behavior is merely private character writ large. — *Stephen Covey*

Don't reserve your best behavior for special occasions. You can't have two sets of manners, two social codes—one for those you admire and want to impress, another for those whom you consider unimportant. You must be the same to all people.

— *Lillian Eichler Watson*

Politeness and consideration for others is like investing pennies and getting dollars back.

— *Thomas Sowell*

The true secret of giving advice is, after you have honestly given it, to be perfectly indifferent whether it is taken or not, and never persist in trying to set people right.

— *Hannah Whitall Smith*

Tact is the knack of making a point without making an enemy. — *Isaac Newton*

I believe in an open mind, but not so open that your brains fall out.

— *Arthur Hays Sulzberger*

I love to be alone. I never found the companion that was so companionable as solitude. — *Henry David Thoreau*

No man is an island, entire of itself; every man is a piece of the continent.

— *John Donne*

Living apart and at peace with myself, I came to realize more vividly the meaning of the doctrine of acceptance. To refrain from giving advice, to refrain from meddling in the affairs of others, to refrain, even though the motives be the highest, from tampering with another's way of life— so simple, yet so difficult for an active spirit. Hands off! — *Henry Miller*

If your happiness depends on what somebody else does, I guess you do have a problem.

— *Richard Bach*

As experience widens, one begins to see how much upon a level all human things are.

— *Joseph Farrell*

As I grow older, I pay less attention to what men say. I just watch what they do.

— *Andrew Carnegie*

Tears shed for self are tears of weakness, but tears shed for others are a sign of strength.

— *Billy Graham*

 I have witnessed the softening of the hardest of hearts by a simple smile.

— GOLDIE HAWN

THE HUMAN SPIRIT

Minds are like parachutes; they work best when open. — *Thomas Dewar*

Too often we underestimate the power of a touch, a smile, a kind word, a listening ear, an honest compliment, or the smallest act of caring, all of which have the potential to turn a life around. — *Leo Buscaglia*

The bird a nest, the spider a web, man friendship. — *William Blake*

To be successful you have to be selfish, or else you never achieve. And once you get to your highest level, then you have to be unselfish. Stay reachable. Stay in touch. Don't isolate. — *Michael Jordan*

I am not in this world to live up to other people's expectations, nor do I feel that the world must live up to mine. — *Fritz Perls*

We judge ourselves by what we feel capable of doing, while others judge us by what we have already done. — *Henry Wadsworth Longfellow*

Beginning today, treat everyone you meet as if they were going to be dead by midnight. Extend them all the care, kindness and understanding you can muster. Your life will never be the same again. — *Og Mandino*

It is not rejection itself that people fear, it is the possible consequences of rejection. Preparing to accept those consequences and viewing rejection as a learning experience that will bring you closer to success, will not only help you to conquer the fear of rejection, but help you to appreciate rejection itself. — *Bo Bennett*

The best way to cheer yourself up is to try to cheer somebody else up. — *Mark Twain*

If you have only one smile in you, give it to the people you love. Don't be surly at home, then go out in the street and start grinning "Good morning" at total strangers. — *Maya Angelou*

Ask yourself: Have you been kind today? Make kindness your daily modus operandi and change your world. — *Annie Lennox*

We cannot hold a torch to light another's path without brightening our own. — *Ben Sweetland*

All of us, at certain moments of our lives, need to take advice and to receive help from other people. — *Alexis Carrel*

I was shy for several years in my early days in Hollywood until I figured out that no one really gave a damn if I was shy or not, and I got over my shyness. — *Lucille Ball*

It is far more impressive when others discover your good qualities without your help. — *Judith Martin*

Always hold your head up, but be careful to keep your nose at a friendly level. — *Max L. Forman*

One must have a good memory to be able to keep the promises one makes. — *Friedrich Nietzsche*

People with courage and character always seem sinister to the rest. — *Hermann Hesse*

I hope that people will finally come to realize that there is only one "race"—the human race—and that we are all members of it. — *Margaret Atwood*

People are unreasonable, illogical, and self-centered. Love them anyway. — *Mother Teresa*

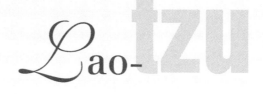

Lao-tzu

Wisdom of the Ages

According to legend, Lao-tzu was curator of the Chinese imperial archives in the 6th century B.C.

Steeped in such a wealth of history and philosophy, Lao-tzu became a wise man himself. Upon retiring, he left civilization. As he passed through a gate in the Great Wall, a border guard asked him to record what he had learned for posterity. Lao-tzu complied and authored a small book of concise and profound thoughts. These writings, now called the *Tao Te Ching,* advocate a passive, intuitive way of behavior—living in harmony with a cosmic unity that underlies everything.

While Lao-tzu is credited with being the founder of Taoism and one of the best known of the Chinese philosophers, scholars disagree as to whether he actually existed. Some theorize that his writings are a collection of teachings from a number of sources.

*

A journey of a thousand miles begins with a single step.

*

He who knows others is wise; he who knows himself is enlightened.

*

To have little is to possess. To have plenty is to be perplexed.

*

In the world there is nothing more submissive and weak than water.
Yet for attacking that which is hard and strong nothing can surpass it.

*

A good traveler has no fixed plans, and is not intent on arriving.

*

To realize that you do not understand is a virtue;
not to realize that you do not understand is a defect.

*

A leader is best when people barely know he exists.
When his work is done, his aim fulfilled, they will say, "We did it ourselves."

Chance and
Destiny

Fortune knocks but once, but misfortune has much more patience. — *Laurence J. Peter*

Life consists not in holding good cards but in playing those you hold well. — *Josh Billings*

The cards are ill shuffled till I have a good hand. — *Jonathan Swift*

Life is like a game of cards. The hand that is dealt you is determinism; the way you play it is free will. — *Jawaharlal Nehru*

In the field of observation, chance favors only the prepared mind. — *Louis Pasteur*

If you don't like something, change it. If you can't change it, change your attitude. Don't complain. — *Maya Angelou*

Make no little plans; they have no magic to stir men's blood. ... Make big plans, aim high in hope and work. — *Daniel H. Burnham*

Take a chance! All life is a chance. The man who goes furthest is generally the one who is willing to do and dare. — *Dale Carnegie*

Luck is what you have left over after you give 100 percent. — *Langston Coleman*

Luck? I don't know anything about luck. I've never banked on it and I'm afraid of people who do. Luck to me is something else: Hard work—and realizing what is opportunity and what isn't. — *Lucille Ball*

Chance is always powerful. Let your hook be always cast; in the pool where you least expect it, there will be a fish. — *Ovid*

The only sure thing about luck is that it will change. — *Bret Harte*

True luck consists not in holding the best of the cards at the table; luckiest is he who knows just when to rise and go home. — *John Hay*

Those who trust to chance must abide by the results of chance. — *Calvin Coolidge*

We must believe in luck. For how else can we explain the success of those we don't like? — *Jean Cocteau*

Luck is not something you can mention in the presence of self-made men. — *E. B. White*

Success is simply a matter of luck. Ask any failure. — *Earl Wilson*

We cannot direct the wind, but we can adjust the sails. — *Bertha Calloway*

We need to learn to set our course by the stars, not by the light of every passing ship. — *Omar N. Bradley*

I am not afraid of storms, for I am learning how to sail my ship. — *Louisa May Alcott*

Even if you're on the right track, you'll get run over if you just sit there. — *Will Rogers*

The Chinese use two brush strokes to write the word *crisis*. One brush stroke stands for danger; the other for opportunity. In a crisis, be aware of the danger—but recognize the opportunity. — *Richard M. Nixon*

THE HUMAN SPIRIT

When one door of happiness closes, another opens;
but often we look so long at the closed door that we
do not see the one which has opened for us.

— HELEN KELLER

Do not count your chickens before they are hatched.

— *Aesop*

The grass is not, in fact, always greener on the other side of the fence. Fences have nothing to do with it. The grass is greenest where it is watered. When crossing over fences, carry water with you and tend the grass wherever you may be.

— *Robert Fulghum*

To look backward for a while is to refresh the eye, to restore it, and to render it the more fit for its prime function of looking forward.

— *Margaret Fairless Barber*

The doors we open and close each day decide the lives we live. — *Flora Whittemore*

I have become my own version of an optimist. If I can't make it through one door, I'll go through another door—or I'll make a door. Something terrific will come no matter how dark the present. — *Joan Rivers*

I don't want to be a passenger in my own life.

— *Diane Ackerman*

No trumpets sound when the important decisions of our life are made. Destiny is made known silently. — *Agnes de Mille*

The important thing is this: to be able at any moment to sacrifice what we are for what we could become. — *Charles Du Bos*

The past is a source of knowledge, and the future is a source of hope. Love of the past implies faith in the future. — *Stephen Ambrose*

Destiny is not a matter of chance, it is a matter of choice; it is not a thing to be waited for, it is a thing to be achieved.

— *William Jennings Bryan*

If you don't run your own life, somebody else will. — *John Atkinson*

If you can find a path with no obstacles, it probably doesn't lead anywhere.

— *Frank A. Clark*

The 50-50-90 rule: Anytime you have a 50-50 chance of getting something right, there's a 90 percent probability you'll get it wrong.

— *Andy Rooney*

We have to believe in free will. We've got no choice. — *Isaac Bashevis Singer*

Of course the game is rigged. Don't let that stop you—if you don't play, you can't win.

— *Robert A. Heinlein*

In reality, serendipity accounts for one percent of the blessings we receive in life, work and love. The other 99 percent is due to our efforts. — *Peter McWilliams*

Shallow men believe in luck. Strong men believe in cause and effect.
— *Ralph Waldo Emerson*

Our problems are man-made, therefore they may be solved by man. And man can be as big as he wants. No problem of human destiny is beyond human beings.
— *John F. Kennedy*

Two roads diverged in a wood, and I—
I took the one less traveled by,
And that has made all the difference.
— *Robert Frost*

If you want a guarantee, buy a toaster.
— *Clint Eastwood*

Hope for the best. Expect the worst.
Life is a play. We're unrehearsed. — *Mel Brooks*

Expect the best. Prepare for the worst.
Capitalize on what comes. — *Zig Ziglar*

Nothing happens to anybody which he is not fitted by nature to bear.
— *Marcus Aurelius*

Ask many of us who are disabled what we would like in life and you would be surprised how few would say, "Not to be disabled." We accept our limitations.
— *Itzhak Perlman*

I have gained this by philosophy: that I do without being commanded what others do only from fear of the law. — *Aristotle*

The price of greatness is responsibility.
— *Winston Churchill*

Success on any major scale requires you to accept responsibility. ... In the final analysis, the one quality that all successful people have ... is the ability to take on responsibility. — *Michael Korda*

To be mature means to face, and not evade, every fresh crisis that comes. — *Fritz Kunkel*

He who is slowest in making a promise is most faithful in its performance.
— *Jean-Jacques Rousseau*

I am free, no matter what rules surround me. If I find them tolerable, I tolerate them; if I find them too obnoxious, I break them. I am free because I know that I alone am morally responsible for everything I do.
— *Robert A. Heinlein*

You are remembered for the rules you break. — *Douglas MacArthur*

Once a word has been allowed to escape, it cannot be recalled. — *Horace*

It is thrifty to prepare today for the wants of tomorrow. — *Aesop*

Men acquire a particular quality by constantly acting a particular way. ... You become just by performing just actions, temperate by performing temperate actions, brave by performing brave actions. — *Aristotle*

The oldest, shortest words—"yes" and "no"—are those which require the most thought. — *Pythagoras*

Do not wait for extraordinary circumstances to do good; try to use ordinary situations.
— *Jean Paul Richter*

THE HUMAN SPIRIT

Right and Wrong

Good judgment comes from experience, and experience comes from bad judgment.

— *Barry LePatner*

Real integrity is doing the right thing, knowing that nobody's going to know whether you did it or not.   — *Oprah Winfrey*

My soul refuses to be satisfied so long as it is a helpless witness of a single wrong or a single misery. But it is not possible for me, a weak, frail, miserable being, to mend every wrong or to hold myself free of blame for all the wrong I see.   — *Mahatma Gandhi*

In matters of style, swim with the current; in matters of principle, stand like a rock.

— *Thomas Jefferson*

Good sense about trivialities is better than nonsense about things that matter.

— *Max Beerbohm*

The character of every act depends upon the circumstances in which it is done.

— *Oliver Wendell Holmes, Jr.*

You should examine yourself daily. If you find faults, you should correct them. When you find none, you should try even harder.

— *Xi Zhi*

I would rather be the man who bought the Brooklyn Bridge than the man who sold it.

— *Will Rogers*

I firmly believe that the Gandhian philosophy of nonviolent resistance is the only logical and moral approach to the solution of the race problem in the United States.   — *Martin Luther King, Jr.*

It is happier to be sometimes cheated than not to trust.   — *Samuel Johnson*

Common sense is the knack of seeing things as they are, and doing things as they ought to be done.   — *Josh Billings*

The time is always right to do what is right.

— *Martin Luther King, Jr.*

A thought which does not result in an action is nothing much, and an action which does not proceed from a thought is nothing at all.   — *Georges Bernanos*

To have a right to do a thing is not at all the same as to be right in doing it.

— *G. K. Chesterton*

Do what you feel in your heart to be right—for you'll be criticized anyway. You'll be damned if you do, and damned if you don't.

— ELEANOR ROOSEVELT

There can be no happiness if the things we believe in are different from the things we do.
— *Freya Stark*

The only correct actions are those that demand no explanation and no apology.
— *Red Auerbach*

Chase after truth like hell and you'll free yourself, even though you never touch its coat-tails.
— *Clarence Darrow*

By the time a man realizes that maybe his father was right, he usually has a son who thinks he's wrong.
— *Charles Wadsworth*

There are few nudities so objectionable as the naked truth.
— *Agnes Repplier*

When I tell the truth, it is not for the sake of convincing those who do not know it, but for the sake of defending those that do.
— *William Blake*

If there's any message to my work, it is ultimately that it's okay to be different, that it's good to be different, that we should question ourselves before we pass judgment on someone who looks different, behaves different, talks different, is a different color.
— *Johnny Depp*

Every minute you are thinking of evil, you might have been thinking of good instead. Refuse to pander to a morbid interest in your own misdeeds. Pick yourself up, be sorry, shake yourself, and go on again.
— *Evelyn Underhill*

Don't ever become a pessimist. . . . A pessimist is correct oftener than an optimist, but an optimist has more fun, and neither can stop the march of events.
— *Robert A. Heinlein*

Never let your sense of morals prevent you from doing what's right.
— *Isaac Asimov*

Like an unchecked cancer,
hate corrodes the personality
and eats away its vital unity.
Hate destroys a man's sense of values
and his objectivity. It causes him to describe
the beautiful as ugly and the ugly as beautiful,
and to confuse the true with the false
and the false with the true.

— MARTIN LUTHER KING, JR.

The **Pleasures** of Living

*Here's a selection of quotes designed to be absorbed lying down
or at least while comfortably reclined—we had a sofa, easy
chair, or hammock in mind, but the choice is up to you.*

Food and Drink

My favorite animal is steak. — *Fran Lebowitz*

Talk of joy: there may be things better than beef stew and baked potatoes and homemade bread—there may be.
— *David Grayson*

I would like to find a stew that will give me heartburn immediately, instead of at three o'clock in the morning. — *John Barrymore*

I want to keep fighting because it is the only thing that keeps me out of the hamburger joints. If I don't fight, I'll eat this planet.
— *George Foreman*

A hot dog at the ballpark is better than steak at the Ritz. — *Humphrey Bogart*

Red meat is *not* bad for you. Now, blue-green meat, *that's* bad for you!
— *Tommy Smothers*

I'm not a vegetarian because I love animals. I'm a vegetarian because I hate plants.
— *A. Whitney Brown*

I know vegetarians don't like to hear this, but God made an awful lot of land that's good for nothing but grazing.
— *Molly Ivins*

I was a vegetarian until I started leaning toward the sunlight. — *Rita Rudner*

Vegetarians are cool. All I eat are vegetarians —except for the occasional mountain lion steak. — *Ted Nugent*

If slaughterhouses had glass walls, everyone would be a vegetarian. — *Paul McCartney*

Life expectancy would grow by leaps and bounds if green vegetables smelled as good as bacon. — *Doug Larson*

Acorns were good until bread was found.
— *Francis Bacon*

Cheese—milk's leap toward immortality.
— *Clifton Fadiman*

What happens to the hole when the cheese is gone? — *Bertolt Brecht*

Fish is the only food that is considered spoiled once it smells like what it is.
— *P. J. O'Rourke*

He was a bold man that first ate an oyster.
— *Jonathan Swift*

"Escargot" is French for "fat crawling bag of phlegm." — *Dave Barry*

I owe it all to little chocolate doughnuts.
— *John Belushi*

Krispy Kreme Doughnuts, everybody loves them. But I thought this was interesting on the box: "Konsult Kardiologist."
— *David Letterman*

The second day of a diet is always easier than the first. By the second day you're off it.
— *Jackie Gleason*

I've been on a diet for two weeks and all I've lost is two weeks. — *Totie Fields*

I feel about airplanes the way I feel about diets. It seems to me they are wonderful things for other people to go on.
— *Jean Kerr*

THE PLEASURES OF LIVING

I was an equal opportunity eater.
Every ethnic group got a shot. — *Bill Clinton*

When we win, I'm so happy I eat a lot.
When we lose, I'm so depressed, I eat a lot.
When we're rained out, I'm so disappointed
I eat a lot. — *Tommy Lasorda*

I haven't trusted polls since I read that
62 percent of women had affairs during
their lunch hour. I've never met a woman in
my life who would give up lunch for sex.
— *Erma Bombeck*

A gourmet who thinks of calories is like a
tart who looks at her watch. — *James Beard*

I was 32 when I started cooking;
up until then, I just ate. — *Julia Child*

I'm at the age where food has taken the
place of sex in my life. In fact, I've just had a
mirror put over my kitchen table.
— *Jackie Gleason*

Last night I dreamed I ate a ten-pound
marshmallow, and when I woke up the pillow
was gone. — *Tommy Cooper*

All the fat guys watch me and say to their
wives, "See, there's a fat guy doing okay.
Bring me another beer." — *Mickey Lolich*

Thin people are beautiful, but fat people
are adorable. — *Jackie Gleason*

My mother was a good recreational cook,
but what she basically believed about
cooking was that if you worked hard
and prospered, someone else would do it
for you. — *Nora Ephron*

The most remarkable thing about my mother
is that for thirty years she served the family
nothing but leftovers. The original meal has
never been found. — *Calvin Trillin*

I no longer prepare food or drink with more
than one ingredient. — *Cyra McFadden*

I don't even butter my bread. I consider
that cooking. — *Katherine Cebrian*

My wife and I tried two or three times in
the last 40 years to have breakfast together,
but it was so disagreeable we had to stop.
— *Winston Churchill*

It's fun to get together and have something
good to eat at least once a day. That's what
human life is all about—enjoying things.
— *Julia Child*

Smell brings to mind . . . a family dinner
of pot roast and sweet potatoes during
a myrtle-mad August in a Midwestern
town. Smells detonate softly in our
memory like poignant land mines hidden
under the weedy mass of years.
— *Diane Ackerman*

My doctor told me to stop
having intimate dinners for four.
Unless there are three other people.

— ORSON WELLES

Eat breakfast like a king, lunch like a prince, and dinner like a pauper. — *Adelle Davis*

At a dinner party one should eat wisely but not too well, and talk well but not too wisely. — *W. Somerset Maugham*

The only man who is really free is the one who can turn down an invitation to dinner without giving an excuse. — *Jules Renard*

At a formal dinner party, the person nearest death should always be seated closest to the bathroom. — *George Carlin*

A crust eaten in peace is better than a banquet partaken in anxiety. — *Aesop*

A banquet is probably the most fatiguing thing in the world except ditchdigging. — *Mark Twain*

I abhor averages. I like the individual case. A man may have six meals one day and none the next, making an average of three meals per day, but that is not a good way to live. — *Louis D. Brandeis*

I come from a family where gravy is considered a beverage. — *Erma Bombeck*

I cook with wine—sometimes I even add it to the food. — *W. C. Fields*

Champagne for my real friends and real pain for my sham friends. — *Tom Waits*

Can't we just get rid of wine lists? Do we really have to be reminded every time we go out to a nice restaurant that we have no idea what we are doing? Why don't they just give us a trigonometry quiz with the menu? — *Jerry Seinfeld*

Great people talk about ideas, average people talk about things, and small people talk about wine. — *Fran Lebowitz*

Wine is a treacherous friend who you must always be on guard for. — *Christian Nestell Bovee*

Water is the only drink for a wise man. — *Henry David Thoreau*

One reason I don't drink is that I want to know when I am having a good time. — *Nancy Astor*

American consumers have no problem with carcinogens, but they will not purchase any product, including floor wax, that has fat in it. — *Dave Barry*

Do not bite at the bait of pleasure till you know there is no hook beneath it. — *Thomas Jefferson*

If it weren't for Philo T. Farnsworth, inventor of television, we'd still be eating frozen radio dinners. — *Johnny Carson*

Tell me what you eat, and I will tell you what you are. — *Anthelme Brillat-Savarin*

Cockroaches and socialites are the only things that can stay up all night and eat anything. — *Herb Caen*

You better cut the pizza in four pieces because I'm not hungry enough to eat six. — *Yogi Berra*

Tomatoes and oregano make it Italian; wine and tarragon make it French. Sour cream makes it Russian; lemon and cinnamon make it Greek. Soy sauce makes it Chinese; garlic makes it good. — *Alice May Brock*

Principles have no real force except when one is well-fed. — *Mark Twain*

Everyday happiness means getting up in the morning, and you can't wait to finish your breakfast. You can't wait to do your exercises. You can't wait to put on your clothes. You can't wait to get out—and you can't wait to come home, because the soup is hot. — *George Burns*

Not all chemicals are bad. Without chemicals such as hydrogen and oxygen, for example, there would be no way to make water, a vital ingredient in beer. — *Dave Barry*

If more of us valued food and cheer and song above hoarded gold, it would be a merrier world. — *J.R.R. Tolkien*

The weather here is gorgeous. It's mild and feels like it's in the eighties. The hot dog vendors got confused because of the weather and thought it was spring, so they accidentally changed the hot dog water in their carts. — *David Letterman*

I believe that if ever I had to practice cannibalism, I might manage if there were enough tarragon around. — *James Beard*

***

Reading and Writing

Man is what he reads. — *Joseph Brodsky*

Always read stuff that will make you look good if you die in the middle of it. — *P. J. O'Rourke*

Reading is to the mind what exercise is to the body. — *Joseph Addison*

A classic is something that everybody wants to have read and nobody wants to read. — *Mark Twain*

Wear the old coat and buy the new book. — *Austin Phelps*

Just the knowledge that a good book is awaiting one at the end of a long day makes that day happier. — *Kathleen Norris*

I am not a speed reader.
I am a speed understander. — *Isaac Asimov*

There are books of which the backs and covers are by far the best parts. — *Charles Dickens*

The man who does not read good books has no advantage over the man who cannot read them. — *Mark Twain*

Readers are plentiful: thinkers are rare. — *Anthony Burgess*

Dorothy Parker

A Slashing Wit

Dorothy Parker used her wit like a whip. She entered professional life as a writer for New York City magazines, such as *Vogue, Vanity Fair,* and *The New Yorker.* There she rubbed shoulders with other famous scribes of the early 20th century and became one of the founders of the literary Algonquin Round Table.

A writer of criticism, poetry, short stories, and screenplays, Parker became one of the most-quoted people of her time—particularly famous for her cynicism, her stinging humor, and a fixation with death.

Parker's was not always a happy life. As a child, she had difficult relationships with her father and stepmother, and she struggled throughout adulthood with alcohol and depression. Despite four suicide attempts, she lived to age 73, when she died of a heart attack in 1967.

*

If you want to know what God thinks of money, just look at the people he gave it to.

*

That woman speaks eighteen languages, and can't say no in any of them.

*

This is not a novel to be tossed aside lightly. It should be thrown with great force.

*

The only ism Hollywood believes in is plagiarism.

*

Women and elephants never forget.

*

I'd rather have a bottle in front of me, than a frontal lobotomy.

*

Razors pain you
Rivers are damp
Acids stain you
And drugs cause cramp.
Guns aren't lawful
Nooses give
Gas smells awful
You might as well live.

Reading without reflecting is like eating without digesting. — *Edmund Burke*

Books think for me. — *Charles Lamb*

An intellectual is a man who takes more words than necessary to tell more than he knows. — *Dwight D. Eisenhower*

An intellectual is a person who has discovered something more interesting than sex. — *Aldous Huxley*

Hold a book in your hand and you're a pilgrim at the gates of a new city. — *Anne Michaels*

There is no mistaking a real book when one meets it. It is like falling in love. — *Christopher Morley*

Reading is like the sex act—done privately, and often in bed. — *Daniel J. Boorstin*

All good books have one thing in common—they are truer than if they had really happened. — *Ernest Hemingway*

The test of literature is, I suppose, whether we ourselves live more intensely for the reading of it. — *Elizabeth Drew*

Never judge a book by its movie. — *J. W. Egan*

Having your book turned into a movie is like seeing your oxen turned into bouillon cubes. — *John le Carré*

Lists of books we reread and books we can't finish tell more about us than about the relative worth of the books themselves. — *Russell Banks*

I read part of it all the way through. — *Samuel Goldwyn*

Books ... are like lobster shells, we surround ourselves with 'em, then we grow out of 'em and leave 'em behind, as evidence of our earlier stages of development. — *Dorothy L. Sayers*

A book is a version of the world. If you do not like it, ignore it; or offer your own version in return. — *Salman Rushdie*

A book is not only a friend, it makes friends for you. When you have possessed a book with mind and spirit, you are enriched. But when you pass it on you are enriched threefold. — *Henry Miller*

Books are not made for furniture, but there is nothing else that so beautifully furnishes a house. — *Henry Ward Beecher*

Don't join the book burners. Don't think you're going to conceal faults by concealing evidence that they ever existed. Don't be afraid to go in your library and read every book. — *Dwight D. Eisenhower*

He who kills a man kills a reasonable creature, but he who destroys a good book kills reason itself. — *John Milton*

In relation to a writer, most readers believe in the Double Standard: they may be unfaithful to him as often as they like, but he must never, never be unfaithful to them. — *W. H. Auden*

If you don't have the time to read, you don't have the time or the tools to write. — *Stephen King*

This is the sixth book I've written, which isn't bad for a guy who's only read two. — *George Burns*

THE PLEASURES OF LIVING

There are three rules for writing a novel. Unfortunately, no one knows what they are.

— *W. Somerset Maugham*

In the case of good books, the point is not to see how many of them you can get through, but how many can get through to you.

— *Mortimer J. Adler*

My stories run up and bite me on the leg— I respond by writing down everything that goes on during the bite. When I finish, the idea lets go and runs off.   — *Ray Bradbury*

Write something to suit yourself and many people will like it; write something to suit everybody and scarcely anyone will care for it.   — *Jesse Stuart*

Some editors are failed writers, but so are most writers.   — *T. S. Eliot*

A good many young writers make the mistake of enclosing a stamped, self-addressed envelope, big enough for the manuscript to come back in. This is too much of a temptation to the editor.

— *Ring Lardner*

Journal writing is a voyage to the interior.

— *Christina Baldwin*

Vigorous writing is concise.

— *William Strunk, Jr.*

There's a great power in words, if you don't hitch too many of them together.

— *Josh Billings*

Simply stated, it is sagacious to eschew obfuscation.   — *Norman R. Augustine*

Pithy sentences are like sharp nails which force truth upon our memory.

— *Denis Diderot*

I consider looseness with words no less of a defect than looseness of the bowels.

— *John Calvin*

When something can be read without effort, great effort has gone into its writing.

— *Enrique Jardiel Poncela*

An intellectual is a man who says a simple thing in a difficult way; an artist is a man who says a difficult thing in a simple way.

— *Charles Bukowski*

Grammar is a piano I play by ear. All I know about grammar is its power.

—*Joan Didion*

You can be a little ungrammatical if you come from the right part of the country.

— *Robert Frost*

Remember: "Y'all" is singular. "All y'all" is plural. "All y'all's" is plural possessive.

— *Kinky Friedman*

When you catch an adjective, kill it. No, I don't mean utterly, but kill most of them— then the rest will be valuable. They weaken when they are close together. They give strength when they are wide apart.   — *Mark Twain*

The adjective is the banana peel of the parts of speech.   — *Clifton Fadiman*

From now on, ending a sentence with a preposition is something up with which I will not put.   — *Winston Churchill*

A synonym is a word you use when you can't spell the word you first thought of.

— *Burt Bacharach*

What's another word for thesaurus?

— *Steven Wright*

Words ought to be a little wild, for they are the assaults of thought on the unthinking.

— *John Maynard Keynes*

Think like a wise man but communicate in the language of the people.

— *William Butler Yeats*

Planning to write is not writing. Outlining, researching, talking to people about what you're doing, none of that is writing. Writing is writing.

— *E. L. Doctorow*

The free-lance writer is a man who is paid per piece or per word or perhaps.

— *Robert Benchley*

If I feel physically as if the top of my head were taken off, I know that is poetry.

— EMILY DICKINSON

I talk to my typewriter and that is what I've been working on for 40 years—how to write for talking.

— *Alistair Cooke*

Love. Fall in love and stay in love. Write only what you love, and love what you write. The key word is love. You have to get up in the morning and write something you love, something to live for.

— *Ray Bradbury*

Every journalist has a novel in him, which is an excellent place for it.

— *Russell Lynes*

Any writer, I suppose, feels that the world into which he was born is nothing less than a conspiracy against the cultivation of his talent.

— *James Baldwin*

If I don't write to empty my mind, I go mad.

— *Lord Byron*

Every book has an intrinsic impossibility, which its writer discovers as soon as his first excitement dwindles.

— *Annie Dillard*

If writers were good businessmen, they'd have too much sense to be writers.

— *Irvin S. Cobb*

I say there're no depressed words, just depressed minds.

— *Bob Dylan*

I can't understand why a person will take a year to write a novel when he can easily buy one for a few dollars.

— *Fred Allen*

You have to know how to accept rejection and reject acceptance.

— *Ray Bradbury*

Writing is not necessarily something to be ashamed of, but do it in private and wash your hands afterwards.

— *Robert A. Heinlein*

For most of history, Anonymous was a woman.

— *Virginia Woolf*

The only reason for being a professional writer is that you can't help it.

— *Leo Rosten*

A critic at best is a waiter at the great table of literature.

— *Louis Dudek*

It's a strange world of language in which skating on thin ice can get you into hot water.
— *Franklin P. Jones*

A good writer is not, per se, a good book critic. No more so than a good drunk is automatically a good bartender.
— *Jim Bishop*

If you can't annoy somebody, there's little point in writing.
— *Kingsley Amis*

What I like in a good author is not what he says but what he whispers.
— *Logan Pearsall Smith*

The ideas I stand for are not mine. I borrowed them from Socrates. I swiped them from Chesterfield. I stole them from Jesus. And I put them in a book. If you don't like their rules, whose would you use?
— *Dale Carnegie*

The skill of writing is to create a context in which other people can think.
— *Edwin Schlossberg*

The reason why so few good books are written is that so few people who can write know anything.
— *Walter Bagehot*

You never have to change anything you got up in the middle of the night to write.
— *Saul Bellow*

Literature is news that stays news.
— *Ezra Pound*

The telephone book is full of facts, but it doesn't contain a single idea.
— *Mortimer J. Adler*

A best-seller was a book which somehow sold well because it was selling well.
— *Daniel J. Boorstin*

"The Ancient Mariner" would not have taken so well if it had been called "The Old Sailor."
— *Samuel Butler*

A good title is the title of a successful book.
— *Raymond Chandler*

The difference between fiction and reality is that fiction has to make sense.
— *Tom Clancy*

Better to write for yourself and have no public, than to write for the public and have no self.
— *Cyril Connolly*

Novelists do not write as birds sing, by the push of nature. It is part of the job that there should be much routine and some daily stuff on the level of carpentry.
— *William Golding*

It was a dark and stormy night....
— *Edward Bulwer-Lytton*

A good novel tells us the truth about its hero; but a bad novel tells us the truth about its author.
— *G. K. Chesterton*

A really good detective never gets married.
— *Raymond Chandler*

I handed in a script last year and the studio didn't change one word. The word they didn't change was on page 87.
— *Steve Martin*

A word is not a crystal, transparent and unchanging, it is the skin of a living thought and may vary greatly in color and content according to the circumstances and time in which it is used.
— *Oliver Wendell Holmes, Jr.*

Always and *never* are two words you should always remember never to use.
— *Wendell Johnson*

Mark Twain

Father of Tom and Huck

He sifted through the American landscape and handed us back verbal nuggets of pure gold.

Samuel Clemens spent his early teen years in Hannibal, Missouri, operating a country newspaper with two brothers. He yearned for wider experience, however, and by age 18 his wanderlust held sway. He became a riverboat pilot and plied that trade for a few years, learning every bend and turn of the Mississippi River. The Civil War ended that career, and Sam drifted to the West, where he split his time between prospecting and journalism. Using the pseudonym Mark Twain—a river-piloting term—Sam eventually gained a nationwide reputation as a humorist.

Clemens put down stakes in New York State and Connecticut. In the 1870s and 1880s, he produced such classic books as *Tom Sawyer, The Prince and the Pauper, Huckleberry Finn,* and *A Connecticut Yankee in King Arthur's Court.* He became the center of a literary universe, and visiting foreign dignitaries made a point of stopping at his home. Despite such success, he struggled with personal woes—including the death of a daughter and disastrous investments—and his later works became increasingly bitter.

He spent much of the 1890s living in Europe and, with his financial problems finally set aright, he died in Connecticut in 1910. He remains one of America's most-quoted writers.

By trying we can easily learn to endure adversity—another man's, I mean.

Cold! If the thermometer had been an inch longer we'd all have frozen to death.

*It is curious—curious that physical courage should be so common in the world,
and moral courage so rare.*

*If you pick up a starving dog and make him prosperous, he will not bite you.
This is the principal difference between a dog and a man.*

*Figures often beguile me, particularly when I have the arranging of them myself;
in which case the remark attributed to Disraeli would often apply with justice
and force: "There are three kinds of lies: lies, damned lies and statistics."*

*An Englishman is a person who does things because they have been done before.
An American is a person who does things because they haven't been done before.*

I don't give a damn for a man that can only spell a word one way.

*The difference between the almost right word and the right word is really
a large matter—it's the difference between the lightning bug and the lightning.*

Ignorance of other writers' work keeps me from discouragement, and I am less well-read than the average bus driver.   — *Garrison Keillor*

The cure for writer's cramp is writer's block.
— *Inigo DeLeon*

Writing fiction, there are no limits to what you write as long as it increases the value of the paper you are writing on.
— *Buddy Ebsen*

I write to discover what I think. After all, the bars aren't open that early.
— *Daniel J. Boorstin*

The reader deserves an honest opinion. If he doesn't deserve it, give it to him anyhow.
— *John Ciardi*

Everywhere I go I find a poet has been there before me.   — *Sigmund Freud*

Chicago sounds rough to the maker of verse. One comfort we have—Cincinnati sounds worse.   — *Oliver Wendell Holmes*

A poem begins in delight and ends in wisdom.   — *Robert Frost*

You don't have to suffer to be a poet; adolescence is enough suffering for anyone.
— *John Ciardi*

A poem is never finished, only abandoned.
— *Paul Valéry*

A poet who reads his verse in public may have other nasty habits.   — *Robert A. Heinlein*

Publishing a volume of verse is like dropping a rose petal down the Grand Canyon and waiting for the echo.   — *Don Marquis*

I gave up on new poetry myself thirty years ago, when most of it began to read like coded messages passing between lonely aliens on a hostile world.
— *Russell Baker*

Always be a poet, even in prose.
— *Charles Baudelaire*

I've read some of your modern free verse and wonder who set it free.
— *John Barrymore*

Writers will happen in the best of families.
— *Rita Mae Brown*

All the king's horses and all the king's men? Are you kidding me? No wonder they couldn't put Humpty together again. Just what did those idiots expect the horses to do, anyway?

— JERRY SEINFELD

THE PLEASURES OF LIVING

Humor

Humor is just another defense against the universe.
— *Mel Brooks*

Laughter is inner jogging. — *Norman Cousins*

Nobody ever died of laughter.
— *Max Beerbohm*

If I had no sense of humor, I should long ago have committed suicide.
— *Mahatma Gandhi*

Humor can be dissected, as a frog can, but the thing dies in the process. — *E. B. White*

Defining and analyzing humor is a pastime of humorless people. — *Robert Benchley*

Look for the ridiculous in everything and you will find it. — *Jules Renard*

I think it's the duty of the comedian to find out where the line is drawn and cross it deliberately. — *George Carlin*

Humor is also a way of saying something serious. — *T. S. Eliot*

When a thing is funny, search it carefully for a hidden truth. — *George Bernard Shaw*

You cannot be mad at somebody who makes you laugh—it's as simple as that.
— *Jay Leno*

I'm nuts and I know it. But so long as I make 'em laugh, they ain't going to lock me up.
— *Red Skelton*

Humor is perhaps a sense of intellectual perspective: an awareness that some things are really important, others not; and that the two kinds are most oddly jumbled in everyday affairs. — *Christopher Morley*

A caricature is putting the face of a joke on the body of a truth. — *Joseph Conrad*

I'm not offended by all the dumb blonde jokes, because I know I'm not dumb . . . and I also know that I'm not blonde.
— *Dolly Parton*

Wit is educated insolence. — *Aristotle*

Hanging is too good for a man who makes puns; he should be drawn and quoted.
— *Fred Allen*

Mark my words, when a society has to resort to the lavatory for its humor, the writing is on the wall. — *Alan Bennett*

It is the ability to take a joke, not make one, that proves you have a sense of humor.
— *Max Eastman*

Men show their characters in nothing more clearly than in what they think laughable.
— *Johann von Goethe*

Wit ought to be a glorious treat like caviar; never spread it about like marmalade.
— *Noël Coward*

Comedy is tragedy plus time. — *Carol Burnett*

Humor is a rubber sword—it allows you to make a point without drawing blood.
— *Mary Hirsch*

A person without a sense of humor is like a wagon without springs. It's jolted by every pebble on the road. — *Henry Ward Beecher*

Woody Allen

Multitalented Funnyman

Intellectual filmmaking, you might think, would be a longer and more tedious process. But no, Woody Allen is as prolific as they come.

Born in Brooklyn in 1935, he got an early start at humor writing, selling one-liners to newspaper columnists when he was just 15. His college career was a flop, but at a young age he was regarded as a gifted comedian, writing scripts for such TV programs as *The Ed Sullivan Show* and *The Tonight Show*.

After a stint as a stand-up comedian, he broke into the film business as the scriptwriter for *What's New, Pussycat?*, which starred Peter Sellers and Peter O'Toole. When he began directing, his early films (*Take the Money and Run* and *Sleeper,* for instance) relied heavily on slapstick, but his comedies took a more highbrow turn with *Annie Hall*. With *Interiors,* he also proved he could deliver a thoughtful drama.

The multitalented director (he's also a musician and a playwright) has been producing films at the rate of almost one per year since 1969. He often casts himself in his movies, typically playing a neurotic New Yorker who is a somewhat successful writer, director, or producer. He may draw a galaxy of stars into his films—the likes of Alan Alda, Judy Davis, Diane Keaton, Michael Caine, John Cusack, Helen Hunt, and scores more—but the actors are always sharing the limelight with Allen's obsessions: New York City and European-style cinema, and his witty and insightful dialogue.

Eighty percent of success is showing up.

*

It seemed the world was divided into good and bad people.
The good ones slept better ... while the bad ones seemed to enjoy
the waking hours much more.

*

I don't want to achieve immortality through my work.
I want to achieve it through not dying.

*

I took a speed-reading course and read War and Peace in twenty minutes.
It involves Russia.

*

If you're not failing every now and again,
it's a sign you're not doing anything very innovative.

*

Love is the answer, but while you're waiting for the answer,
sex raises some pretty interesting questions.

*

Time is nature's way of keeping everything from happening at once.

*

94.5% of all statistics are made up.

I'm a classic example of all humorists—only funny when I'm working. — *Peter Sellers*

Our comedies are not to be laughed at. — *Samuel Goldwyn*

When someone who is known for being comedic does something straight, it's always "a big breakthrough" or a "radical departure." Why is it no one ever says that if a straight actor does comedy? Are they presuming comedy is easier? — *Carol Burnett*

A sense of humor is just common sense, dancing. — *Clive James*

That is the saving grace of humor—if you fail no one is laughing at you. — *A. Whitney Brown*

A little nonsense now and then, is cherished by the wisest men. — *Roald Dahl*

Ahhh. A man with a sharp wit. Someone ought to take it away from him before he cuts himself. — *Peter da Silva*

Tragedy is when I cut my finger. Comedy is when you fall into an open sewer and die. — *Mel Brooks*

***

Movies

The length of a film should be directly related to the endurance of the human bladder. — *Alfred Hitchcock*

Pictures are for entertainment, messages should be delivered by Western Union. — *Samuel Goldwyn*

There are some movies that I would like to forget, for the rest of my life. But even those movies teach me things. — *Antonio Banderas*

A wide screen just makes a bad film twice as bad. — *Samuel Goldwyn*

An actress can only play a woman. I'm an actor, I can play anything. — *Whoopi Goldberg*

We have our factory, which is called a stage. We make a product, we color it, we title it and we ship it out in cans. — *Cary Grant*

I think most of the people involved in any art always secretly wonder whether they are really there because they're good or there because they're lucky. — *Katharine Hepburn*

Disney has the best casting. If he doesn't like an actor he just tears him up. — *Alfred Hitchcock*

A James Cagney love scene is one where he lets the other guy live. — *Bob Hope*

If my films make one more person miserable, I'll feel I have done my job. — *Woody Allen*

Acting is the most minor of gifts and not a very high-class way to earn a living. After all, Shirley Temple could do it at the age of four.

— *Katharine Hepburn*

I went into the business for the money, and the art grew out of it. If people are disillusioned by that remark, I can't help it. It's the truth.

— *Charlie Chaplin*

Perhaps it sounds ridiculous, but the best thing that young filmmakers should do is to get hold of a camera and some film and make a movie of any kind at all.

— *Stanley Kubrick*

Anybody can direct, but there are only eleven good writers.

— *Mel Brooks*

Film is one of the three universal languages, the other two: mathematics and music.

— *Frank Capra*

All art is autobiographical. The pearl is the oyster's autobiography.

— *Federico Fellini*

A director once said to me, "I was an actor once, but I didn't like it. It took so much concentration, a fire could break out in the audience when I was onstage and I wouldn't notice it," and I said, "That's why you're a director." As an actor, you're going to be aware of it. You use everything. If a fire breaks out, that feeds you.

— *Robert Duvall*

* * *

Television

Television—a medium. So called because it is neither rare nor well done.

— *Ernie Kovacs*

I find television very educating. Every time somebody turns on the set, I go into the other room and read a book.

— *Groucho Marx*

Television is more interesting than people. If it were not, we would have people standing in the corners of our rooms.

— *Alan Corenk*

Television enables you to be entertained in your home by people you wouldn't have in your home.

— *David Frost*

In California, they don't throw their garbage away—they make it into TV shows.

— *Woody Allen*

Seeing a murder on television ... can help work off one's antagonisms. And if you haven't any antagonisms, the commercials will give you some.

— *Alfred Hitchcock*

Imitation is the sincerest form of television.

— *Fred Allen*

A TV licence is a licence to print money.

— *Roy Thomson*

It is difficult to produce a television documentary that is both incisive and probing when every twelve minutes one is interrupted by twelve dancing rabbits singing about toilet paper.

— *Rod Serling*

Said in the Cinema

Great movie lines—some serious, some ironic, and some funny or even silly—are a telling transcription of our civilization. Here are a few particularly memorable ones. Lights, camera, action!

I've wrestled with reality for 35 years, Doctor, and I'm happy to state I finally won out over it.

⤳ ELWOOD P. DOWD (Jimmy Stewart) in *Harvey*

So this is how liberty dies. With thunderous applause.

⤳ SEN. PADMÉ AMIDALA (Natalie Portman) in *Star Wars: Episode III—Revenge of the Sith*

Do you spend time with your family? Good. Because a man that doesn't spend time with his family can never be a real man.

⤳ DON CORLEONE (Marlon Brando) in *The Godfather*

I want you to get up right now, sit up, go to your windows, open them and stick your head out and yell, "I'm as mad as hell and I'm not going to take this anymore!"

⤳ HOWARD BEALE (Peter Finch) in *Network*

You can't handle the truth!

⤳ COL. NATHAN R. JESSEP (Jack Nicholson) in *A Few Good Men*

I shall always be a common flower girl to Professor Higgins, because he always treats me like a common flower girl, and always will. But I know that I shall always be a lady to Colonel Pickering, because he always treats me like a lady, and always will.

⤳ ELIZA DOOLITTLE (Audrey Hepburn) in *My Fair Lady*

*Momma always said life was like a box of chocolates.
You never know what you're gonna get.*

➤ FORREST GUMP (Tom Hanks) in *Forrest Gump*

*You don't understand. I coulda had class. I coulda been a
contender. I could've been somebody, instead of a bum,
which is what I am, let's face it.*

➤ TERRY MALLOY (Marlon Brando)
in *On the Waterfront*

*If I ever go looking for my heart's desire again, I won't look
any further than my own backyard. Because if it isn't there,
I never really lost it to begin with!*

➤ DOROTHY GALE (Judy Garland)
in *The Wizard of Oz*

*I want to say one word to you. Just one word. ...
Are you listening? ... Plastics.*

➤ MR. MCGUIRE (Walter Brooke) in *The Graduate*

They're not gonna catch us. We're on a mission from God.

➤ ELWOOD BLUES (Dan Aykroyd)
in *The Blues Brothers*

*Where I'm going, you can't follow. What I've got to do, you
can't be any part of. Ilsa, I'm no good at being noble, but it
doesn't take much to see that the problems of three little
people don't amount to a hill of beans in this crazy world.
Someday you'll understand that. Now, now ... Here's looking
at you, kid.*

➤ RICK BLAINE (Humphrey Bogart)
in *Casablanca*

*Don't you think that everyone looks back on their childhood
with a certain amount of bitterness and regret? It doesn't
have to ruin your life!*

➤ ETHEL THAYER (Katharine Hepburn)
in *On Golden Pond*

*None of you ever knew George Gipp. He was long before your
time, but you all know what a tradition he is at Notre Dame.
And the last thing he said to me, "Rock," he said, "sometime
when the team is up against it and the breaks are beating the
boys, tell them to go out there with all they've got and win just
one for the Gipper. I don't know where I'll be then, Rock," he
said, "but I'll know about it and I'll be happy."*

➤ KNUTE ROCKNE (Pat O'Brien)
in *Knute Rockne All American*

Remember, George: No man is a failure who has friends.

         CLARENCE (Henry Travers) in *It's a Wonderful Life*

The trouble with kids is they always figure they're smarter than their parents—never stop to think if their old man could get by for 50 years and feed 'em and clothe 'em—he maybe had something up here to get by with—things that seem like brain twisters to you might be very simple for him.

         CONSTABLE KOCKENLOCKER (William Demarest)
         in *The Miracle of Morgan's Creek*

You risk your skin catching killers and the juries turn them loose so they can come back and shoot at you again. If you're honest you're poor your whole life, and in the end you wind up dying all alone on some dirty street. For what? For nothing. For a tin star.

         MARTIN HOWE (Lon Chaney, Jr.) in *High Noon*

Coal mining may be your life, but it's not mine. I'm never going down there again. I wanna go into space.

         HOMER HICKAM (Jake Gyllenhaal) in *October Sky*

For the past 50 years or so I've been getting more and more worried about Christmas. Seems we're all so busy trying to beat the other fellow in making things go faster and look shinier and cost less that Christmas and I are sort of getting lost in the shuffle.

         KRIS KRINGLE (Edmund Gwenn)
         in *Miracle on 34th Street*

I could never answer to a whistle. Whistles are for dogs and cats and other animals, but not for children and definitely not for me. It would be too ... humiliating.

         MARIA VON TRAPP (Julie Andrews)
         in *The Sound of Music*

Gentlemen, you can't fight in here—this is the War Room!

         DR. STRANGELOVE (Peter Sellers)
         in *Dr. Strangelove or:*
         How I Learned to Stop Worrying and Love the Bomb

Theater

Most of my nightmares involve me forgetting my lines in a stage play. — *Robert Englund*

The remarkable thing about Shakespeare is that he really is very good, in spite of all the people who say he is very good.
— *Robert Graves*

The structure of a play is always the story of how the birds come home to roost.
— *Arthur Miller*

Acting is merely the art of keeping a large group of people from coughing.
— *Ralph Richardson*

The play was a great success, but the audience was a disaster. — *Oscar Wilde*

Broadway has been very good to me. But then, I've been very good to Broadway.
— *Ethel Merman*

If all the world's a stage, I want to operate the trapdoor. — *Paul Beatty*

If you really want to help the American theater, don't be an actress, dahling. Be an audience. — *Tallulah Bankhead*

All the world's a stage and most of us are desperately unrehearsed. — *Sean O'Casey*

Critics are like eunuchs in a harem; they know how it's done, they've seen it done every day, but they're unable to do it themselves. — *Brendan Behan*

✳✳✳

Music

Music is the divine way to tell beautiful, poetic things to the heart. — *Pablo Casals*

Music is the soundtrack of your life.
— *Dick Clark*

I have never thought of writing for reputation and honor. What I have in my heart must come out; that is the reason why I compose. — *Ludwig van Beethoven*

Music can be made anywhere, is invisible and does not smell. — *W. H. Auden*

Music is the only language in which you cannot say a mean or sarcastic thing.
— *John Erskine*

There's nothing remarkable about it. All one has to do is hit the right keys at the right time and the instrument plays itself.
— *Johann Sebastian Bach*

I can't listen to that much Wagner. I start getting the urge to conquer Poland.
— *Woody Allen*

Too many pieces of music finish too long after the end. — *Igor Stravinsky*

Every composer knows the anguish and despair occasioned by forgetting ideas which one had no time to write down.
— *Hector Berlioz*

Inspiration is wonderful when it happens, but the writer must develop an approach for the rest of the time. . . . The wait is simply too long. — *Leonard Bernstein*

So long as the human spirit thrives on this planet, music in some living form will accompany and sustain it and give it expressive meaning. — *Aaron Copland*

My music is best understood by children and animals. — *Igor Stravinsky*

There are two golden rules for an orchestra: start together and finish together. The public doesn't give a damn what goes on in between.
— *Thomas Beecham*

The whole problem can be stated quite simply by asking, "Is there a meaning to music?" My answer would be, "Yes." And "Can you state in so many words what the meaning is?" My answer to that would be, "No." — *Aaron Copland*

The notes I handle no better than many pianists. But the pauses between the notes—ah, that is where the art resides!
— *Artur Schnabel*

Music is well said to be the speech of angels. — *Thomas Carlyle*

An intellectual snob is someone who can listen to the "William Tell Overture" and not think of the Lone Ranger. — *Dan Rather*

The difference between a violin and a viola is that a viola burns longer. — *Victor Borge*

The first question I ask myself when something doesn't seem to be beautiful is why do I think it's not beautiful? And very shortly you discover that there is no reason.
— *John Cage*

I understand the inventor of the bagpipes was inspired when he saw a man carrying an indignant, asthmatic pig under his arm. Unfortunately, the man-made sound never equaled the purity of the sound achieved by the pig. — *Alfred Hitchcock*

People are wrong when they say that opera is not what it used to be. It is what it used to be. That is what is wrong with it.
— *Noël Coward*

When an opera star sings her head off, she usually improves her appearance.
— *Victor Borge*

I don't mind what language an opera is sung in so long as it is a language I don't understand. — *Edward Appleton*

No opera plot can be sensible, for people do not sing when they are feeling sensible.
— *W. H. Auden*

If a thing isn't worth saying, you sing it.
— *Pierre Beaumarchais*

No operatic star has yet died soon enough for me. — *Thomas Beecham*

I wish they'd had electric guitars in cotton fields back in the good old days. A whole lot of things would've been straightened out.
— *Jimi Hendrix*

THE PLEASURES OF LIVING

Brass bands are all very well in their place—outdoors and several miles away.
— *Thomas Beecham*

Pure entertainment is not an egotistical lady singing boring songs onstage for two hours and people in tuxes clapping whether they like it or not. It's the real performers on the street who can hold people's attention and keep them from walking away.
— *Andy Kaufman*

What is soul? It's like electricity. We don't really know what it is, but it's a force that can light a room.
— *Ray Charles*

I merely took the energy it takes to pout and wrote some blues.
— *Duke Ellington*

You do not merely want to be considered just the best of the best. You want to be considered the only ones who do what you do.
— *Jerry Garcia*

 Sometimes you have to play for a long time to be able to play like yourself.

— MILES DAVIS

It was when I found out I could make mistakes that I knew I was on to something.
— *Ornette Coleman*

Music is your own experience, your thoughts, your wisdom. If you don't live it, it won't come out of your horn.
— *Charlie Parker*

Jazz is the big brother of the blues. If a guy's playing blues like we play, he's in high school. When he starts playing jazz it's like going on to college, to a school of higher learning.
— *B. B. King*

My son does not appreciate classical musicians such as the Stones; he is more into bands with names like Heave and Squatting Turnips.
— *Dave Barry*

Making the simple complicated is commonplace. Making the complicated simple, awesomely simple, that's creativity.
— *Charles Mingus*

What I wanted to hear didn't exist, so it was necessary for me to go out and create it.
— *Richard Thompson*

Man, if you gotta ask you'll never know.
— *Louis Armstrong, asked what jazz is*

If you play a tune and a person don't tap their feet, don't play the tune.
— *Count Basie*

It seems to me that those songs that have been any good, I have nothing much to do with the writing of them. The words have just crawled down my sleeve and come out on the page.
— *Joan Baez*

The only thing better than singing is more singing.
— *Ella Fitzgerald*

I see my body as an instrument, rather than an ornament.
— *Alanis Morissette*

All music is folk music. I ain't never heard no horse sing a song.
— *Louis Armstrong*

Said in a SONG

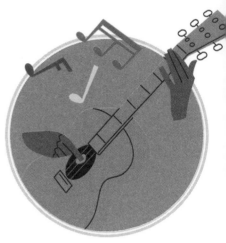

Well-chosen words have a power all of their own, but when you combine them with music—well, they can become permanently imprinted on your psyche. Here's a handful of popular lyrics. Browse them, and you're sure to find a familiar soundtrack for your life.

You may say I'm a dreamer
But I'm not the only one,
I hope someday you'll join us
And the world will live as one.

↝ JOHN LENNON, "Imagine"

Amazing grace! How sweet the sound
That saved a wretch like me!
I once was lost, but now am found
Was blind, but now I see.

↝ JOHN NEWTON, "Amazing Grace"

Freedom's just another word for nothin' left to lose
Nothin' ain't worth nothin' but it's free.

↝ KRIS KRISTOFFERSON,
"Me and Bobby McGee"

God bless America
Land that I love
Stand beside her and guide her
Through the night with a light
From above.

↝ IRVING BERLIN, "Good Bless America"

Yes, 'n' how many times can a man turn his head
And pretend that he just doesn't see?

↝ BOB DYLAN, "Blowin' in the Wind"

I've looked at life from both sides now
From up and down, and still somehow
It's life's illusions I recall
I really don't know life at all.

↝ JONI MITCHELL, "Both Sides Now"

Hear that lonesome whippoorwill?
He sounds too blue to fly
The midnight train is whining low
I'm so lonesome I could cry.

↝ HANK WILLIAMS,
"I'm So Lonesome I Could Cry"

I used to be disgusted
Now I try to be amused.

↝ ELVIS COSTELLO, "Red Shoes"

All you touch and all you see
Is all your life will ever be.

↝ PINK FLOYD, "Breathe"

Shower the people you love with love
Show them the way that you feel
Things are gonna work out fine if you only will.
　　　　JAMES TAYLOR, "Shower the People"

What the world needs now is love, sweet love
It's the only thing that there's just too little of.
　　　　BURT BACHARACH AND HAL DAVID,
　　　　　　"What the World Needs Now Is Love"

Summertime
And the livin' is easy
Fish are jumpin'
And the cotton is high.
　　　　GEORGE GERSHWIN, "Summertime"

I've lived a life that's full
I've traveled each and every highway
But more, much more than this
I did it my way.
　　　　PAUL ANKA, "My Way"

The love you take is equal to the love you make.
　　　　JOHN LENNON AND PAUL MCCARTNEY,
　　　　　　"The End"

When my soul was in the lost-and-found
You came along to claim it.
　　　　CAROLE KING, "A Natural Woman"

When you're weary, feeling small
When tears are in your eyes,
I will dry them all
I'm on your side
When times get rough
And friends just can't be found
Like a bridge over troubled water
I will lay me down.
　　　　PAUL SIMON,
　　　　　"Bridge Over Troubled Water"

You may be right
I may be crazy.
But it just may be a lunatic you're looking for.
　　　　BILLY JOEL, "You May Be Right"

To right the unrightable wrong
To love pure and chaste from afar
To try when your arms are too weary
To reach the unreachable star.
　　　　JOE DARION, "The Impossible Dream"

No one to walk with
All by myself
No one to talk with
But I'm happy on the shelf
Ain't misbehavin'
I'm savin' my love for you.
　　　　FATS WALLER, "Ain't Misbehavin'"

You're my favorite mistake.
　　　　SHERYL CROW, "My Favorite Mistake"

If the phone doesn't ring it's me.
　　　　JIMMY BUFFETT,
　　　　　"If the Phone Doesn't Ring It's Me"

And it seems to me you lived your life
Like a candle in the wind
Never fading with the sunset
When the rain set in
And your footsteps will always fall here
Along England's greenest hills
Your candle's burned out long before
Your legend ever will.
　　　　ELTON JOHN AND BERNIE TAUPIN,
　　　　　"Candle in the Wind 1997,"
　　　　　for Princess Diana's funeral

No two people on earth are alike, and it's got to be that way in music or it isn't music.

— *Billie Holiday*

After about three lessons the voice teacher said, "Don't take voice lessons. Do it your way." — *Johnny Cash*

Onstage I make love to 25,000 people; then I go home alone. — *Janis Joplin*

A lot of pop music is about stealing pocket money from children. — *Ian Anderson*

Canned music is like audible wallpaper.

— *Alistair Cooke*

The music business is a cruel and shallow money trench, a long plastic hallway where thieves and pimps run free, and good men die like dogs. There's also a negative side.

— *Hunter S. Thompson*

Talking about music is like dancing about architecture. — *Steve Martin*

I am out to sing songs that will prove to you that this is your world and that if it has hit you pretty hard and knocked you for a dozen loops, no matter what color, what size you are, how you are built, I am out to sing the songs that make you take pride in yourself and in your work. And the songs that I sing are made up for the most part by all sorts of folks just about like you.

— *Woody Guthrie*

I like to sing. I write music. Country songs. You have to if you're in Nashville. It's part of the lease. You sign a lease that says, "I will write country songs and pay my rent on time." — *Jim Varney*

***

Visual Arts

Art is a collaboration between God and the artist, and the less the artist does the better.

— *André Gide*

The artist, a traveler on this earth, leaves behind imperishable traces of his being.

— *François Delsarte*

The artist should be a seeing-eye dog for a myopic civilization. — *Jacob Getlar Smith*

Every artist dips his brush in his own soul, and paints his own nature into his pictures.

— *Henry Ward Beecher*

Artists can color the sky red because they know it's blue. Those of us who aren't artists must color things the way they really are or people might think we're stupid.

— *Jules Feiffer*

Art is not about thinking something up. It is the opposite—getting something down.

— *Julia Cameron*

Every time I paint a portrait I lose a friend.

— *John Singer Sargent*

> Abstract art: a product of the untalented sold by the unprincipled to the utterly bewildered.
>
> — AL CAPP

I said to myself, I have things in my head that are not like what anyone has taught me—shapes and ideas so near to me—so natural to my way of being and thinking that it hasn't occurred to me to put them down. I decided to start anew, to strip away what I had been taught. *— Georgia O'Keeffe*

Art is either plagiarism or revolution.

— Paul Gauguin

Art is not a mirror but a hammer.

—John Grierson

I believe that if it were left to artists to choose their own labels, most would choose none.

— Ben Shahn

There is no abstract art. You must always start with something. Afterward you can remove all traces of reality. *— Pablo Picasso*

I saw the angel in the marble and I carved until I set him free. *— Michelangelo*

One may have a blazing hearth in one's soul and yet no one ever comes to sit by it. Passersby see only a wisp of smoke from the chimney and continue on the way.

— Vincent van Gogh

Skill without imagination is craftsmanship and gives us many useful objects such as wickerwork picnic baskets. Imagination without skill gives us modern art.

— Tom Stoppard

The artist is nothing without the gift, but the gift is nothing without work.

— Emile Zola

All the arts we practice are apprenticeship. The big art is our life. *— M. C. Richards*

The murals in restaurants are on par with the food in museums. *— Peter De Vries*

Are you really sure that a floor can't also be a ceiling? *— M. C. Escher*

Art is making something out of nothing and selling it. *— Frank Zappa*

Modern art is what happens when painters stop looking at girls and persuade themselves that they have a better idea. *—John Ciardi*

Art is anything you can get away with.

— Marshall McLuhan

An artist cannot fail; it is a success to be one.

— Charles Horton Cooley

One picture is worth a thousand words.

— Fred R. Barnard

If I could say it in words there would be no reason to paint. *— Edward Hopper*

Painting: The art of protecting flat surfaces from the weather and exposing them to the critic. *— Ambrose Bierce*

It is a gratification to me to know that I am ignorant of art, and ignorant also of surgery. Because people who understand art find nothing in pictures but blemishes, and surgeons and anatomists see no beautiful women in all their lives, but only a ghastly stack of bones with Latin names to them, and a network of nerves and muscles and tissues inflamed by disease.   — *Mark Twain*

My garden is my most beautiful masterpiece.
     — *Claude Monet*

A good photograph is knowing where to stand.   — *Ansel Adams*

It's the way to educate your eyes. Stare. Pry, listen, eavesdrop. Die knowing something. You are not here long.   — *Walker Evans*

When one buys some of my artwork I hope it is because they will wish to learn from it and not because they think it will match their drapes!   — *Christian Cardell Corbet*

Architecture is the art of how to waste space.   — *Philip Johnson*

Designed by architects with honorable intentions but hands of palsy. — *Jimmy Breslin*

A doctor can bury his mistakes but an architect can only advise his client to plant vines.   — *Frank Lloyd Wright*

I have often thought that if photography were difficult in the true sense of the term—meaning that the creation of a simple photograph would entail as much time and effort as the production of a good water-color or etching—there would be a vast improvement in total output. The sheer ease with which we can produce a superficial image often leads to creative disaster.
     — *Ansel Adams*

The creative act lasts but a brief moment, a lightning instant of give-and-take, just long enough for you to level the camera and to trap the fleeting prey in your little box.
     — *Henri Cartier-Bresson*

It takes a lot of imagination to be a good photographer. You need less imagination to be a painter because you can invent things. But in photography everything is so ordinary; it takes a lot of looking before you learn to see the extraordinary.
     — *David Bailey*

***

Sex

I only like two kinds of men: domestic and foreign.   — *Mae West*

Women need a reason to have sex. Men just need a place.   — *Billy Crystal*

I never hated a man enough to give him his diamonds back.   — *Zsa Zsa Gabor*

Remember, if you smoke after sex you're doing it too fast.   — *Woody Allen*

Hosting the Oscars is like making love to a beautiful woman—it's something I only get to do when Billy Crystal's out of town.

— *Steve Martin*

The reason most people sweat is so they will not catch fire while they are making love.

— *Don Rose*

My best birth control now is just to leave the lights on.

— *Joan Rivers*

Once in his life, every man is entitled to fall madly in love with a gorgeous redhead.

— *Lucille Ball*

Give me golf clubs, fresh air and a beautiful partner, and you can keep the clubs and the fresh air.

— *Jack Benny*

In less enlightened times, the best way to impress women was to own a hot car. But women wised up and realized it was better to buy their own hot cars so they wouldn't have to ride around with jerks.

— *Scott Adams*

I'm tired of all this nonsense about beauty being only skin-deep. That's deep enough. What do you want, an adorable pancreas?

— *Jean Kerr*

I'm looking for Miss Right, or at least Miss Right Now.

— *Robin Williams*

I wonder what fool it was that first invented kissing.

— *Jonathan Swift*

Any woman who thinks the way to a man's heart is through his stomach is aiming about 10 inches too high.

— *Adrienne E. Gusoff*

Remember, men, we're fighting for this woman's honor, which is probably more than she ever did.

— *Groucho Marx*

Macho does not prove mucho.

— *Zsa Zsa Gabor*

Love is an exploding cigar we willingly smoke.

— *Lynda Barry*

Sex alleviates tension. Love causes it.

— *Woody Allen*

A man can sleep around, no questions asked, but if a woman makes nineteen or twenty mistakes she's a tramp.

— *Joan Rivers*

Let thy maidservant be faithful, strong, and homely.

— *Benjamin Franklin*

It is better to be unfaithful than faithful without wanting to be.

— *Brigitte Bardot*

It's hard for me to get used to these changing times. I can remember when the air was clean and sex was dirty.

— *George Burns*

It's the good girls who keep diaries; the bad girls never have the time.

— *Tallulah Bankhead*

The sound of a kiss is not so loud as that of a cannon, but its echo lasts a great deal longer.

— *Oliver Wendell Holmes*

Don't have sex, man. It leads to kissing and pretty soon you have to start talking to them.

— *Steve Martin*

A relationship, I think, is like a shark, you know? It has to constantly move forward or it dies. And I think what we got on our hands is a dead shark.

— *Woody Allen*

I don't think it's the nature of any man to be monogamous. Men are propelled by genetically ordained impulses over which they have no control to distribute their seed.

— *Marlon Brando*

Men seldom make passes at girls who wear glasses.

— *Dorothy Parker*

A girl can wait for the right man to come along but in the meantime that still doesn't mean she can't have a wonderful time with all the wrong ones.

— *Cher*

One man's folly is another man's wife.

— *Helen Rowland*

Picasso had his pink period and his blue period. I am in my blonde period right now.

— *Hugh Hefner*

I'm always looking for meaningful one-night stands.

— *Dudley Moore*

Most of us spend the first six days of each week sowing wild oats, then we go to church on Sunday and pray for a crop failure.

— *Fred Allen*

People who throw kisses are hopelessly lazy.

— *Bob Hope*

The only unnatural sex act is that which you cannot perform.

— *Alfred Kinsey*

There's no place for the state in the bedrooms of the nation.

— *Pierre Elliot Trudeau*

A kiss is a lovely trick designed by nature to stop speech when words become superfluous.

— *Ingrid Bergman*

I could dance with you till the cows come home ... but I would rather dance with the cows till you come home.

— *Groucho Marx*

A woman making up her lips is like a soldier preparing his machine gun.

— *Sigmund Freud*

In my sex fantasy, nobody ever loves me for my mind.

— *Nora Ephron*

If all the girls who attended the Yale prom were laid end to end, I wouldn't be a bit surprised.

— *Dorothy Parker*

Sex: the thing that takes up the least amount of time and causes the most amount of trouble.

— *John Barrymore*

Sex is one of the most wholesome, beautiful and natural experiences that money can buy.

— *Steve Martin*

When I'm good I'm very, very good, but when I'm bad I'm better.

— *Mae West*

Happiness is watching the TV at your girlfriend's house during a power failure.

— *Bob Hope*

Men should be like Kleenex—soft, strong and disposable.

— *Cher*

Brevity is the soul of lingerie.

— *Dorothy Parker*

Sex without love is an empty experience, but as empty experiences go it's a pretty good one.

— *Woody Allen*

I think onstage nudity is disgusting, shameful and damaging to all things American. But if I were 22 with a great body, it would be artistic, tasteful, patriotic and a progressive religious experience.

— *Shelley Winters*

I often think that a slightly exposed shoulder emerging from a long satin nightgown packs more sex than two naked bodies in bed.

— *Bette Davis*

Pornography is rather like trying to find out about a Beethoven symphony by having somebody tell you about it and perhaps hum a few bars.

— *Robertson Davies*

THE PLEASURES OF LIVING

I seriously object to seeing on the screen what belongs in the bedroom.

— *Samuel Goldwyn*

In America sex is an obsession, in other parts of the world it is a fact. — *Marlene Dietrich*

Women are the only exploited group in history to have been idealized into powerlessness. — *Erica Jong*

A woman without a man is like a fish without a bicycle. — *Gloria Steinem*

***

Relaxation

Time you enjoy wasting was not wasted.

—*John Lennon*

If you can spend a perfectly useless afternoon in a perfectly useless manner, you have learned how to live. — *Lin Yutang*

Spend the afternoon.
You can't take it with you. — *Annie Dillard*

There is no pleasure in having nothing to do; the fun is in having lots to do and not doing it. — *Mary Wilson Little*

Good friends, good books and a sleepy conscience: this is the ideal life.

— *Mark Twain*

Arranging a bowl of flowers in the morning can give a sense of quiet in a crowded day— like writing a poem, or saying a prayer.

— *Anne Morrow Lindbergh*

Most men pursue pleasure with such breathless haste that they hurry past it.

— *Soren Kierkegaard*

It's all right letting yourself go as long as you can let yourself back. — *Mick Jagger*

It is in his pleasure that a man really lives; it is from his leisure that he constructs the true fabric of self. — *Agnes Repplier*

No man needs a vacation so much as the man who has just had one. — *Elbert Hubbard*

If people concentrated on the really important things in life, there'd be a shortage of fishing poles. — *Doug Larson*

There must be quite a few things a hot bath won't cure, but I don't know many of them.

— *Sylvia Plath*

It was such a lovely day I thought it a pity to get up. — *W. Somerset Maugham*

I don't generally feel anything until noon, then it's time for my nap.

— *Oliver Wendell Holmes*

Lying in bed would be an altogether perfect and supreme experience if only one had a colored pencil long enough to draw on the ceiling. — *G. K. Chesterton*

I can think of nothing less pleasurable than a life devoted to pleasure. — *John D. Rockefeller*

Happiness is as a butterfly which, when pursued, is always beyond our grasp, but which if you will sit down quietly, may alight upon you.

— NATHANIEL HAWTHORNE

One of the most adventurous things left us is to go to bed. For no one can lay a hand on our dreams.
— *E. V. Lucas*

Far from idleness being the root of all evil, it is rather the only true good.
— *Soren Kierkegaard*

You have to allow a certain amount of time in which you are doing nothing in order to have things occur to you, to let your mind think.
— *Mortimer J. Adler*

Dreaming permits each and every one of us to be quietly and safely insane every night of our lives.
— *William Dement*

People seem to enjoy things more when they know a lot of other people have been left out of the pleasure.
— *Russell Baker*

Give me the luxuries of life and I will willingly do without the necessities.
— *Frank Lloyd Wright*

***

Travel

If God wanted us to fly, He would have given us tickets.
— *Mel Brooks*

If you don't know where you are going, any road will take you there.
— *Lewis Carroll*

The traveler sees what he sees, the tourist sees what he has come to see.
— *G. K. Chesterton*

Not all who wander are lost.
— *J.R.R. Tolkien*

No place is boring, if you've had a good night's sleep and have a pocket full of unexposed film.
— *Robert Adams*

I am not a great cook, I am not a great artist, but I love art, and I love food, so I am the perfect traveler.
— *Michael Palin*

Wheresoever you go, go with all your heart.
— *Confucius*

Maps encourage boldness. They're like cryptic love letters. They make anything seem possible.
— *Mark Jenkins*

THE PLEASURES OF LIVING

The worst thing about being a tourist
is having other tourists recognize you as
a tourist.   — *Russell Baker*

To travel hopefully is a better thing than
to arrive.   — *Robert Louis Stevenson*

The everyday kindness of the back roads
more than makes up for the acts of greed in
the headlines.   — *Charles Kuralt*

The country has charms only for those not
obliged to stay there.   — *Edouard Manet*

Travel is only glamorous in retrospect.
                — *Paul Theroux*

When you get there, there isn't any
there there.   — *Gertrude Stein*

If we don't change direction soon, we'll end
up where we're going.   — *Professor Irwin Corey*

Remember, no matter where you go,
there you are.   — *Earl Mac Rauch*

How often I found where I should be going
only by setting out for somewhere else.
              — *R. Buckminster Fuller*

Airplane travel is nature's way of making you
look like your passport photo.   — *Al Gore*

Of course great hotels have always been
social ideas, flawless mirrors to the particular
societies they service.   — *Joan Didion*

There is nothing like returning to a place
that remains unchanged to find the ways in
which you yourself have altered.
              — *Nelson Mandela*

My favorite thing is to go where I've
never been.   — *Diane Arbus*

Certainly, travel is more than the seeing of
sights; it is a change that goes on, deep and
permanent, in the ideas of living.
              — *Miriam Beard*

Happiness is not a station you arrive at, but a
manner of traveling.   — *Margaret Lee Runbeck*

We hit the sunny beaches where we occupy
ourselves keeping the sun off our skin, the
salt water off our bodies and the sand out of
our belongings.   — *Erma Bombeck*

When you travel, remember that a foreign
country is not designed to make you comfortable. It is designed to make its own
people comfortable.   — *Clifton Fadiman*

Everyone carries his own inch-rule of
taste, and amuses himself by applying it,
triumphantly, wherever he travels.
              — *Henry Adams*

You can find your way across this country
using burger joints the way a navigator
uses stars.   — *Charles Kuralt*

People, when they first come to America,
whether as travelers or settlers, become
aware of a new and agreeable feeling: that
the whole country is their oyster.
              — *Alistair Cooke*

In America there are two classes of travel—
first class, and with children. — *Robert Benchley*

Thanks to the Interstate Highway System, it
is now possible to travel from coast to coast
without seeing anything.   — *Charles Kuralt*

If you are lucky enough to have lived in
Paris as a young man, then wherever you go
for the rest of your life it stays with you, for
Paris is a moveable feast. — *Ernest Hemingway*

Venice is like eating an entire box of chocolate liqueurs in one go. — *Truman Capote*

Santa Claus has the right idea; visit people once a year.
— *Victor Borge*

Fish and visitors stink after three days.
— *Benjamin Franklin*

His shortcoming is his long staying.
— *Benjamin Disraeli*

Some cause happiness wherever they go; others whenever they go. — *Oscar Wilde*

It is equally offensive to speed a guest who would like to stay and to detain one who is anxious to leave.
— *Homer*

Texas does not, like any other region, simply have indigenous dishes. It proclaims them. It congratulates you, on your arrival, at having escaped from the slop pails of the other 49 states.
— *Alistair Cooke*

***

Home

Never give a party if you will be the most interesting person there. — *Mickey Friedman*

All great change in America begins at the dinner table. — *Ronald Reagan*

As a child my family's menu consisted of two choices: take it or leave it.
— *Buddy Hackett*

Household tasks are easier and quicker when they are done by somebody else.
— *James Thorpe*

Cleaning your house while your kids are still growing is like shoveling the walk before it stops snowing. — *Phyllis Diller*

A place for everything and everything in its place. — *Isabella Mary Beeton*

There is no need to do any housework at all. After the first four years the dirt doesn't get any worse. — *Quentin Crisp*

The home is the chief school of human virtues. — *William Ellery Channing*

Space and light and order. Those are the things that men need just as much as they need bread or a place to sleep. — *Le Corbusier*

What the New Yorker calls home would seem like a couple of closets to most Americans, yet he manages not only to live there but also to grow trees and cockroaches right on the premises. — *Russell Baker*

May your walls know joy. May every room hold laughter and every window open to great possibility.

— *Maryanne Radmacher-Hershey*

THE PLEASURES OF LIVING

Traditions

Cooking Tip: Wrap turkey leftovers in aluminum foil and throw them out.

— *Nicole Hollander*

We're having something a little different this year for Thanksgiving. Instead of a turkey, we're having a swan. You get more stuffing.

— *George Carlin*

The consequences of hearing "Little Drummer Boy" while eating a piece of fruitcake are not pretty, and while I'm not one who goes in for alarming the American people, I know of a young man from a fine family who swallowed a chunk of fruitcake in the same instant that a choir rum-tum-tummed, and that was years ago and we have never spoken of him since.

— *Garrison Keillor*

The excellence of a gift lies in its appropriateness rather than in its value.

— *Charles Dudley Warner*

There is one day that is ours. Thanksgiving Day is the one day that is purely American.

— *O. Henry*

I celebrated Thanksgiving in an old-fashioned way. I invited everyone in my neighborhood to my house, we had an enormous feast, and then I killed them and took their land. — *Jon Stewart*

There is nothing funny about Halloween. This sarcastic festival reflects, rather, an infernal demand for revenge by children on the adult world. — *Jean Baudrillard*

Fatherhood is pretending the present you love most is soap-on-a-rope.

— *Bill Cosby*

The worst gift is a fruitcake.
There is only one fruitcake in the entire world,
and people keep sending it to each other.

— JOHNNY CARSON

Sports and **Achievement**

Here we celebrate the achievements of human brain and brawn.
I'll bet you I can read 'em faster than you. Ready, set, go!

Winning

Winning isn't everything,
but wanting to win is. — *Vince Lombardi*

A champion is someone who gets up when
he can't. — *Jack Dempsey*

If you think you can win, you can win. Faith
is necessary to victory. — *William Hazlitt*

When you win, say nothing.
When you lose, say less. — *Paul Brown*

Win as if you were used to it,
lose as if you enjoyed it for a change.
— *Ralph Waldo Emerson*

Anybody can win unless there happens to be
a second entry. — *George Ade*

In real life, it is the hare who wins. Every
time. Look around you. And in any case it is
my contention that Aesop was writing for
the tortoise market. Hares have no time to
read. They are too busy winning the game.
— *Anita Brookner*

If at first you do succeed—try to hide
your astonishment. — *Harry Banks*

Act as if it were impossible to fail.
— *Dorothea Brande*

The first man gets the oyster, the second
man gets the shell. — *Andrew Carnegie*

The moment of victory is much too short
to live for that and nothing else.
— *Martina Navratilova*

A winner never whines. — *Paul Brown*

The will to win is important, but the will to
prepare is vital. — *Joe Paterno*

A minute's success pays the failure of years.
— *Robert Browning*

If winning isn't everything, why do they
keep score? — *Vince Lombardi*

There is nothing to winning, really. That is,
if you happen to be blessed with a keen eye,
an agile mind, and no scruples whatsoever.
— *Alfred Hitchcock*

There is . . . nothing greater than touching
the shore after crossing some great body of
water knowing that I've done it with my
own two arms and legs.
— *Diana Nyad*

You hit home runs not by chance
but by preparation. — *Roger Maris*

One should always play fairly when one has
the winning cards. — *Oscar Wilde*

If you don't win, you're going to be fired.
If you do win, you've only put off the day
you're going to be fired. — *Leo Durocher*

Success is not the result of spontaneous
combustion. You must set yourself on fire.
— *Reggie Leach*

A fellow told me he was going to hang-
glider school. He said, "I've been going for
three months." I said, "How many successful
jumps do you need to make before you
graduate?" He said, "All of them."
— *Red Skelton*

Sweat plus sacrifice equals success.
— *Charlie Finley*

Success is the ability to go from one failure to another with no loss of enthusiasm.
— *Winston Churchill*

Every man who is high up likes to think that he has done it all himself, and the wife smiles and lets it go at that. — *James M. Barrie*

The guy who takes a chance, who walks the line between the known and unknown, who is unafraid of failure, will succeed.
— *Gordon Parks*

Ability may get you to the top, but it takes character to keep you there. — *John Wooden*

You will get all you want in life if you help enough other people get what they want.

— ZIG ZIGLAR

The penalty for success is to be bored by the people who used to snub you.
— *Nancy Astor*

It is not enough to succeed. Others must fail.
— *Gore Vidal*

Concentrate your energies, your thoughts and your capital. The wise man puts all his eggs in one basket and watches the basket.
— *Andrew Carnegie*

The thermometer of success is merely the jealousy of the malcontents. — *Salvador Dalí*

I always turn to the sports pages first, which records people's accomplishments. The front page has nothing but man's failures.
— *Earl Warren*

The toughest thing about success is that you've got to keep on being a success. Talent is only a starting point in this business. You've got to keep on working that talent. Someday I'll reach for it and it won't be there. — *Irving Berlin*

The measure of success is not whether you have a tough problem to deal with, but whether it is the same problem you had last year. — *John Foster Dulles*

Congratulate yourselves if you have done something strange and extravagant and broken the monotony of a decorous age.
— *Ralph Waldo Emerson*

When you do the common things in life in an uncommon way, you will command the attention of the world.
— *George Washington Carver*

The only time you don't fail is the last time you try anything—and it works.
— *William Strong*

To be successful in show business, all you need are fifty good breaks.
— *Walter Matthau*

This stammer got me a home in Beverly Hills, and I'm not about to screw with it now.
— *Bob Newhart*

$\mathcal{Y}$ogi Berra

Catcher in the Wry

His logic-defying aphorisms have more twists in them than a cartful of pretzels.

Lawrence Peter Berra was born in St. Louis in 1925. He picked up the nickname Yogi from a young friend who thought he walked like a Hindu snake charmer he had seen in a movie.

Berra played minor-league baseball in the early 1940s before he traded in his catcher's mitt for a Navy uniform to fight in World War II. He served during the D-day invasion, in North Africa, and in Italy. He returned to the diamond after the war and in 1946 was signed by the New York Yankees.

For a wild-swinging batter, he was notoriously hard to strike out. He was on winning World Series teams a record 10 times. In 1972 he was elected to the National Baseball Hall of Fame.

Aside from his stellar career as a baseball player and then as a coach and manager, Berra is also legendary for his humility, his kindness, his generosity, and his wit—in particular his delightful, twists of logic that have made him the most-quoted athlete in history.

*

It's déjà vu all over again.

*

Baseball is 90 percent mental; the other half is physical.

*

If the people don't want to come out to the ballpark, nobody's going to stop them.

*

When you come to a fork in the road, take it.

*

Never answer an anonymous letter.

*

A nickel ain't worth a dime anymore.

*

You can observe a lot by watching.

*

Half the lies they tell about me aren't true.

*

It ain't over till it's over.

The secret of successful managing is to keep the five guys who hate you away from the four guys who haven't made up their minds.
— *Casey Stengel*

Yellow cat, black cat, as long as it catches mice it is a good cat. — *Deng Xiaoping*

The secret of all success is to know how to deny yourself. Prove that you can control yourself, and you are an educated man; and without this all other education is good for nothing. — *R. D. Hitchcock*

Creativity can solve almost any problem. The creative act, the defeat of habit by originality, overcomes everything.
— *George Lois*

A man is a success if he gets up in the morning and goes to bed at night and in between does what he wants to do.
— *Bob Dylan*

The real power behind whatever success I have now was something I found within myself—something that's in all of us, I think, a little piece of God just waiting to be discovered. — *Tina Turner*

Success is liking yourself, liking what you do, and liking how you do it. — *Maya Angelou*

Nothing recedes like success.
— *Walter Winchell*

My mother drew a distinction between achievement and success. She said that "achievement is the knowledge that you have studied and worked hard and done the best that is in you. Success is being praised by others, and that's nice, too, but not as important or satisfying. Always aim for achievement and forget about success."
— *Helen Hayes*

***

*L*osing

I've missed more than 9,000 shots in my career. I've lost almost 300 games. Twenty-six times, I've been trusted to take the game-winning shot and missed. I've failed over and over and over again in my life. And that is why I succeed. — *Michael Jordan*

You can learn little from victory. You can learn everything from defeat.
— *Christy Mathewson*

You can learn a line from a win and a book from a defeat. — *Paul Brown*

What would you attempt to do if you knew you could not fail? — *Robert Schuller*

You build on failure. You use it as a stepping stone. Close the door on the past. You don't try to forget the mistakes, but you don't dwell on it. You don't let it have any of your energy, or any of your time, or any of your space. — *Johnny Cash*

Through the years of experience I have found that air offers less resistance than dirt.
— *Jack Nicklaus*

Try again. Fail again. Fail better.
— *Samuel Beckett*

He who never made a mistake never made a discovery. — *Samuel Smiles*

Not admiring a mistake is a bigger mistake.
— *Robert Half*

Most ball games are lost, not won.
— *Casey Stengel*

Every strike brings me closer to the next home run. — *Babe Ruth*

You miss 100 percent of the shots you never take. — *Wayne Gretzky*

Ninety-nine percent of the failures come from people who have the habit of making excuses. — *George Washington Carver*

I had a mother who taught me there is no such thing as failure. It is just a temporary postponement of success. — *Buddy Ebsen*

That's what learning is, after all: not whether we lose the game, but how we lose and how we've changed because of it, and what we take away from it that we never had before, to apply to other games. Losing, in a curious way, is winning. — *Richard Bach*

We can't all be heroes, because somebody has to sit on the curb and applaud when they go by. — *Will Rogers*

I always wanted to be somebody, but now I realize I should have been more specific.
— *Lily Tomlin*

Mistakes, obviously, show us what needs improving. Without mistakes, how would we know what we had to work on?
— *Peter McWilliams*

I can accept failure, but I can't accept not trying. — *Michael Jordan*

A man can fail many times, but he isn't a failure until he begins to blame somebody else. — *John Burroughs*

There's nothing like rejection to make you do an inventory of yourself.
— *James Lee Burke*

Your best teacher is your last mistake.
— *Ralph Nader*

Mistakes are a part of being human. Appreciate your mistakes for what they are: precious life lessons that can only be learned the hard way. Unless it's a fatal mistake, which, at least, others can learn from.
— *Al Franken*

The only real mistake is the one from which we learn nothing. — *John Powell*

Laughing at our mistakes can lengthen our own life. Laughing at someone else's can shorten it. — *Cullen Hightower*

If all else fails, immortality can always be assured by spectacular error.
— *John Kenneth Galbraith*

Only the mediocre are always at their best.
— *Jean Giraudoux*

I think that comedy really tells you how it is. The other thing about comedy is, that you don't even know if you're failing in drama, but you do know when you're failing in comedy. When you go to a comedy and you don't hear anybody laughing, you know that you've failed.
— *Carl Reiner*

If you live long enough, you'll make mistakes.
But if you learn from them, you'll be a better person.
It's how you handle adversity, not how it affects you.
The main thing is never quit, never quit, never quit.

— BILL CLINTON

You find out your mistakes from an audience that pays admission. — *Edgar Bergen*

I've done the calculation and your chances of winning the lottery are identical whether you play or not. — *Fran Lebowitz*

It was on the 10th day of May—1884— that I confessed to age by mounting spectacles for the first time, and in the same hour I renewed my youth, to outward appearance, by mounting a bicycle for the first time. The spectacles stayed on.
— *Mark Twain*

Defeat is not the worst of failures. Not to have tried is the true failure.
— *George E. Woodberry*

Mistakes are the portals of discovery.
— *James Joyce*

Show me a guy who's afraid to look bad, and I'll show you a guy you can beat every time. — *Lou Brock*

Argue for your limitations, and sure enough they're yours. — *Richard Bach*

You may have a fresh start any moment you choose, for this thing that we call "failure" is not the falling down, but the staying down.
— *Mary Pickford*

The only way to prove that you're a good sport is to lose. — *Ernie Banks*

Never confuse a single defeat with a final defeat. — *F. Scott Fitzgerald*

I never questioned the integrity of an umpire. Their eyesight, yes. — *Leo Durocher*

Show me someone without an ego, and I'll show you a loser. — *Donald Trump*

Many of life's failures are people who did not realize how close they were to success when they gave up. — *Thomas Alva Edison*

Talent without discipline is like an octopus on roller skates. There's plenty of movement, but you never know if it's going to be forward, backwards, or sideways.
— *H. Jackson Brown, Jr.*

We didn't lose the game; we just ran out of time. — *Vince Lombardi*

If you know you are going to fail, then fail gloriously. — *Cate Blanchett*

The minute you start talking about what you're going to do if you lose, you have lost.
— *George Shultz*

People fail forward to success. — *Mary Kay Ash*

Show me a thoroughly satisfied man,
and I'll show you a failure.
— *Thomas Alva Edison*

The man who goes alone can start today;
but he who travels with another must wait
till the other is ready, and it may be a long
time before they get off.
— *Henry David Thoreau*

If at first you don't succeed, try again. Then
quit. No use being a fool about it.
— *Scott Adams*

A great deal of talent is lost to the world for
want of a little courage. Every day sends to
their graves obscure men whose timidity
prevented them from making a first effort.
— *Sydney Smith*

If at first you don't succeed, failure may be
your style.
— *Quentin Crisp*

Nice guys finish last, but we get to sleep in.
— *Evan Davis*

***

Competition

If I were playing third base and my
mother were rounding third with the run
that was going to beat us, I'd trip her. Oh,
I'd pick her up and brush her off and say,
"Sorry, Mom," but nobody beats me.
— *Leo Durocher*

My motto was always to keep swinging.
Whether I was in a slump or feeling badly
or having trouble off the field, the only
thing to do was keep swinging.
— *Hank Aaron*

Ability is what you're capable of doing.
Motivation determines what you do.
Attitude determines how well you do it.
— *Lou Holtz*

Slow and steady wins the race.   — *Aesop*

Float like a butterfly, sting like a bee.
— *Muhammad Ali*

Build up your weaknesses until they become
your strong points.
— *Knute Rockne*

The secret of joy in work is contained in
one word—excellence. To know how to do
something well is to enjoy it.   — *Pearl S. Buck*

Good, better, best. Never let it rest. Till your
good is better and your better, best.
— *Motto of J. Furphy & Sons*

It takes 20 years to build a reputation and
five minutes to ruin it. If you think about
that, you'll do things differently.
— *Warren Buffett*

I am easily satisfied with the very best.
— *Winston Churchill*

Some people regard discipline as a chore.
For me, it is a kind of order that sets me
free to fly.
— *Julie Andrews*

The riches of the game are in the thrills, not the money. — *Ernie Banks*

Never let the fear of striking out get in your way. — *Babe Ruth*

Motivation is when your dreams put on work clothes. — *Milton Berle*

Take time to deliberate, but when the time for action has arrived, stop thinking and go in. — *Napoleon Bonaparte*

An ant on the move does more than a dozing ox. — *Lao-tzu*

The most effective way to do it, is to do it. — *Amelia Earhart*

It is easy to sit up and take notice. What is difficult is getting up and taking action. — *Honoré de Balzac*

When you build bridges you can keep crossing them. — *Rick Pitino*

A little knowledge that acts is worth infinitely more than much knowledge that is idle. — *Kahlil Gibran*

Don't think. Thinking is the enemy of creativity. It's self-conscious and anything self-conscious is lousy. You cannot try to do things. You simply must do things.

— *Ray Bradbury*

Anyone who has gumption knows what it is, and anyone who hasn't can never know what it is. So there is no need of defining it. — *L. M. Montgomery*

Opportunity dances with those already on the dance floor. — *H. Jackson Brown, Jr.*

How important it is for us to recognize and celebrate our heroes and she-roes! — *Maya Angelou*

Nurture your minds with great thoughts. To believe in the heroic makes heroes. — *Benjamin Disraeli*

True heroism is remarkably sober, very undramatic. It is not the urge to surpass all others at whatever cost, but the urge to serve others, at whatever cost. — *Arthur Ashe*

As you get older it is harder to have heroes, but it is sort of necessary. — *Ernest Hemingway*

We all have idols. Play like anyone you care about but try to be yourself while you're doing so. — *B. B. King*

A man who builds his own pedestal had better use strong cement. — *Anna Quindlen*

Everyone is necessarily the hero of his own life story. — *John Barth*

The real hero is always a hero by mistake; he dreams of being an honest coward like everybody else. — *Umberto Eco*

A hero is no braver than an ordinary man, but he is braver five minutes longer. — *Ralph Waldo Emerson*

A hero is someone who has given his or her life to something bigger than oneself. — *Joseph Campbell*

For when the One Great Scorer comes
To write against your name,
He marks—not that you won or lost—
But how you played the game.

— *Grantland Rice*

Have no fear of perfection,
you'll never reach it.   — *Salvador Dalí*

Never ascribe to an opponent motives
meaner than your own.   — *James M. Barrie*

I don't hate anyone, at least not for more
than 48 minutes, barring overtime.

— *Charles Barkley*

The dumber a pitcher is, the better. When
he gets smart and begins to experiment
with a lot of different pitches, he's in trouble.
All I ever had was a fastball, a curve and a
changeup and I did pretty good.

— *Dizzy Dean*

People who live in the past generally are
afraid to compete in the present. I've got my
faults, but living in the past is not one of
them. There's no future in it.

— *Sparky Anderson*

Don't look back: Something may be gaining
on you.   — *Satchel Paige*

There is always some kid who may be seeing me
for the first or last time—I owe him my best.

— JOE DIMAGGIO

I wouldn't ever set out to hurt anyone deliberately unless it was, you know, important
—like a league game or something.

— *Dick Butkus*

Son, what kind of pitch would you like
to miss?   — *Dizzy Dean*

Some guys are admired for coming to play,
as the saying goes. I prefer those who come
to kill.   — *Leo Durocher*

The pitcher has got only a ball. I've got a
bat. So the percentage in weapons is in my
favor and I let the fellow with the ball do
the fretting.   — *Hank Aaron*

I've always tried to go a step past wherever
people expected me to end up.

— *Beverly Sills*

A catcher and his body are like the outlaw
and his horse. He's got to ride that nag till
it drops.   — *Johnny Bench*

You gotta be careful with your body. Your
body is like a bar of soap. The more you use
it, the more it wears down.   — *Richie Allen*

The world is all gates, all opportunities,
strings of tension waiting to be struck.

— *Ralph Waldo Emerson*

Push yourself again and again. Don't give
an inch until the final buzzer sounds.

— *Larry Bird*

Both tears and sweat are salty, but they
render a different result. Tears will get you
sympathy; sweat will get you change.

— *Jesse Jackson*

Oliver Wendell Holmes

Doctor of Letters

A poet's typical income being what it is, it helps if you're also a working physician. So it was for one of the most highly regarded American poets of the 19th century, Oliver Wendell Holmes.

Holmes first sprang to prominence with the publication of "Old Ironsides," the ode that led to preservation of the battleship U.S.S. *Constitution*. He was also a prominent doctor, however. He studied medicine in Paris, received his medical degree from Harvard, taught anatomy and physiology at Dartmouth College, and at age 33 became the first dean of Harvard Medical School. He should not be confused with his son, Oliver Wendell Holmes, Jr., a noted U.S. Supreme Court Justice.

Holmes was a popular speaker at Boston events, and known for his series of "Breakfast-Table" sketches, imaginary conversations set in a boardinghouse. The sketches, a showcase for his opinions and humor, were published in the *Atlantic Monthly* magazine and later collected into the book *The Autocrat of the Breakfast-Table*. He published three novels and two biographies.

*

Man's mind, once stretched by a new idea, never regains its original dimensions.

*

Take a music bath once or twice a week for a few seasons,
and you will find that it is to the soul what the water bath is to the body.

*

Don't flatter yourself that friendship authorizes you to say disagreeable things
to your intimates. The nearer you come into relation with a person,
the more necessary do tact and courtesy become. Except in cases of necessity,
which are rare, leave your friend to learn unpleasant things from his enemies;
they are ready enough to tell them.

*

Knowledge and timber shouldn't be much used till they are seasoned.

*

A person is always startled when he hears himself seriously called
an old man for the first time.

*

A pun does not commonly justify a blow in return.
But if a blow were given for such cause, and death ensued,
the jury would be judges both of the facts and of the pun, and might,
if the latter were of an aggravated character,
return a verdict of justifiable homicide.

*

Some people are so heavenly minded that they are no earthly good.

*

The young man knows the rules, but the old man knows the exceptions.

Every man in the world is better than someone else. And not as good as someone else.

— *William Saroyan*

Success is the sum of small efforts—repeated day in and day out.

— *Robert Collier*

I skate to where the puck is going to be, not to where it has been.

— *Wayne Gretzky*

In skating over thin ice our safety is in our speed.

— *Ralph Waldo Emerson*

You know it's going to hell when the best rapper out there is white and the best golfer is black.

— *Charles Barkley*

The secret of my success was clean living and a fast outfield.

— *Lefty Gomez*

Never keep up with the Joneses. Drag them down to your level.

— *Quentin Crisp*

There is no sudden leap into the stratosphere. There is only advancing step by step, slowly and tortuously, up the pyramid towards your goals.

— *Ben Stein*

I never could have done what I have done without the habits of punctuality, order, and diligence, without the determination to concentrate myself on one subject at a time.

— *Charles Dickens*

I've always taken risks, and never worried what the world might really think of me.

— CHER

Remember that nobody will ever get ahead of you as long as he is kicking you in the seat of the pants.

— *Walter Winchell*

Courage is being scared to death— but saddling up anyway.

—*John Wayne*

Courage is grace under pressure.

— *Ernest Hemingway*

When it's third and ten, you can take the milk drinkers and I'll take the whiskey drinkers every time.

— *Max McGee*

When you are in any contest you should work as if there were—to the very last minute—a chance to lose it.

— *Dwight D. Eisenhower*

I've learned my song, and I sing it.

— *Bob Barker*

Whoever wants to know the heart and mind of America had better learn baseball, the rules and realities of the game—and do it by watching first some high school or small-town teams.

— *Jacques Barzun*

I know I'm never as good or bad as one single performance. I've never believed in my critics or my worshippers, and I've always been able to leave the game at the arena.

— *Charles Barkley*

Your talent is God's gift to you. What you do with it is your gift back to God.

— *Leo Buscaglia*

Maybe all one can do is hope to end up with the right regrets. — *Arthur Miller*

Life's too short for chess. — *Henry James Byron*

Chess is as elaborate a waste of human intelligence as you can find outside an advertising agency. — *Raymond Chandler*

Avoid the crowd. Do your own thinking independently. Be the chess player, not the chess piece. — *Ralph Charell*

Every game ever invented by mankind is a way of making things hard for the fun of it! — *John Ciardi*

Applause is the spur of noble minds, the end and aim of weak ones. — *Edmund Burke*

I'm just a ballplayer with one ambition, and that is to give all I've got to help my ball club win. I've never played any other way. — *Joe DiMaggio*

Boxing is just show business with blood. — *Frank Bruno*

Concentration is the ability to think about absolutely nothing when it is absolutely necessary. — *Ray Knight*

People who don't take risks generally make about two big mistakes a year. People who do take risks generally make about two big mistakes a year. — *Peter F. Drucker*

To play it safe is not to play. — *Robert Altman*

Avoid having your ego so close to your position that when your position falls, your ego goes with it. — *Colin Powell*

Gentlemen, start your egos. — *Billy Crystal*

It ain't braggin' if you can back it up. — *Dizzy Dean*

Ambition is a dream with a V–8 engine. — *Elvis Presley*

The mind is the limit. As long as the mind can envision the fact that you can do something, you can do it—as long as you really believe 100 percent. — *Arnold Schwarzenegger*

People take different roads seeking fulfillment and happiness. Just because they're not on your road doesn't mean they've gotten lost. — *H. Jackson Brown, Jr.*

Soar, eat ether, see what has never been seen; depart, be lost, but climb. — *Edna St. Vincent Millay*

You can't help someone get up a hill without getting closer to the top yourself. — *H. Norman Schwarzkopf*

In heaven an angel is nobody in particular. — *George Bernard Shaw*

When a true genius appears in this world, you may know him by this sign, that the dunces are all in confederacy against him. — *Jonathan Swift*

Golf

It took me seventeen years to get 3,000 hits in baseball. I did it in one afternoon on the golf course. — *Hank Aaron*

It is nothing new or original to say that golf is played one stroke at a time. But it took me many years to realize it. — *Bobby Jones*

These greens are so fast I have to hold my putter over the ball and hit it with the shadow. — *Sam Snead*

Golf is played by 20 million mature American men whose wives think they are out having fun. —*Jim Bishop*

The only time my prayers are never answered is on the golf course. — *Billy Graham*

I know I am getting better at golf because I am hitting fewer spectators. — *Gerald R. Ford*

Golf is a good walk spoiled. — *Mark Twain*

The reason the pro tells you to keep your head down is so you can't see him laughing. — *Phyllis Diller*

One advantage of golf over bowling is that you never lose a bowling ball. — *Don Carter*

Achievement is largely the product of steadily raising one's levels of aspiration and expectation. —*Jack Nicklaus*

Never break your putter and your driver in the same round or you're dead. — *Tommy Bolt*

Golf is the cruelest game, because eventually it will drag you out in front of the whole school, take your lunch money and slap you around. — *Rick Reilly*

Although golf was originally restricted to wealthy, overweight Protestants, today it's open to anybody who owns hideous clothing. — *Dave Barry*

Golf is more fun than walking naked in a strange place, but not much. — *Buddy Hackett*

If you think it's hard to meet new people, try picking up the wrong golf ball. —*Jack Lemmon*

If you watch a game, it's fun.
If you play at it, it's recreation.
If you work at it, it's golf.

— BOB HOPE

Adversity

It ain't the heat, it's the humility.   — *Yogi Berra*

Impossible is a word to be found only in the dictionary of fools.   — *Napoleon Bonaparte*

Circumstances hell! I make circumstances!
— *Bruce Lee*

There has never been a great athlete who died not knowing what pain is.   — *Bill Bradley*

If I were to say, "God, why me?" about the bad things, then I should have said, "God, why me?" about the good things that happened in my life.   — *Arthur Ashe*

You can turn painful situations around through laughter. If you can find humor in anything, even poverty, you can survive it.
— *Bill Cosby*

Anything inside that immobilizes me, gets in my way, keeps me from my goals, is all mine.
— *Wayne Dyer*

Before you give up hope, turn back and read the attacks that were made on Lincoln.
— *Bruce Barton*

Our doubts are traitors, and make us lose the good we oft might win, by fearing to attempt.   — *William Shakespeare*

I'm not a dreamer . . . but I believe in miracles. I have to.   — *Terry Fox*

The more I heard that I couldn't make it, the more I was determined to do it. I never liked being told that I'm not good enough to do this or that.   — *Archie Griffin*

If you are distressed by anything external, the pain is not due to the thing itself, but to your estimate of it; and this you have the power to revoke at any moment.
— *Marcus Aurelius*

All the adversity I've had in my life, all my troubles and obstacles, have strengthened me. . . . You may not realize it when it happens, but a kick in the teeth may be the best thing in the world for you.   — *Walt Disney*

In every adversity there lies the seed of an equivalent advantage. In every defeat is a lesson showing you how to win the victory next time.   — *Robert Collier*

A successful man is one who can lay a firm foundation with the bricks others have thrown at him.   — *David Brinkley*

Comfort and prosperity have never enriched the world as much as adversity has.
— *Billy Graham*

Whatever women do they must do twice as well as men to be thought half as good. Luckily this is not difficult.
— *Charlotte Whitton*

Don't let life discourage you; everyone who got where he is had to begin where he was.
— *Richard L. Evans*

It's not the load that breaks you down, it's the way you carry it.   — *Lena Horne*

We find no real satisfaction or happiness in life without obstacles to conquer and goals to achieve.   — *Maxwell Maltz*

Success is how high you bounce when you hit bottom.   — *George S. Patton*

Challenges are what make life interesting; overcoming them is what makes life meaningful. — *Joshua J. Marine*

Each handicap is like a hurdle in a steeple-chase, and when you ride up to it, if you throw your heart over, the horse will go along, too. — *Lawrence Bixby*

The way of the pioneer is always rough. — *Harvey S. Firestone*

Great things are done when men and mountains meet. — *William Blake*

He who limps is still walking. — *Joan Rivers*

It does not matter how slowly you go so long as you do not stop. — *Confucius*

A ball player has to be kept hungry to become a big leaguer. That's why no boy from a rich family has ever made the big leagues. — *Joe DiMaggio*

Football isn't a contact sport, it's a collision sport. Dancing is a contact sport. — *Duffy Daugherty*

We are continually faced with a series of great opportunities brilliantly disguised as insoluble problems. — *John W. Gardner*

Fans don't boo nobodies. — *Reggie Jackson*

Be bold. If you're going to make an error, make a doozy, and don't be afraid to hit the ball. — *Billie Jean King*

Where there is a will, there is a way. If there is a chance in a million that you can do something, anything, to keep what you want from ending, do it. Pry the door open or, if need be, wedge your foot in that door and keep it open. — *Pauline Kael*

To swear off making mistakes is very easy. All you have to do is swear off having ideas. — *Leo Burnett*

Accept that some days you are the pigeon and some days the statue. — *Scott Adams*

Some days you're a bug, some days you're a windshield. — *Price Cobb*

If you find a good solution and become attached to it, the solution may become your next problem. — *Robert Anthony*

Arithmetic is where the answer is right and everything is nice and you can look out of the window and see the blue sky— or the answer is wrong and you have to start over and try again and see how it comes out this time. — *Carl Sandburg*

Guys ask me, don't I get burned out? How can you get burned out doing something you love? I ask you, have you ever got tired of kissing a pretty girl? — *Tommy Lasorda*

Often we can achieve an even better result when we stumble yet are willing to start over, when we don't give up after a mistake, when something doesn't come easily but we throw ourselves into trying, when we're not afraid to appear less than perfectly polished. — *Susan Salzberg*

Most people give up just when they're about to achieve success. They quit on the one yard line. They give up at the last minute of the game one foot from a winning touchdown. — *H. Ross Perot*

The difference between perseverance and obstinacy is that one comes from a strong will, and the other from a strong won't. — *Henry Ward Beecher*

I have found it advisable
not to give too much heed
to what people say
when I am trying to accomplish
something of consequence.
Invariably they proclaim it can't be done.
I deem that the very best time
to make the effort.

— CALVIN COOLIDGE

Noise proves nothing. Often a hen who has merely laid an egg cackles as if she had laid an asteroid. — *Mark Twain*

The greatest enemy of progress is not stagnation, but false progress. — *Sydney J. Harris*

Adversity has the same effect on a man that severe training has on the pugilist: It reduces him to his fighting weight. — *Josh Billings*

You can't choose the ways in which you'll be tested. — *Robert J. Sawyer*

Incompetents invariably make trouble for people other than themselves.
— *Larry McMurtry*

In a real dark night of the soul, it is always three o'clock in the morning, day after day.
— *F. Scott Fitzgerald*

You have to run as fast as you can just to stay where you are. If you want to get anywhere, you'll have to run much faster.
— *Lewis Carroll*

If one cannot catch the bird of paradise, better take a wet hen. — *Nikita Khrushchev*

The majority of men meet with failure because of their lack of persistence in creating new plans to take the place of those which fail. — *Napoleon Hill*

Be master of your petty annoyances and conserve your energies for the big, worthwhile things. It isn't the mountain ahead that wears you out—it's the grain of sand in your shoe. — *Robert Service*

If they can make penicillin out of moldy bread, they can sure make something out of you. — *Muhammad Ali*

I couldn't wait for success, so I went ahead without it. — *Jonathan Winters*

Don't say you don't have enough time. You have exactly the same number of hours per day that were given to Helen Keller, Pasteur, Michelangelo, Mother Teresa, Leonardo da Vinci, Thomas Jefferson, and Albert Einstein.
— *H. Jackson Brown, Jr.*

Fresh air is good if you do not take too much of it; most of the achievements and pleasures of life are in bad air.

— *Oliver Wendell Holmes*

Be content with your lot; one cannot be first in everything.

— *Aesop*

Nothing is built on stone; all is built on sand, but we must build as if the sand were stone.

— *Jorge Luis Borges*

If you can't stand the heat, get out of the kitchen.

— *Harry S. Truman*

***

Scientific Endeavor

When a distinguished but elderly scientist states that something is possible, he is almost certainly right. When he states that something is impossible, he is very probably wrong.

— *Arthur C. Clarke*

I have learned to use the word *impossible* with the greatest caution.

— *Wernher von Braun*

Never interrupt someone doing what you said couldn't be done.

— *Amelia Earhart*

The world is moving so fast these days that the man who says it can't be done is generally interrupted by someone doing it.

— *Harry Emerson Fosdick*

We live in a time when the words *impossible* and *unsolvable* are no longer part of the scientific community's vocabulary. Each day we move closer to trials that will not just minimize the symptoms of disease and injury but eliminate them.

— *Christopher Reeve*

It is difficult to say what is impossible, for the dream of yesterday is the hope of today and the reality of tomorrow.

— *Robert H. Goddard*

The church says that the earth is flat, but I know that it is round. For I have seen the shadow on the moon and I have more faith in the shadow than in the church.

— *Ferdinand Magellan*

The limits of the possible can only be defined by going beyond them into the impossible.

— *Arthur C. Clarke*

The best scientist is open to experience and begins with romance—the idea that anything is possible.

— *Ray Bradbury*

The greatest obstacle to discovery is not ignorance—it is the illusion of knowledge.

— *Daniel J. Boorstin*

In science, "fact" can only mean "confirmed to such a degree that it would be perverse to withhold provisional assent." I suppose that apples might start to rise tomorrow, but the possibility does not merit equal time in physics classrooms.

— *Stephen Jay Gould*

Leave the beaten track occasionally and dive into the woods. Every time you do so you will be certain to find something that you have never seen before. Follow it up, explore all around it, and before you know it, you will have something worth thinking about to occupy your mind. All really big discoveries are the results of thought.

— *Alexander Graham Bell*

Just because something doesn't do what you planned it to do doesn't mean it's useless.

— *Thomas Alva Edison*

When Thomas Edison worked late into the night on the electric light, he had to do it by gas lamp or candle. I'm sure it made the work seem that much more urgent.

— *George Carlin*

That's one small step for man, one giant leap for mankind.

— *Neil Armstrong, stepping onto the moon*

We must not forget that when radium was discovered no one knew that it would prove useful in hospitals. The work was one of pure science. And this is a proof that scientific work must not be considered from the point of view of the direct usefulness of it. It must be done for itself, for the beauty of science, and then there is always the chance that a scientific discovery may become like the radium a benefit for humanity.

— *Marie Curie*

A good scientist is a person with original ideas. A good engineer is a person who makes a design that works with as few original ideas as possible. There are no prima donnas in engineering. — *Freeman Dyson*

The more original a discovery, the more obvious it seems afterwards. — *Arthur Koestler*

What was most significant about the lunar voyage was not that men set foot on the moon but that they set eye on the earth.

— *Norman Cousins*

"Obvious" is the most dangerous word in mathematics. — *E. T. Bell*

If quantum mechanics hasn't profoundly shocked you, you haven't understood it yet.

— *Niels Bohr*

Never measure the height of a mountain until you have reached the top. Then you will see how low it was. — *Dag Hammarskjöld*

When I was young, I said to God, "God, tell me the mystery of the universe." But God answered, "That knowledge is for me alone." So I said, "God, tell me the mystery of the peanut." Then God said, "Well, George, that's more nearly your size."

— *George Washington Carver*

If I have seen further it is by standing on the shoulders of giants. — *Isaac Newton*

Millions saw the apple fall, but Newton was the one who asked why. — *Bernard Baruch*

It is inexcusable for scientists to torture animals; let them make their experiments on journalists and politicians. — *Henrik Ibsen*

When I find myself in the company of scientists, I feel like a shabby curate who has strayed by mistake into a room full of dukes.

— *W. H. Auden*

When you make the finding yourself—even if you're the last person on earth to see the light—you'll never forget it. — *Carl Sagan*

Science is nothing but developed perception, interpreted intent, common sense rounded out and minutely articulated.

— *George Santayana*

No sooner does man discover intelligence than he tries to involve it in his own stupidity.

— *Jacques Yves Cousteau*

Every great advance in science has issued from a new audacity of imagination.

— *John Dewey*

The best way to have a good idea is to have lots of ideas. — *Linus Pauling*

Science is facts; just as houses are made of stones, so is science made of facts; but a pile of stones is not a house and a collection of facts is not necessarily science.

— *Henri Poincaré*

Science is one thing, wisdom is another. Science is an edged tool, with which men play like children, and cut their own fingers.

— *Arthur Eddington*

Build a better mousetrap
and the world will beat a path to your door.

— RALPH WALDO EMERSON

We have been God-like in our planned breeding of our domesticated plants and animals, but we have been rabbit-like in our unplanned breeding of ourselves.

— *Arnold Toynbee*

Most advances in science come when a person for one reason or another is forced to change fields. — *Peter Borden*

Machines take me by surprise with great frequency. — *Alan Turing*

It is a capital mistake to theorize before one has data. — *Arthur Conan Doyle*

If I have a thousand ideas and only one turns out to be good, I am satisfied. — *Alfred Nobel*

A fact is a simple statement that everyone believes. It is innocent, unless found guilty. A hypothesis is a novel suggestion that no one wants to believe. It is guilty, until found effective. — *Edward Teller*

Let me tell you the secret that has led me to my goal. My strength lies solely in my tenacity. — *Louis Pasteur*

Man is the best computer we can put aboard a spacecraft . . . and the only one that can be mass-produced with unskilled labor.

— *Wernher von Braun*

The universe is not required to be in perfect harmony with human ambition.

— *Carl Sagan*

New knowledge is the most valuable commodity on earth. The more truth we have to work with, the richer we become.
— *Kurt Vonnegut*

As our own species is in the process of proving, one cannot have superior science and inferior morals. The combination is unstable and self-destroying.
— *Arthur C. Clarke*

A problem well stated is a problem half solved.
— *Charles F. Kettering*

Bear in mind the simple rule, X squared to the power of two minus five over the seven point eight three times nineteen is approximately equal to the cube root of MCC squared divided by X minus a quarter of a third percent. Keep that in mind, and you can't go very far wrong.
— *Eric Idle*

In science the credit goes to the man who convinces the world, not the man to whom the idea first occurs.
— *Francis Darwin*

Nothing you can't spell will ever work.
— *Will Rogers*

Anything that won't sell, I don't want to invent. Its sale is proof of utility, and utility is success.
— *Thomas Alva Edison*

Research is the process of going up alleys to see if they are blind.
— *Marston Bates*

Basic research is what I am doing when I don't know what I am doing.
— *Wernher von Braun*

Supposing is good, but finding out is better.
— *Mark Twain*

The great tragedy of science—the slaying of a beautiful hypothesis by an ugly fact.
— *Thomas H. Huxley*

It is a good morning exercise for a research scientist to discard a pet hypothesis every day before breakfast. It keeps him young.
— *Konrad Lorenz*

A scientific truth does not triumph by convincing its opponents and making them see the light, but rather because its opponents eventually die and a new generation grows up that is familiar with it.
— *Max Planck*

Every revolutionary idea seems to evoke three stages of reaction. They may be summed up by the phrases:
(1) It's completely impossible.
(2) It's possible, but it's not worth doing.
(3) I said it was a good idea all along.
— *Arthur C. Clarke*

I can't understand why people are frightened of new ideas. I'm frightened of the old ones.
— *John Cage*

One of the greatest pains to human nature is the pain of a new idea.
— *Walter Bagehot*

Ideas are like rabbits. You get a couple and learn how to handle them, and pretty soon you have a dozen.
— *John Steinbeck*

I don't believe in intuition. When you get sudden flashes of perception, it is just the brain working faster than usual. But you've been getting ready to know it for a long time, and when it comes, you feel you've known it always.
— *Katherine Anne Porter*

Follow the path of the unsafe, independent thinker. Expose your ideas to the dangers of controversy. Speak your mind and fear less the label of "crackpot" than the stigma of conformity. And on issues that seem important to you, stand up and be counted at any cost.
— *Thomas J. Watson*

Albert Einstein

Universal Truths

There probably was not a more powerful thinker in the 20th century—or any century, for that matter—than theoretical physicist Albert Einstein.

With physical tools no more complicated than pencil and paper, he revolutionized the way that scientists think about time, space, and matter. His intellectual tools were beyond compare, of course—including a deep, intuitive understanding of the workings of nature combined with the so-called thought experiments that he used to develop theories.

The wild-haired wonder was no slouch when it came to putting pencil and paper to more traditional uses, too: namely, writing about the complexities of life in a way that we all can understand. A humanist and a Jew, he was an outspoken advocate of peace and social justice. Here's a small sampling of musings from the intellectual giant.

*

*I know not with what weapons World War III will be fought,
but World War IV will be fought with sticks and stones.*

*

*The important thing is not to stop questioning.
Curiosity has its own reason for existing. One cannot help but be in awe
when he contemplates the mysteries of eternity, of life, of the marvelous structure
of reality. It is enough if one tries merely to comprehend
a little of this mystery every day.
Never lose a holy curiosity.*

*

Before God we are all equally wise—and equally foolish.

*

*Do not worry about your difficulties in mathematics.
I can assure you mine are still greater.*

*

Imagination is more important than knowledge.

*

*The release of atomic energy has not created a new problem.
It has merely made more urgent the necessity of solving an existing one.*

Skeptical scrutiny is the means, in both science and religion, by which deep insights can be winnowed from deep nonsense.

— *Carl Sagan*

Perfect as the wing of a bird may be, it will never enable the bird to fly if unsupported by the air. Facts are the air of science. Without them a man of science can never rise.

— *Ivan Pavlov*

Since we cannot know all that there is to be known about anything, we ought to know a little about everything. — *Blaise Pascal*

Mathematics, rightly viewed, possesses not only truth, but supreme beauty—a beauty cold and austere, like that of sculpture.

— *Bertrand Russell*

As a rule we disbelieve all the facts and theories for which we have no use.

— *William James*

An inventor is simply a fellow who doesn't take his education too seriously.

— *Charles F. Kettering*

The American, by nature, is optimistic. He is experimental, an inventor and a builder who builds best when called upon to build greatly.

— *John F. Kennedy*

The beginning of knowledge is the discovery of something we do not understand.

— *Frank Herbert*

A discovery is said to be an accident meeting a prepared mind. — *Albert Szent-Györgyi*

Results! Why, man, I have gotten a lot of results. I know several thousand things that won't work. — *Thomas Alva Edison*

Do you realize if it weren't for Edison we'd be watching TV by candlelight? — *Al Boliska*

Talent hits a target no one else can hit; genius hits a target no one else can see.

— *Arthur Schopenhauer*

If we value the pursuit of knowledge, we must be free to follow wherever that search may lead us. The free mind is not a barking dog, to be tethered on a 10-foot chain.

— *Adlai E. Stevenson*

The saddest aspect of life right now is that science gathers knowledge faster than society gathers wisdom. — *Isaac Asimov*

Science may have found a cure for most evils; but it has found no remedy for the worst of them all—the apathy of human beings.

— *Helen Keller*

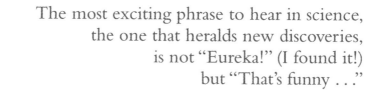

The most exciting phrase to hear in science, the one that heralds new discoveries, is not "Eureka!" (I found it!) but "That's funny . . ."

— ISAAC ASIMOV

When you are courting a nice girl an hour seems like a second. When you sit on a red-hot cinder a second seems like an hour. That's relativity.

— *Albert Einstein*

We can lick gravity, but sometimes the paperwork is overwhelming.

— *Wernher von Braun*

Archaeology is the peeping Tom of the sciences. It is the sandbox of men who care not where they are going; they merely want to know where everyone else has been.

— *Jim Bishop*

The purpose of anthropology is to make the world safe for human differences.

— *Ruth Benedict*

God runs electromagnetics by wave theory on Monday, Wednesday, and Friday, and the Devil runs them by quantum theory on Tuesday, Thursday, and Saturday.

— *William Bragg*

I believe that a scientist looking at non-scientific problems is just as dumb as the next guy.

— *Richard Feynman*

***

Goals and Mind-Set

When I was a small boy growing up in Kansas, a friend of mine and I went fishing and as we sat there in the warmth of a summer afternoon on a riverbank we talked about what we wanted to do when we grew up. I told him that I wanted to be a real major-league baseball player, a genuine professional like Honus Wagner. My friend said that he'd like to be President of the United States. Neither of us got our wish.

— *Dwight D. Eisenhower*

The fight is won or lost far away from witnesses—behind the lines, in the gym, and out there on the road, long before I dance under those lights.

— *Muhammad Ali*

There are no secrets to success. It is the result of preparation, hard work, and learning from failure.

— *Colin Powell*

When you are not practicing, remember, someone somewhere is practicing, and when you meet him he will win.

— *Ed Macauley*

If you train hard, you'll not only be hard, you'll be hard to beat.

— *Herschel Walker*

I skate to where the puck is going to be, not where it's been.

— *Wayne Gretzky*

Before anything else, preparation is the key to success.

— *Alexander Graham Bell*

An idealist believes the short run doesn't count. A cynic believes the long run doesn't matter. A realist believes that what is done or left undone in the short run determines the long run.

— *Sydney J. Harris*

I don't know if I practiced more than any-body, but I sure practiced enough. I still wonder if somebody—somewhere—was practicing more than me. — *Larry Bird*

As a general rule the most successful man in life is the man who has the best information.
— *Benjamin Disraeli*

Whoever wants to reach a distant goal must take small steps. — *Saul Bellow*

Arriving at one goal is the starting point to another. — *Fyodor Dostoyevsky*

A goal without a plan is just a wish.
— *Antoine de Saint-Exupéry*

A rock pile ceases to be a rock pile the moment a single man contemplates it, bear-ing within him the image of a cathedral.
— *Antoine de Saint-Exupéry*

A successful individual typically sets his next goal somewhat but not too much above his last achievement. In this way he steadily raises his level of aspiration. — *Kurt Lewin*

Keep away from people who try to belittle your ambitions. Small people always do that, but the really great make you feel that you, too, can become great. — *Mark Twain*

The indispensable first step to getting the things you want out of life is this: decide what you want. — *Ben Stein*

Give me a museum, and I'll fill it.
— *Pablo Picasso*

A man without ambition is dead.
A man with ambition but no love is dead.
A man with ambition and love for his bless-ings here on earth is ever so alive. Having been alive, it won't be so hard in the end to lie down and rest. — *Pearl Bailey*

The reason most people never reach their goals is that they don't define them, or ever seriously consider them as believable or achievable. Winners can tell you where they are going, what they plan to do along the way, and who will be sharing the adventure with them. — *Denis Watley*

The discipline you learn and character you build from setting and achieving a goal can be more valuable than the achievement of the goal itself. — *Bo Bennett*

Establishing goals is all right if you don't let them deprive you of interesting detours.
— *Doug Larson*

If you don't make things happen then things will happen to you. — *Robert Collier*

Be like a postage stamp. Stick to one thing until you get there. — *Josh Billings*

There is no point at which you can say, "Well, I'm successful now. I might as well take a nap." — *Carrie Fisher*

Creativity is . . . seeing something that doesn't exist already. You need to find out how you can bring it into being and that way be a playmate with God. — *Michele Shea*

148

No bird soars too high if he soars with his own wings.
— *William Blake*

Intelligence without ambition is a bird without wings.
— *Salvador Dalí*

Nothing contributes so much to tranquilizing the mind as a steady purpose—a point on which the soul may fix its intellectual eye.
— *Mary Shelley*

We succeed only as we identify in life, or in war, or in anything else, a single overriding objective, and make all other considerations bend to that one objective.
— *Dwight D. Eisenhower*

To achieve great things, two things are needed; a plan, and not quite enough time.
— *Leonard Bernstein*

I hope that I may always desire more than I can accomplish.
— *Michelangelo*

If everything seems under control, you're just not going fast enough.
— *Mario Andretti*

Concentration comes out of a combination of confidence and hunger.
— *Arnold Palmer*

A somebody was once a nobody who wanted to and did.
— *John Burroughs*

It's never too late to be who you might have been.
— *George Eliot*

If we are to have magical bodies, we must have magical minds.
— *Wayne Dyer*

The big question is whether you are going to be able to say a hearty yes to your adventure.
— *Joseph Campbell*

Attitude is a little thing that makes a big difference.
— *Winston Churchill*

The secret to my success is that I bit off more than I could chew and chewed as fast as I could.
— *Paul Hogan*

Champions aren't made in gyms. Champions are made from something they have deep inside them: a desire, a dream, a vision. They have to have last-minute stamina, they have to be a little faster, they have to have the skill and the will. But the will must be stronger than the skill.
— *Muhammad Ali*

All our dreams can come true, if we have the courage to pursue them.
— *Walt Disney*

Follow your bliss and doors will open where there were no doors before.
— *Joseph Campbell*

Nothing is as real as a dream. The world can change around you, but your dream will not. Responsibilities need not erase it. Duties need not obscure it. Because the dream is within you, no one can take it away.
— *Tom Clancy*

I have learned, as a rule of thumb, never to ask whether you can do something. Say, instead, that you are doing it. Then fasten your seat belt. The most remarkable things follow.
— *Julia Cameron*

You have to believe in yourself, that's the secret. Even when I was in the orphanage, when I was roaming the street trying to find enough to eat, even then I thought of myself as the greatest actor in the world. I had to feel the exuberance that comes from utter confidence in yourself. Without it, you go down to defeat.
— *Charlie Chaplin*

A thinker sees his own actions as experiments and questions—as attempts to find out something. Success and failure are for him answers above all.
— *Friedrich Nietzsche*

Some of the world's greatest feats were accomplished by people not smart enough to know they were impossible.

— *Doug Larson*

You have to recognize when the right place and the right time fuse and take advantage of that opportunity. There are plenty of opportunities out there. You can't sit back and wait.

— *Ellen Metcalf*

A ship in harbor is safe, but that is not what ships are built for.

— *John A. Shedd*

If the highest aim of a captain were to preserve his ship, he would keep it in port forever.

— *Saint Thomas Aquinas*

Only those who dare to fail greatly can ever achieve greatly.

— *Robert F. Kennedy*

I'm a big believer in the fact that life is about preparation, preparation, preparation.

— *Johnnie Cochran*

Genius ain't anything more than elegant common sense.

— *Josh Billings*

Intelligence recognizes what has happened. Genius recognizes what will happen.

— *John Ciardi*

The big secret in life is that there is no big secret. Whatever your goal, you can get there if you're willing to work.

— *Oprah Winfrey*

Success usually comes to those who are too busy to be looking for it.

— *Henry David Thoreau*

If your ship doesn't come in, swim out to it!

— *Jonathan Winters*

Be always sure you are right— then go ahead.

— *Davy Crockett*

Never mistake motion for action.

— *Ernest Hemingway*

Do not be awestruck by other people and try to copy them. Nobody can be you as efficiently as you can. — *Norman Vincent Peale*

There is a difference between conceit and confidence. Conceit is bragging about yourself. Confidence means you believe you can get the job done.

— *Johnny Unitas*

Success is that old ABC—ability, breaks, and courage.

— *Charles Luckman*

We are limited but we can push back the borders of our limitations. — *Stephen Covey*

Go West, young man, and grow up with the country.

— *Horace Greeley*

To be a good actor you have to be something like a criminal, to be willing to break the rules to strive for something new.

— *Nicolas Cage*

Once in seven years I burn all my sermons; for it is a shame if I cannot write better sermons now than I did seven years ago.

— *John Wesley*

The hardest thing in life is to know which bridge to cross and which to burn.

— *David Russell*

Begin doing what you want to do now. We are not living in eternity. We have only this moment, sparkling like a star in our hand and melting like a snowflake. Let us use it before it is too late. — *Marie Beyon Ray*

An unfulfilled vocation drains the color from a man's entire existence.

— *Honoré de Balzac*

Shoot for the moon. Even if you miss, you'll land among the stars. — *Les Brown*

The best advice I got from my aunt, the great singer Rosemary Clooney, and from my dad, who was a game show host and news anchor, was: Don't wake up at 70 years old sighing over what you *should* have tried. Just do it, be willing to fail, and at least you gave it a shot. — *George Clooney*

The thing to remember is that the future comes one day at a time. — *Dean Acheson*

There are many paths to the top of the mountain, but only one view. — *Harry Millner*

Confidence is the hinge on the door to success. — *Mary O'Hare Dumas*

Do something. If it doesn't work, do something else. No idea is too crazy. — *Jim Hightower*

We must be willing to get rid of the life we've planned, so as to have the life that is waiting for us. — *Joseph Campbell*

Always be a first-rate version of yourself, instead of a second-rate version of somebody else.

— JUDY GARLAND

Do not go where the path may lead, go instead where there is no path and leave a trail. — *Ralph Waldo Emerson*

Learn to limit yourself, to content yourself with some definite thing, and some definite work; dare to be what you are, and learn to resign with a good grace all that you are not and to believe in your own individuality. — *Henri-Frédéric Amiel*

A great preservative against angry and mutinous thoughts, and all impatience and quarreling, is to have some great business and interest in your mind, which, like a sponge shall suck up your attention and keep you from brooding over what displeases you. — *Joseph Rickaby*

You've gotta find a way to get out of your own way, so you can progress in life. — *Steve Carlton*

Everybody keeps telling me how surprised they are with what I've done. But I'm telling you honestly that it doesn't surprise me. I knew I could do it. — *Ralph Waldo Emerson*

Our attitudes control our lives. Attitudes are a secret power working twenty-four hours a day, for good or bad. It is of paramount importance that we know how to harness and control this great force. — *Irving Berlin*

I don't want to be called "the greatest" or "one of the greatest." Let other guys claim to be the best. I just want to be known as a clown, because to me that's the height of my profession. It means you can do everything— sing, dance and, above all, make people laugh. — *Red Skelton*

If you always do what interests you, at least one person is pleased. — *Katharine Hepburn*

If you can believe it, the mind can achieve it.
— *Ronnie Lott*

Life engenders life. Energy creates energy. It is by spending oneself that one becomes rich.
— *Sarah Bernhardt*

I am not a has-been. I am a will be.
— *Lauren Bacall*

Faith in oneself is the best and safest course.
— *Michelangelo*

***

Wealth

Money and success don't change people; they merely amplify what is already there.
— *Will Smith*

I'd like to live like a poor man— only with lots of money.   — *Pablo Picasso*

It isn't necessary to be rich and famous to be happy. It's only necessary to be rich.
— *Alan Alda*

A large income is the best recipe for happiness I ever heard of.   — *Jane Austen*

Money doesn't always bring happiness. People with $10 million are no happier than people with $9 million.   — *Hobart Brown*

A rich man's joke is always funny.
— *Thomas Edward Brown*

Of the billionaires I have known, money just brings out the basic traits in them. If they were jerks before they had money, they are simply jerks with a billion dollars.
— *Warren Buffett*

It is pretty hard to tell what does bring happiness; poverty and wealth have both failed.
— *Kin Hubbard*

If you can count your money, you don't have a billion dollars.   — *J. Paul Getty*

The only thing I like about rich people is their money.   — *Nancy Astor*

When a man tells you that he got rich through hard work, ask him: "Whose?"
— *Don Marquis*

The secret to success is to know something nobody else knows.   — *Aristotle Onassis*

It's far better to buy a wonderful company at a fair price than a fair company at a wonderful price.   — *Warren Buffett*

No one can possibly achieve any real and lasting success or "get rich" in business by being a conformist.   — *J. Paul Getty*

The entire essence of America is the hope to first make money—then make money with money—then make lots of money with lots of money.   — *Paul Erdman*

No one can earn a million dollars honestly.
— *William Jennings Bryan*

Gentlemen prefer bonds.   *— Andrew Mellon*

Money can't buy friends, but it can get you a better class of enemy.   *— Spike Milligan*

I enjoy being a highly overpaid actor.

— Roger Moore

Do not be fooled into believing that because a man is rich he is necessarily smart. There is ample proof to the contrary.

— Julius Rosenwald

No matter how rich you become, how famous or powerful, when you die the size of your funeral will still pretty much depend on the weather.   *— Michael Pritchard*

I have always said that if I were a rich man I would employ a professional praiser.

— Osbert Sitwell

Some are born great, some achieve greatness, and some hire public relations officers.

— Daniel J. Boorstin

Never pay the slightest attention to what a company president ever says about his stock.

— Bernard Baruch

Poverty is an anomaly to rich people; it is very difficult to make out why people who want dinner do not ring the bell.

— Walter Bagehot

I find it interesting that the meanest life, the poorest existence, is attributed to God's will, but as human beings become more affluent, as their living standard and style begin to ascend the material scale, God descends the scale of responsibility at commensurate speed.

— Maya Angelou

About the only difference between the poor and the rich, is this, the poor suffer misery, while the rich have to enjoy it.   *— Josh Billings*

I don't know much about being a millionaire, but I'll bet I'd be darling at it.

— Dorothy Parker

The surest way to remain poor is to be an honest man.   *— Napoleon Bonaparte*

Though I am grateful for the blessings of wealth, it hasn't changed who I am. My feet are still on the ground. I'm just wearing better shoes.   *— Oprah Winfrey*

An unhurried sense of time is in itself a form of wealth.   *— Bonnie Friedman*

Money is like manure. You have to spread it around or it smells.   *— J. Paul Getty*

The more money an American accumulates, the less interesting he becomes.   *— Gore Vidal*

A wise man should have money in his head, but not in his heart.   *— Jonathan Swift*

You can't have everything.
Where would you put it?

— STEVEN WRIGHT

If you see yourself as prosperous, you will be. If you see yourself as continually hard up, that is exactly what you will be.

— *Robert Collier*

So you think that money is the root of all evil. Have you ever asked what is the root of all money?

— *Ayn Rand*

To suppose, as we all suppose, that we could be rich and not behave as the rich behave, is like supposing that we could drink all day and keep absolutely sober.

— *Logan Pearsall Smith*

Every man serves a useful purpose: A miser, for example, makes a wonderful ancestor.

— *Laurence J. Peter*

We can have democracy in this country, or we can have great wealth concentrated in the hands of a few, but we can't have both.

— *Louis D. Brandeis*

The advantage of a classical education is that it enables you to despise the wealth which it prevents you from achieving.   — *Russell Green*

Many an optimist has become rich by buying out a pessimist.   — *Robert G. Allen*

People working in the private sector should try to save money. There remains the possibility that it may someday be valuable again.   — *Norman R. Augustine*

There's no reason to be the richest man in the cemetery. You can't do any business from there.   — *Colonel Harland Sanders*

The rich are different from you and me because they have more credit.

— *John Leonard*

The first wealth is health.

— *Ralph Waldo Emerson*

There is nothing wrong with men possessing riches. The wrong comes when riches possess men.   — *Billy Graham*

When you have told anyone you have left him a legacy the only decent thing to do is to die at once.   — *Samuel Butler*

The best way to realize the pleasure of feeling rich is to live in a smaller house than your means would entitle you to have.

— *Edward Clarke*

Anyone who lives within their means suffers from a lack of imagination.   — *Oscar Wilde*

Americans have always been able to handle austerity and even adversity. Prosperity is what is doing us in.   — *James Reston*

What's the quickest way to become a millionaire? Borrow fivers off everyone you meet.   — *Richard Branson*

People who go broke in a big way never miss any meals. It is the poor jerk who is shy a half slug who must tighten his belt.

— *Robert A. Heinlein*

You cannot sift out the poor from the community. The poor are indispensable to the rich.   — *Henry Ward Beecher*

The easiest way for your children to learn about money is for you not to have any.

— *Katharine Whitehorn*

I have enough money to last me the rest of my life, unless I buy something.

— *Jackie Mason*

Just for Fun

The way to make coaches think you're in shape in the spring is to get a tan.

— *Whitey Ford*

The trouble is not that players have sex the night before a game. It's that they stay out all night looking for it.

— *Casey Stengel*

The only reason I don't like playing in the World Series is I can't watch myself play.

— *Reggie Jackson*

I think there are only three things America will be known for 2,000 years from now when they study this civilization: the Constitution, jazz music, and baseball.

— *Gerald Early*

If I ever find a pitcher who has heat, a good curve, and a slider, I might seriously consider marrying him, or at least proposing.

— *Sparky Anderson*

He hits from both sides of the plate. He's amphibious.

— *Yogi Berra*

If it weren't for baseball, many kids wouldn't know what a millionaire looked like.

— *Phyllis Diller*

When we played softball, I'd steal second base, feel guilty and go back.

— *Woody Allen*

I like the job I have, but if I had to live my life over again, I would like to have ended up a sports writer.

— *Richard M. Nixon*

Karate is a form of martial arts in which people who have had years and years of training can, using only their hands and feet, make some of the worst movies in the history of the world.

— *Dave Barry*

Football is a game designed to keep coal miners off the streets.

— *Jimmy Breslin*

Football is a mistake. It combines the two worst elements of American life. Violence and committee meetings.

— *George F. Will*

Thanksgiving dinners take 18 hours to prepare. They are consumed in 12 minutes. Half-times take 12 minutes. This is not coincidence.

— *Erma Bombeck*

If you do big things they print your face, and if you do little things they only print your thumbs.

— *Bugs Baer*

There is a fine line between fishing and just standing on the shore like an idiot.

— *Steven Wright*

Cricket is basically baseball on Valium.

— *Robin Williams*

In order to acquire a growing and lasting respect in society, it is a good thing, if you possess great talent, to give, early in your youth, a very hard kick to the right shin of the society that you love. After that, be a snob.

— *Salvador Dalí*

The early bird gets the worm. The early worm . . . gets eaten.

— *Norman R. Augustine*

Our **Darker** Side

Yes, we humans have a few foibles, as these quotes remind us.
However, amid the despair and criticism, you'll be surprised at
how often you find a glimmer of hope and humor.

Greed

Suburbia is where the developer bulldozes out the trees, then names the streets after them. — *Bill Vaughan*

The salary of the chief executive of a large corporation is not a market award for achievement. It is frequently in the nature of a warm personal gesture by the individual to himself.

— *John Kenneth Galbraith*

The fellow that agrees with everything you say is either a fool or he is getting ready to skin you. — *Kin Hubbard*

The darkest hour in any man's life is when he sits down to plan how to get money without earning it. — *Horace Greeley*

Selfishness is that detestable vice which no one will forgive in others, and no one is without himself. — *Henry Ward Beecher*

As long as people will accept crap, it will be financially profitable to dispense it.

— *Dick Cavett*

We are all selfish and I no more trust myself than others with a good motive.

— *Lord Byron*

The more you have, the more you are occupied, the less you give. But the less you have the more free you are. Poverty for us is a freedom. It is not mortification, a penance. It is joyful freedom. There is no television here, no this, no that. But we are perfectly happy.

— *Mother Teresa*

Another good thing about being poor is that when you are seventy your children will not have you declared legally insane in order to gain control of your estate. — *Woody Allen*

Free will is an illusion. People always choose the perceived path of greatest pleasure.

— *Scott Adams*

I was thrown out of college for cheating on the metaphysics exam; I looked into the soul of the boy sitting next to me.

— *Woody Allen*

The more laws and order are made prominent, the more thieves and robbers there will be. — *Lao-tzu*

The difference between a divorce and a legal separation is that a legal separation gives a husband time to hide his money.

— *Johnny Carson*

The road to Easy Street goes through the sewer. — *John Madden*

People who are always making allowances for themselves soon go bankrupt.

— *Mary Pettibone Poole*

Nothing is illegal if one hundred businessmen decide to do it.

— ANDREW YOUNG

Deception

A man's most open actions have a secret side to them.
— *Joseph Conrad*

It's better to be quotable than to be honest.
— *Tom Stoppard*

Complainant received immediate lacerations of the credibility.
— *Jimmy Breslin*

You can fool some of the people all of the time, and all of the people some of the time, but you cannot fool all of the people all of the time.
— *Abraham Lincoln*

A bizarre sensation pervades a relationship of pretense. No truth seems true. A simple morning's greeting and response appear loaded with innuendo and fraught with implications. Each nicety becomes more sterile and each withdrawal more permanent.
— *Maya Angelou*

It is a profitable thing, if one is wise, to seem foolish.
— *Aeschylus*

Charm is a way of getting the answer yes without having asked any clear question.
— *Albert Camus*

There is nothing as deceptive as an obvious fact.
— *Arthur Conan Doyle*

Many a secret that cannot be pried out by curiosity can be drawn out by indifference.
— *Sydney J. Harris*

Illusions commend themselves to us because they save us pain and allow us to enjoy pleasure instead. We must therefore accept it without complaint when they sometimes collide with a bit of reality against which they are dashed to pieces.
— *Sigmund Freud*

It is hard to believe that a man is telling the truth when you know that you would lie if you were in his place.
— *H. L. Mencken*

Never trust the advice of a man in difficulties.
— *Aesop*

Nobody speaks the truth when there's something they must have.
— *Elizabeth Bowen*

A man always has two reasons for doing anything: a good reason and the real reason.
— *J. P. Morgan*

Never trust a person who says "frankly," "candidly," or "to be honest." He probably is none of those things.
— *Roger Simon*

A person who trusts no one can't be trusted.
— *Jerome Blattner*

He's mad that trusts in the tameness of a wolf.
— *William Shakespeare*

Americans detest all lies except lies spoken in public or printed lies.
— *Edgar Watson Howe*

I detest that man who hides one thing in the depths of his heart, and speaks for another.
— *Homer*

It takes a wise man to handle a lie. A fool had better remain honest.
— *Norman Douglas*

People may or may not say what they mean ... but they always say something designed to get what they want.
— *David Mamet*

When you want to fool the world,
tell the truth. — *Otto von Bismarck*

When you have eliminated the impossible,
whatever remains, however improbable,
must be the truth. — *Arthur Conan Doyle*

Respect for the truth comes close to being
the basis for all morality. — *Frank Herbert*

There are a terrible lot of lies going around
the world, and the worst of it is half of them
are true. — *Winston Churchill*

It is always the best policy to speak
the truth, unless, of course, you are an
exceptionally good liar. — *Jerome K. Jerome*

A truth that's told with bad intent
Beats all the lies you can invent. — *William Blake*

Any fool can tell the truth, but it requires a
man of some sense to know how to lie well. — *Samuel Butler*

The pure and simple truth is rarely pure and
never simple. — *Oscar Wilde*

I have a theory that the truth is never told
during the nine-to-five hours. — *Hunter S. Thompson*

It is discouraging how many people are
shocked by honesty and how few by deceit. — *Noël Coward*

Oh what a tangled web we weave,
When first we practice to deceive! — *Walter Scott*

In the spider-web of facts, many a truth
is strangled. — *Paul Eldridge*

Each time you are honest and conduct yourself with honesty, a success force will drive
you toward greater success. Each time you
lie, even with a little white lie, there are
strong forces pushing you toward failure. — *Joseph Sugarman*

The best measure of a man's honesty isn't
his income tax return. It's the zero adjust on
his bathroom scale. — *Arthur C. Clarke*

The truth does not change according to our
ability to stomach it. — *Flannery O'Connor*

Truth is always strange, stranger than fiction. — *Lord Byron*

I never deny.
I never contradict.
I sometimes forget. — *Benjamin Disraeli*

The cruelest lies are often told in silence. — *Robert Louis Stevenson*

The world wants to be deceived. — *Sebastian Brant*

Of course I lie to people.
But I lie altruistically—for our mutual good.
The lie is the basic building block of good
manners. That may seem mildly shocking to
a moralist—but then what isn't? — *Quentin Crisp*

Those that think it permissible to tell white
lies soon grow color-blind. — *Austin O'Malley*

Fair speech may hide a foul heart. — *J.R.R. Tolkien*

Sin has many tools, but a lie is the handle
which fits them all. — *Edmund Burke*

Men occasionally stumble over the truth,
but most of them pick themselves up
and hurry off as if nothing ever happened.

—WINSTON CHURCHILL

Truth is so rare that it is delightful to tell it.
— *Emily Dickinson*

Exaggeration is a blood relation to falsehood
and nearly as blamable. — *Hosea Ballou*

As scarce as truth is, the supply has always
been in excess of the demand. — *Josh Billings*

If someone betrays you once, it's their fault;
if they betray you twice, it's your fault.
— *Eleanor Roosevelt*

Never assume the obvious is true.
— *William Safire*

The eye sees only what the mind is prepared
to comprehend. — *Robertson Davies*

No man is happy without a delusion of
some kind. Delusions are as necessary to our
happiness as realities. — *Christian Nestell Bovee*

Lying to ourselves is more deeply ingrained
than lying to others. — *Fyodor Dostoyevsky*

A little inaccuracy sometimes saves tons
of explanation. — *Saki*

What really flatters a man is that you think
him worth flattering. — *George Bernard Shaw*

Flattery is like cologne water, to be smelt of,
not swallowed. — *Josh Billings*

A flatterer is a friend who is your inferior,
or pretends to be so. — *Aristotle*

The power of hiding ourselves from one
another is mercifully given, for men are wild
beasts, and would devour one another but
for this protection. — *Henry Ward Beecher*

Delusions of grandeur make me feel a lot
better about myself. — *Jane Wagner*

If we all worked on the assumption that
what is accepted as true is really true, there
would be little hope of advance.
— *Orville Wright*

They used to photograph Shirley Temple
through gauze. They should photograph me
through linoleum. — *Tallulah Bankhead*

Trying to squash a rumor is like trying to
unring a bell. — *Shana Alexander*

The great masses of the people . . . will more
easily fall victims to a great lie than to a
small one. — *Adolf Hitler*

Wittiest Insults

Nobody likes a perpetual grump. But a finely crafted, cleverly phrased insult has its own special kind of beauty. A friendly warning, however: Don't try this at home.

She runs the gamut of emotions from A to B.
    ↶ DOROTHY PARKER on Katharine Hepburn

I never forget a face, but in your case I'll be glad to make an exception.
    ↶ GROUCHO MARX

Her virtue was that she said what she thought, her vice that what she thought didn't amount to much.
    ↶ PETER USTINOV

His lack of education is more than compensated for by his keenly developed moral bankruptcy.
    ↶ WOODY ALLEN

I didn't attend the funeral, but I sent a nice letter saying that I approved of it.
    ↶ MARK TWAIN

I heard his library burned down and both books were destroyed—and one of them hadn't even been colored in yet.
    ↶ ROBERTSON DAVIES

He has all the characteristics of a dog—except loyalty.
    ↶ SAM HOUSTON

He has all the virtues I dislike and none of the vices I admire.
    ↶ WINSTON CHURCHILL

If you have any trouble sounding condescending, find a Unix user to show you how it's done.
    ↶ SCOTT ADAMS

What's on your mind, if you will allow the overstatement?
~ FRED ALLEN

My wife has a slight impediment in her speech.
Every now and then she stops to breathe.
~ JIMMY DURANTE

Sometimes when you look in his eyes you get the
feeling that someone else is driving.
~ DAVID LETTERMAN

She is the original good time that was had by all.
~ BETTE DAVIS

It is guaranteed to put all teeth on edge, including
George Washington's, wherever they might be.
~ VINCENT CANBY

He can compress the most words into the smallest
ideas of any man I ever met.
~ ABRAHAM LINCOLN

I do not know the American gentleman, God forgive
me for putting two such words together.
~ CHARLES DICKENS

No one can have a higher opinion of him than I
have, and I think he's a dirty little beast.
~ W. S. GILBERT

You must come again when you have less time.
~ WALTER SICKERT

I don't like country music, but I don't mean to denigrate those who do.
And for the people who like country music, denigrate means put down.
~ BOB NEWHART

Jerry Ford is a nice guy, but he played too much
football with his helmet off.
~ LYNDON BAINES JOHNSON

Who picks your clothes—Stevie Wonder?
~ DON RICKLES

I may be drunk, Miss, but in the morning I will
be sober and you will still be ugly.
~ WINSTON CHURCHILL

Crime

Behind every great fortune there is a crime.
— *Honoré de Balzac*

Crime is terribly revealing. Try and vary your methods as you will, your tastes, your habits, your attitude of mind, and your soul is revealed by your actions. — *Agatha Christie*

Obviously crime pays, or there'd be no crime. — *G. Gordon Liddy*

I have a suggestion that I think would help fight serious crime. Signs. There are lots of signs for minor infractions: "No Smoking," "Stay Off the Grass," "Keep Out," and they seem to work fairly well. I think we should also have signs for major crimes: "Murder Strictly Prohibited," "No Raping People," "Thank You for Not Kidnapping Anyone." It's certainly worth a try. I'm convinced Watergate would never have happened if there had just been a sign in the Oval Office that said, "Malfeasance of Office Is Strictly Against the Law," or "Thank You for Not Undermining the Constitution."
— *George Carlin*

Everybody has a little bit of Watergate in him.
— *Billy Graham*

Anytime four New Yorkers get into a cab together without arguing, a bank robbery has just taken place. — *Johnny Carson*

New York now leads the world's great cities in the number of people around whom you shouldn't make a sudden move.
— *David Letterman*

It is ridiculous to set a detective story in New York City. New York City is itself a detective story. — *Agatha Christie*

People say New Yorkers can't get along. Not true. I saw two New Yorkers, complete strangers, sharing a cab. One guy took the tires and the radio; the other guy took the engine. — *David Letterman*

There is a new billboard outside Times Square. It keeps an up-to-the-minute count of gun-related crimes in New York. Some goofball is going to shoot someone just to see the numbers move. — *David Letterman*

I love New York City; I've got a gun.
— *Charles Barkley*

In England, if you commit a crime, the police don't have a gun and you don't have a gun. If you commit a crime, the police will say, "Stop, or I'll say stop again."
— *Robin Williams*

Thus the metric system did not really catch on in the States, unless you count the increasing popularity of the nine-millimeter bullet. — *Dave Barry*

In films murders are always very clean. I show how difficult it is and what a messy thing it is to kill a man. — *Alfred Hitchcock*

The only difference between doctors and lawyers is that lawyers merely rob you, whereas doctors rob you and kill you, too.
— *Anton Chekhov*

The illegal we do immediately. The unconstitutional takes a little longer.
— *Henry Kissinger*

Poverty is the parent of revolution and crime. — *Aristotle*

OUR DARKER SIDE

There are worse crimes than burning books. One of them is not reading them.

— *Ray Bradbury*

The number one rule of thieves is that nothing is too small to steal. — *Jimmy Breslin*

A thief believes everybody steals.

— *Edward W. Howe*

What a crazy world we live in! Trying to treat addiction as a legal problem, and trying to treat criminal misbehaviors using guns as a medical problem! Beam me up, Scotty. Ain't no intelligent life down here.

— *Julie Cochrane*

Pick my left pocket of its silver dime, but spare the right—it holds my golden time!

— *Oliver Wendell Holmes*

The guilty think all talk is of themselves.

— *Geoffrey Chaucer*

The towels were so thick there I could hardly close my suitcase. — *Yogi Berra*

We may not all break the Ten Commandments, but we are certainly all capable of it. Within us lurks the breaker of all laws, ready to spring out at the first real opportunity. — *Isadora Duncan*

The good should be grateful to the bad— for providing the world with a basis for comparison. — *Sven Halla*

The cost of living is going up and the chance of living is going down. — *Flip Wilson*

***

Vice

First you take a drink, then the drink takes a drink, then the drink takes you.

— *F. Scott Fitzgerald*

Always do sober what you said you'd do drunk. That will teach you to keep your mouth shut. — *Ernest Hemingway*

I think a man ought to get drunk at least twice a year just on principle, so he won't let himself get snotty about it.

— *Raymond Chandler*

Sometimes too much drink is barely enough.

— *Mark Twain*

If you were to ask me if I'd ever had the bad luck to miss my daily cocktail, I'd have to say that I doubt it; where certain things are concerned, I plan ahead. — *Louis Buñuel*

Actually, it only takes one drink to get me loaded. Trouble is, I can't remember if it's the thirteenth or fourteenth. — *George Burns*

I have taken more out of alcohol than alcohol has taken out of me. — *Winston Churchill*

A woman drove me to drink and I didn't even have the decency to thank her.

— *W. C. Fields*

I am not a heavy drinker. I can sometimes go for hours without touching a drop.
— *Noël Coward*

My makeup wasn't smeared, I wasn't disheveled, I behaved politely, and I never finished off a bottle, so how could I be alcoholic? — *Betty Ford*

Scientists announced that they have located the gene for alcoholism. Scientists say they found it at a party, talking way too loudly.
— *Conan O'Brien*

If you drink, don't drive. Don't even putt.
— *Dean Martin*

Maybe the French will get a manned craft into space if they can get a rocket strong enough to lift a bottle of wine.
— *David Brinkley*

I feel sorry for people who do not drink. When they wake up in the morning it is as good as they are going to feel all day.
— *Frank Sinatra*

Our national drug is alcohol. We tend to regard the use of any other drug with special horror. — *William S. Burroughs*

The worst thing about some men is that when they are not drunk they are sober.
— *William Butler Yeats*

Sure I eat what I advertise. Sure I eat Wheaties for breakfast. A good bowl of Wheaties with bourbon can't be beat.
— *Dizzy Dean*

When I read about the evils of drinking, I gave up reading. — *Henny Youngman*

I am a drinker with writing problems.
— *Brendan Behan*

When you stop drinking, you have to deal with this marvelous personality that started you drinking in the first place.
— *Jimmy Breslin*

I drink too much. The last time I gave a urine sample it had an olive in it.
— *Rodney Dangerfield*

I always keep a supply of stimulant handy in case I see a snake—which I also keep handy.
— *W. C. Fields*

I envy people who drink. At least they have something to blame everything on.
— *Oscar Levant*

I'm a Method actor. I spent years training for the drinking and carousing I had to do in this film. — *George Clooney*

The trouble with jogging is that the ice falls out of your glass. — *Martin Mull*

An alcoholic is someone you don't like who drinks as much as you do. — *Dylan Thomas*

You are not drunk if you can lie on the floor without holding on. — *Dean Martin*

I exercise self-control and never touch a beverage stronger than gin before breakfast.
— *W. C. Fields*

People who drink to drown their sorrow should be told that sorrow knows how to swim. — *Ann Landers*

Drinking makes such fools of people, and people are such fools to begin with that it's compounding a felony. · — *Robert Benchley*

I hate to advocate drugs, alcohol, violence, or insanity to anyone, but they've always worked for me. — *Hunter S. Thompson*

OUR DARKER SIDE

Drug misuse is not a disease, it is a decision, like the decision to step out in front of a moving car. You would call that not a disease but an error of judgment. — *Philip K. Dick*

There are three side effects of acid: enhanced long-term memory, decreased short-term memory, and I forget the third.
— *Timothy Leary*

Dope never helped anybody sing better or play music better or do anything better. All dope can do for you is kill you—and kill you the long, slow, hard way.
— *Billie Holiday*

Cocaine is God's way of saying you're making too much money. — *Robin Williams*

Reality is just a crutch for people who can't cope with drugs. — *Robin Williams*

If you can remember anything about the '60s, you weren't really there. — *Paul Kantner*

Cocaine isn't habit forming. I should know—I've been using it for years.
— *Tallulah Bankhead*

Sometimes a cigar is just a cigar.
— *Sigmund Freud*

To cease smoking is the easiest thing I ever did. I ought to know, I've done it a thousand times. — *Mark Twain*

Smoking is one of the leading causes of statistics. — *Fletcher Knebel*

I like to play blackjack. I'm not addicted to gambling, I'm addicted to sitting in a semi-circle. — *Mitch Hedberg*

To many, total abstinence is easier than perfect moderation. — *Saint Augustine*

I'm glad I don't have to explain to a man from Mars why each day I set fire to dozens of little pieces of paper, and then put them in my mouth. — *Mignon McLaughlin*

Every form of addiction is bad, no matter whether the narcotic be alcohol, morphine or idealism. — *Carl Jung*

Nothing is more desirable than to be released from an affliction, but nothing is more frightening than to be divested of a crutch.
— *James Baldwin*

The problem with people who have no vices is that generally you can be pretty sure they're going to have some pretty annoying virtues. — *Elizabeth Taylor*

I know a man who gave up smoking, drinking, sex, and rich food. He was healthy right up to the day he killed himself.
— *Johnny Carson*

Total abstinence is so excellent a thing that it cannot be carried to too great an extent. In my passion for it I even carry it so far as to totally abstain from total abstinence itself.
— *Mark Twain*

Chains of habit are too light to be felt until they are too heavy to be broken.
— *Warren Buffett*

The wages of sin are death, but by the time taxes are taken out, it's just sort of a tired feeling. — *Paula Poundstone*

It is good to be without vices, but it is not good to be without temptations. — *Walter Bagehot*

Abstainer: A weak person who yields to the temptation of denying himself a pleasure. — *Ambrose Bierce*

My problem lies in reconciling my gross habits with my net income. — *Errol Flynn*

I generally avoid temptation unless I can't resist it. — *Mae West*

Lead me not into temptation; I can find the way myself. — *Rita Mae Brown*

Men are more easily governed through their vices than through their virtues. — *Napoleon Bonaparte*

A bad habit never disappears miraculously; it's an undo-it-yourself project. — *Abigail Van Buren*

Hate the sin, love the sinner. — *Mahatma Gandhi*

Underneath this flabby exterior is an enormous lack of character. — *Oscar Levant*

Between two evils, I always pick the one I never tried before. — *Mae West*

It is not heroin or cocaine that makes one an addict, it is the need to escape from a harsh reality. There are more television addicts, more baseball and football addicts, more movie addicts, and certainly more alcohol addicts in this country than there are narcotics addicts. — *Shirley Chisholm*

***

*L*aziness

I don't think necessity is the mother of invention—invention, in my opinion, arises directly from idleness, possibly also from laziness. To save oneself trouble. — *Agatha Christie*

People are not lazy. They simply have impotent goals—that is, goals that do not inspire them. — *Tony Robbins*

The day will happen whether or not you get up. — *John Ciardi*

Failure is not the only punishment for laziness; there is also the success of others. — *Jules Renard*

I like this place and willingly could waste my time in it. — *William Shakespeare*

The most wasted of all days is one without laughter. — *e.e. cummings*

A day wasted on others is not wasted on one's self. — *Charles Dickens*

Getting caught is the mother of invention.
— *Robert Byrne*

A man who dares to waste one hour of time has not discovered the value of life.
— *Charles Darwin*

Idleness is not doing nothing. Idleness is being free to do anything.
— *Floyd Dell*

A man is not idle because he is absorbed in thought. There is a visible labor and there is an invisible labor.
— *Victor Hugo*

Indifference and neglect often do much more damage than outright dislike.
— *J. K. Rowling*

Ambition is a poor excuse for not having sense enough to be lazy.
— *Edgar Bergen*

Never go to a doctor whose office plants have died.
— *Erma Bombeck*

I have noticed that the people who are late are often so much jollier than the people who have to wait for them.
— *E. V. Lucas*

Blessed is he who expects nothing, for he shall never be disappointed.
— *Jonathan Swift*

One of the advantages of being disorderly is that one is constantly making exciting discoveries.
— *A. A. Milne*

There are two cardinal sins from which all the others spring: impatience and laziness.
— *Franz Kafka*

***

Enemies

You shall judge a man by his foes as well as by his friends.
— *Joseph Conrad*

If you hate a person, you hate something in him that is part of yourself. What isn't part of ourselves doesn't disturb us.
— *Hermann Hesse*

Let my enemies devour each other.
— *Salvador Dalí*

In the end, we will remember not the words of our enemies, but the silence of our friends.
— *Martin Luther King, Jr.*

True friends stab you in the front.
— *Oscar Wilde*

Often we have no time for our friends but all the time in the world for our enemies.
— *Leon Uris*

You must not fight too often with one enemy, or you will teach him all your art of war.
— *Napoleon Bonaparte*

He hasn't an enemy in the world— but all his friends hate him.
— *Eddie Cantor*

It is hard to fight an enemy who has outposts in your head.
— *Sally Kempton*

A wise man gets more use from his enemies than a fool from his friends.
— *Baltasar Gracian*

The best weapon against an enemy is another enemy.
— *Friedrich Nietzsche*

We often give our enemies the means of our own destruction.
— *Aesop*

A man may learn wisdom even from a foe.
— *Aristophanes*

It is easier to forgive an enemy than to forgive a friend.
— *William Blake*

Enemies are so stimulating.
— *Katharine Hepburn*

When my enemies stop hissing, I shall know I'm slipping.
— *Maria Callas*

If you want to make enemies, try to change something.
— *Woodrow Wilson*

Beware the wrath of a patient adversary.
— *John C. Calhoun*

When I got through with him, he was all covered wit' blood—my blood.
— *Jimmy Durante*

Time wounds all heels.
— *Jane Ace*

Gossip is when you hear something you like about someone you don't.
— *Earl Wilson*

The surest way to make a monkey of a man is to quote him.
— *Robert Benchley*

There is only one way to defeat the enemy, and that is to write as well as one can. The best argument is an undeniably good book.
— *Saul Bellow*

***

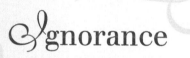

Ignorance

There is more stupidity around than hydrogen and it has a longer shelf life.
— *Frank Zappa*

Only two things are infinite, the universe and human stupidity, and I'm not sure about the former.
— *Albert Einstein*

In view of the fact that God limited the intelligence of man, it seems unfair that He did not also limit his stupidity.
— *Konrad Adenauer*

There's nothing more dangerous than a resourceful idiot.
— *Scott Adams*

The difference between stupid and intelligent people—and this is true whether or not they are well-educated—is that intelligent people can handle subtlety.
— *Neal Stephenson*

Aristotle was famous for knowing everything. He taught that the brain exists merely to cool the blood and is not involved in the process of thinking. This is true only of certain persons.
— *Will Cuppy*

He may look like an idiot and talk like an idiot but don't let that fool you. He really is an idiot.
— *Groucho Marx*

Stupidity is an elemental force for which no earthquake is a match. — *Karl Kraus*

Common sense is not so common. — *Voltaire*

Stupidity has a knack of getting its way. — *Albert Camus*

I think there is only one quality worse than hardness of heart and that is softness of head. — *Theodore Roosevelt*

Too often we . . . enjoy the comfort of opinion without the discomfort of thought. — *John F. Kennedy*

The trouble with the world is that the stupid are cocksure and the intelligent are full of doubt. — *Bertrand Russell*

Nothing defines humans better than their willingness to do irrational things in the pursuit of phenomenally unlikely payoffs. This is the principle behind lotteries, dating, and religion. — *Scott Adams*

If knowledge can create problems, it is not through ignorance that we can solve them. — *Isaac Asimov*

A fellow who is always declaring he's no fool usually has his suspicions. — *Wilson Mizner*

No man likes to have his intelligence or good faith questioned, especially if he has doubts about it himself. — *Henry B. Adams*

Ignorance per se is not nearly as dangerous as ignorance of ignorance. — *Sydney J. Harris*

It has yet to be proven that intelligence has any survival value. — *Arthur C. Clarke*

Facts do not cease to exist because they are ignored. — *Aldous Huxley*

Rogues are preferable to imbeciles because they sometimes take a rest. — *Alexandre Dumas*

A man with one watch knows what time it is. A man with two watches is never sure. — *Albert Einstein*

Little-minded people's thoughts move in such small circles that five minutes' conversation gives you an arc long enough to determine their whole curve. — *Oliver Wendell Holmes*

If there are no stupid questions, then what kind of questions do stupid people ask? Do they get smart just in time to ask questions? — *Scott Adams*

Behind every argument is someone's ignorance. — *Louis D. Brandeis*

My mother said I must always be intolerant of ignorance but understanding of illiteracy. That some people, unable to go to school, were more educated and more intelligent than college professors. — *Maya Angelou*

One man alone can be pretty dumb sometimes, but for real bona fide stupidity, there ain't nothin' can beat teamwork. — *Edward Abbey*

The first man to compare the cheeks of a young woman to a rose was obviously a poet; the first to repeat it was possibly an idiot. — *Salvador Dalí*

If a little knowledge is dangerous, where is the man who has so much as to be out of danger? — *Thomas H. Huxley*

Groucho Marx

Master of One-Liners

We remember him now as the lovable, cigar-waving maniac with an absurd greasepaint mustache. But Julius Henry "Groucho" Marx started his show-biz career as a sweet-faced 15-year-old.

The Marx Brothers (Chico, Harpo, Groucho, Gummo, and Zeppo) staged musical and comedy vaudeville shows in New York in the early 20th century. By 1929, they had transitioned to movies, and they made 13 films over the next 20 years, including *Animal Crackers, A Night at the Opera, Horse Feathers,* and *Duck Soup.* The brothers also appeared individually in another 20 movies. They sometimes tested and fine-tuned their material in front of live audiences before committing a script to film.

By the 1930s, the Marx Brothers were also finding more and more work in the increasingly popular medium of radio—a perfect forum for Groucho's sarcastic wit. As a broadcaster, Groucho was best known as the host of the radio comedy quiz show *You Bet Your Life,* which morphed into a television show and aired until 1961.

Groucho was famous for ad-libbed jokes and insults. While he peppered his banter with sexual innuendo, he never used profanity and did not want to be known as a "dirty" comedian.

*

Go, and never darken my towels again.

*

I don't want to belong to any club that will accept me as a member.

*

I've had a perfectly wonderful evening. But this wasn't it.

*

Outside of a dog, a book is man's best friend.
Inside of a dog it's too dark to read.

*

Time flies like an arrow. Fruit flies like a banana.

*

One morning I shot an elephant in my pajamas.
How he got in my pajamas, I don't know.
Then we tried to remove the tusks....
But they were embedded so firmly we couldn't budge them.
Of course, in Alabama the Tuscaloosa,
but that is entirely ir-elephant to what I was talking about.

*

Why don't you bore a hole in yourself and let the sap run out?

Genuine ignorance is profitable because it is likely to be accompanied by humility, curiosity, and open mindedness; whereas ability to repeat catch-phrases, cant terms, familiar propositions, gives the conceit of learning and coats the mind with varnish waterproof to new ideas. — *John Dewey*

Never attribute to malice what can be adequately explained by stupidity.

— *Nick Diamos*

The trouble ain't that people are ignorant; it's that they know so much that ain't so.

— *Josh Billings*

I'm not sure I want popular opinion on my side—I've noticed those with the most opinions often have the fewest facts.

— *Bethania McKenstry*

Some people are born on third base and go through life thinking they hit a triple.

— *Barry Switzer*

An ignorant person is one who doesn't know what you have just found out.

— *Will Rogers*

There are lots of people who mistake their imagination for their memory. — *Josh Billings*

He that cannot reason is a fool. He that will not is a bigot. He that dare not is a slave.

— ANDREW CARNEGIE

We can have facts without thinking but we cannot have thinking without facts.

— *John Dewey*

I have never met a man so ignorant that I couldn't learn something from him.

— *Galileo*

Few people think more than two or three times a year; I have made an international reputation for myself by thinking once or twice a week. — *George Bernard Shaw*

Most human beings have an almost infinite capacity for taking things for granted.

— *Aldous Huxley*

I am patient with stupidity but not with those who are proud of it. — *Edith Sitwell*

Memory is the thing you forget with.

— *Alexander Chase*

Most of the arguments to which I am a party fall somewhat short of being impressive, owing to the fact that neither I nor my opponent knows what we are talking about.

— *Robert Benchley*

Ignorance gives one a large range of probabilities. — *George Eliot*

Against logic there is no armor like ignorance. — *Laurence J. Peter*

A man thinks that by mouthing hard words he understands hard things.

— *Herman Melville*

OUR DARKER SIDE

Assumptions allow the best in life to
pass you by. — *John Sales*

The human mind treats a new idea the same
way the body treats a strange protein; it
rejects it. — *P. B. Medawar*

Not to engage in the pursuit of ideas is to
live like ants instead of like men.
— *Mortimer J. Adler*

A great many people think they are
thinking when they are merely
re-arranging their prejudices.
— *William James*

Ignorance and superstition ever bear a close
and mathematical relation to each other.
— *James Fenimore Cooper*

It is better to keep your mouth shut and
appear stupid than to open it and remove
all doubt. — *Mark Twain, paraphrasing Lincoln*

The best way to convince a fool that he is
wrong is to let him have his own way.
— *Josh Billings*

There are two ways to slide easily through
life; to believe everything or to doubt everything. Both ways save us from thinking.
— *Alfred Korzybski*

Half the world is composed of idiots, the
other half of people clever enough to take
indecent advantage of them. — *Walter Kerr*

There are no right answers to
wrong questions. — *Ursula K. Le Guin*

Any fool can criticize, condemn,
and complain—and most fools do.
— *Dale Carnegie*

To talk to someone who does not listen is
enough to tense the devil. — *Pearl Bailey*

✳✳✳

$\mathscr{H}$ypocrisy

When a man says he approves of something
in principle, it means he hasn't the slightest
intention of putting it into practice.
— *Otto von Bismarck*

I didn't really say everything I said.
— *Yogi Berra*

The sad truth is that excellence makes
people nervous. — *Shana Alexander*

What I just said is the fundamental, end-all,
final, not-subject-to-opinion absolute truth,
depending on where you're standing.
— *Steve Martin*

The reason people blame things on the
previous generations is that there's only
one other choice. — *Doug Larson*

Some people like my advice so much
that they frame it upon the wall instead of
using it. — *Gordon R. Dickson*

People often grudge others what they
cannot enjoy themselves. — *Aesop*

Too many people spend money they haven't earned, to buy things they don't want, to impress people they don't like.   — *Will Smith*

It's innocence when it charms us, ignorance when it doesn't.   — *Mignon McLaughlin*

Most people have seen worse things in private than they pretend to be shocked at in public.   — *Edgar Watson Howe*

The trouble with most of us is that we would rather be ruined by praise than saved by criticism.   — *Norman Vincent Peale*

Absurdity: A statement or belief manifestly inconsistent with one's own opinion.   — *Ambrose Bierce*

If a man is offered a fact which goes against his instincts, he will scrutinize it closely, and unless the evidence is overwhelming, he will refuse to believe it. If, on the other hand, he is offered something which affords a reason for acting in accordance to his instincts, he will accept it even on the slightest evidence.   — *Bertrand Russell*

Fanaticism consists in redoubling your effort when you have forgotten your aim.   — *George Santayana*

The greatest of faults, I should say, is to be conscious of none.   — *Thomas Carlyle*

If I weren't earning $3 million a year to dunk a basketball, most people on the street would run in the other direction if they saw me coming.   — *Charles Barkley*

Gossip is what no one claims to like, but everybody enjoys.   — *Joseph Conrad*

A lot of people mistake a short memory for a clear conscience.   — *Doug Larson*

There is nobody so irritating as somebody with less intelligence and more sense than we have.   — *Don Herold*

Nothing is more responsible for the good old days than a bad memory.   — *Franklin P. Adams*

If there is anything the nonconformist hates worse than a conformist, it's another non-conformist who doesn't conform to the prevailing standard of nonconformity.   — *Bill Vaughan*

The meanest, most contemptible kind of praise is that which first speaks well of a man, and then qualifies it with a "but."   — *Henry Ward Beecher*

People ask for criticism, but they only want praise.   — *W. Somerset Maugham*

I simply cannot understand the passion that some people have for making themselves thoroughly uncomfortable and then boasting about it afterwards.   — *Patricia Moyes*

There's always somebody who is paid too much, and taxed too little—and it's always somebody else.   — *Cullen Hightower*

Between friends differences in taste or opinion are irritating in direct proportion to their triviality.   — *W. H. Auden*

Rudeness is the weak man's imitation of strength.   — *Eric Hoffer*

Hollywood is a place where they'll pay you a thousand dollars for a kiss and fifty cents for your soul.   — *Marilyn Monroe*

Hollywood grew to be the most flourishing factory of popular mythology since the Greeks.   — *Alistair Cooke*

OUR DARKER SIDE

California is like an artificial limb the rest of the country doesn't really need. You can quote me on that. — *Saul Bellow*

Tip the world over on its side and everything loose will land in Los Angeles. — *Frank Lloyd Wright*

You can take all the sincerity in Hollywood, place it in the navel of a firefly and still have room enough for three caraway seeds and a producer's heart. — *Fred Allen*

***

$\mathcal{A}$nger and Hatred

A riot is the language of the unheard. — *Martin Luther King, Jr.*

Abuse a man unjustly, and you will make friends for him. — *Edgar Watson Howe*

Nothing inspires forgiveness quite like revenge. — *Scott Adams*

If we were to wake up some morning and find that everyone was the same race, creed and color, we would find some other cause for prejudice by noon. — *George Aiken*

Remember, a chip on the shoulder is a sure sign of wood higher up. — *Brigham Young*

Hatred is self-punishment. Hatred is the coward's revenge for being intimidated. — *Hosea Ballou*

As long as you hate, there will be people to hate. — *George Harrison*

Prejudice comes from being in the dark; sunlight disinfects it. — *Muhammad Ali*

Holding anger is a poison. It eats you from inside. We think that hating is a weapon that attacks the person who harmed us. But hatred is a curved blade. And the harms we do, we do to ourselves. — *Mitch Albom*

Many people lose their tempers merely from seeing you keep yours. — *Frank Moore Colby*

The worst-tempered people I have ever met were those who knew that they were wrong. — *David Letterman*

I know that there are people who do not love their fellow man, and I hate people like that! — *Tom Lehrer*

Fear of something is at the root of hate for others, and hate within will eventually destroy the hater. — *George Washington Carver*

The mind of a bigot is like the pupil of the eye. The more light you shine on it, the more it will contract. — *Oliver Wendell Holmes, Jr.*

The price of hating other human beings is loving oneself less. — *Eldridge Cleaver*

I do not want people to be agreeable, as it saves me the trouble of liking them. — *Jane Austen*

The person who does not enjoy his own company is usually right. — *Coco Chanel*

In nine times out of ten, the slanderous tongue belongs to a disappointed person. — *George Bancroft*

Inside every cynical person, there is a disappointed idealist. — *George Carlin*

I certainly did feel inferior. Because of class. Because of strength. Because of height. I guess if I'd been able to hit somebody in the nose, I wouldn't have been a comic. — *Dudley Moore*

Someday we'll look back on this moment and plow into a parked car. — *Evan Davis*

I don't have pet peeves, I have whole kennels of irritation. — *Whoopi Goldberg*

My loathings are simple: stupidity, oppression, crime, cruelty, soft music. — *Vladimir Nabokov*

I hate mankind, for I think myself one of the best of them, and I know how bad I am. — *James Boswell*

He who angers you conquers you. — *Elizabeth Kenny*

Never forget what a man says to you when he is angry. — *Henry Ward Beecher*

Temper is a weapon that we hold by the blade. — *James M. Barrie*

We boil at different degrees. — *Clint Eastwood*

Never leave a message in haste or anger. — *Jeff Davidson*

I like long walks, especially when they are taken by people who annoy me. — *Noël Coward*

Conflict cannot survive without your participation. — *Wayne Dyer*

When someone is impatient and says,
"I haven't got all day,"
I always wonder, How can that be?
How can you not have all day?

— GEORGE CARLIN

OUR DARKER SIDE

Worry and Fear

Never play cards with a man called Doc, never eat at a place called Mom's, and never sleep with a woman whose troubles are worse than your own. — *Nelson Algren*

If you can't sleep, then get up and do something instead of lying there and worrying. It's the worry that gets you, not the loss of sleep. — *Dale Carnegie*

Worry never robs tomorrow of its sorrow, it only saps today of its joy. — *Leo Buscaglia*

Pessimists are not boring. Pessimists are right. Pessimists are superfluous. — *Elias Canetti*

If I knew what I was so anxious about, I wouldn't be so anxious. — *Mignon McLaughlin*

Indecision may, or may not, be my problem. — *Jimmy Buffett*

Ninety-two percent of the stuff told you in confidence you couldn't get anyone else to listen to. — *Franklin P. Adams*

Anxiety is love's greatest killer. It makes others feel as you might when a drowning man holds on to you. You want to save him, but you know he will strangle you with his panic. — *Anaïs Nin*

It takes a real storm in the average person's life to make him realize how much worrying he has done over the squalls. — *Bruce Barton*

It makes no sense to worry about things you have no control over because there's nothing you can do about them, and why worry about things you do control? The activity of worrying keeps you immobilized. — *Wayne Dyer*

Nowadays men lead lives of noisy desperation. — *James Thurber*

As a cure for worrying, work is better than whiskey. — *Ralph Waldo Emerson*

The reason why worry kills more people than work is that more people worry than work. — *Robert Frost*

What worries you masters you. — *Haddon W. Robinson*

A ruffled mind makes a restless pillow. — *Charlotte Brontë*

Little things affect little minds. — *Benjamin Disraeli*

You probably wouldn't worry about what people think of you if you could know how seldom they do. — *Olin Miller*

Most people would rather be certain they're miserable than risk being happy. — *Robert Anthony*

A cynic is not merely one who reads bitter lessons from the past, he is one who is prematurely disappointed in the future. — *Sydney J. Harris*

A frightened captain makes a frightened crew. — *Lister Sinclair*

People are never more insecure than when they become obsessed with their fears at the expense of their dreams. — *Norman Cousins*

Timeless Tombstones

Perhaps you *can't* take it with you. You can, however, leave behind a few choice words for the living to remember you by. The following folks and their loved ones obviously put a lot of thought into these epitaphs before the words were, as they say, chiseled in stone.

"That's all folks."
⚮ MEL BLANC

I had a lover's quarrel with the world.
⚮ ROBERT FROST

Here lies a man named Zeke, second fastest draw in Cripple Creek.
⚮ Gunfighter, Silver City, Nevada

She did it the hard way.
⚮ BETTE DAVIS

Here lies the body of our Anna, done to death by a banana.
It wasn't the fruit that laide her low, but the skin of the
thing that made her go.
⚮ ANNA HOPEWELL, Enosburg Falls, Vermont

And away we go.
⚮ JACKIE GLEASON

A star on earth—a star in heaven.
⚮ KAREN CARPENTER

Murdered by a traitor and a coward whose
name is not worthy to appear here.

~ JESSE JAMES

Here lies the body of Jonathan Blake.
Stepped on the gas instead of the brake.

~ JONATHAN BLAKE Uniontown, Pennsylvania

Good friend, for Jesus' sake forbear,
To dig the dust enclosed here.
Blest be the man that spares these stones,
But cursed be he that moves my bones.

~ WILLIAM SHAKESPEARE

I told you I was sick.

~ B. P. ROBERTS, Key West, Florida

Truth and history
21 men.
The boy bandit king—
He died as he lived.

~ BILLY THE KID (William H. Bonney)

Everybody loves somebody sometime.

~ DEAN MARTIN

A gentle man and a gentleman.

~ JACK DEMPSEY

A tomb now suffices him for whom the
world was not enough.

~ ALEXANDER THE GREAT

Gone but not forgiven.

~ An adulterous husband, Atlanta, Georgia

181

I've developed a new philosophy—
I only dread one day at a time.

— CHARLES M. SCHULZ

While we are focusing on fear, worry, or hate, it is not possible for us to be experiencing happiness, enthusiasm or love. — *Bo Bennett*

Fear defeats more people than any other one thing in the world. — *Ralph Waldo Emerson*

To use fear as the friend it is, we must retrain and reprogram ourselves. ...
We must persistently and convincingly tell ourselves that the fear is here—with its gift of energy and heightened awareness—so we can do our best and learn the most in the new situation.

— *Peter McWilliams*

Fear is a disease that eats away at logic and makes man inhuman. — *Marian Anderson*

I'm really a timid person—I was beaten up by Quakers. — *Woody Allen*

There are only three sins—causing pain, causing fear, and causing anguish. The rest is window dressing. — *Roger Caras*

Fear is that little darkroom where negatives are developed.

— *Michael Pritchard*

For the most part, fear is nothing but an illusion. When you share it with someone else, it tends to disappear. — *Marilyn C. Barrick*

Do the thing you fear to do and keep on doing it ... that is the quickest and surest way ever yet discovered to conquer fear.

— *Dale Carnegie*

Many a man is praised for his reserve and so-called shyness when he is simply too proud to risk making a fool of himself.

—*J. B. Priestley*

None of us, I am sure, knows what is the pain of hunger, but one day I learned it from a little child. I found the child in the street and I saw in her face that terrible hunger that I have seen in many eyes. Without questioning her, I gave her a piece of bread, and then I saw that the little child was eating the bread crumb by crumb. And I said to her, "Eat the bread." And that little one looked at me and said, "I am afraid because when the bread is finished, I will be hungry again."

— *Mother Teresa*

OUR DARKER SIDE

Ill Feelings

A good friend can tell you what is the matter with you in a minute. He may not seem such a good friend after telling.
— *Arthur Brisbane*

Egotist: A person ... more interested in himself than in me.
— *Ambrose Bierce*

The nice thing about egotists is that they don't talk about other people.
— *Lucille S. Harper*

Talk to a man about himself, and he will listen for hours.
— *Benjamin Disraeli*

A bore is a fellow who opens his mouth and puts his feats in it.
— *Henry Ford*

People always call it luck when you've acted more sensibly than they have.
— *Anne Tyler*

The cynic knows the price of everything and the value of nothing.
— *Oscar Wilde*

Cynicism is an unpleasant way of saying the truth.
— *Lillian Hellman*

Winston Churchill—50 percent genius, 50 percent bloody fool.
— *Clement Attlee*

Bad taste is simply saying the truth before it should be said.
— *Mel Brooks*

Let a smile be your umbrella, and you'll end up with a face full of rain.
— *George Carlin*

Start every day off with a smile and get it over with.
— *W. C. Fields*

A lie gets halfway around the world before the truth has a chance to get its pants on.
— *Winston Churchill*

My initial response was to sue her for defamation of character, but then I realized that I had no character.
— *Charles Barkley*

There will be a time when loud-mouthed, incompetent people seem to be getting the best of you. When that happens, you only have to be patient and wait for them to self-destruct. It never fails.
— *Richard Rybolt*

If you can't say anything good about someone, sit right here by me.
— *Alice Roosevelt Longworth*

You cannot be lonely if you like the person you're alone with.
— *Wayne Dyer*

The future ain't what it used to be.
— *Yogi Berra*

Nostalgia isn't what it used to be.
— *Peter De Vries*

The world is full of people whose notion of a satisfactory future is, in fact, a return to the idealized past.
— *Robertson Davies*

I am not ashamed of my grandparents for having been slaves. I am only ashamed of myself for having at one time been ashamed.
— *Ralph Ellison*

Man invented language to satisfy his deep need to complain.
— *Lily Tomlin*

No good deed goes unpunished.
— *Clare Booth Luce*

I have a very strong feeling that the opposite of love is not hate—it's apathy. It's not giving a damn.
— *Leo Buscaglia*

If something is boring after 2 minutes, try it for 4. If still boring, then 8. Then 16. Then 32. Eventually one discovers that it is not boring at all. — *John Cage*

Cynicism is not realistic and tough. It's unrealistic and kind of cowardly because it means you don't have to try. — *Peggy Noonan*

There is no such thing on earth as an uninteresting subject; the only thing that can exist is an uninterested person. — *G. K. Chesterton*

Boredom: the desire for desires. — *Leo Tolstoy*

* * *

*M*ental Problems

Anyone who goes to a psychiatrist ought to have his head examined. — *Samuel Goldwyn*

Freud: If it's not one thing, it's your mother. — *Robin Williams*

If you have an ounce of common sense and one good friend you don't need an analyst. — *Joan Crawford*

He's turned his life around. He used to be depressed and miserable. Now he's miserable and depressed. — *David Frost*

When dealing with the insane, the best method is to pretend to be sane. — *Hermann Hesse*

Nobody realizes that some people expend tremendous energy merely to be normal. — *Albert Camus*

There's a fine line between the Method actor and the schizophrenic. — *Nicolas Cage*

The place where optimism most flourishes is the lunatic asylum. — *Havelock Ellis*

There's a fine line between genius and insanity. I have erased this line. — *Oscar Levant*

Every man is wise when attacked by a mad dog; fewer when pursued by a mad woman; only the wisest survive when attacked by a mad notion. — *Robertson Davies*

A paranoid is someone who knows a little of what's going on. — *William S. Burroughs*

Everything we think of as great has come to us from neurotics. It is they and they alone who found religions and create great works of art. The world will never realize how much it owes to them, and what they have suffered in order to bestow their gifts on it. — *Marcel Proust*

A mistake which is commonly made about neurotics is to suppose that they are interesting. It is not interesting to be always unhappy, engrossing with oneself, malignant and ungrateful, and never quite in touch with reality. — *Cyril Connolly*

Sometimes the appropriate response to reality is to go insane. — *Philip K. Dick*

OUR DARKER SIDE

I am accustomed to sleep and in my dreams to imagine the same things that lunatics imagine when awake. — *René Descartes*

Insanity: doing the same thing over and over again and expecting different results. — *Albert Einstein*

Insanity in individuals is something rare—but in groups, parties, nations and epochs, it is the rule. — *Friedrich Nietzsche*

In a mad world only the mad are sane. — *Akira Kurosawa*

Sanity is a cozy lie. — *Susan Sontag*

Sanity is a madness put to good use. — *George Santayana*

Show me a sane man and I will cure him for you. — *Carl Jung*

Insane people are always sure that they are fine. It is only the sane people who are willing to admit that they are crazy. — *Nora Ephron*

All are lunatics, but he who can analyze his delusions is called a philosopher. — *Ambrose Bierce*

There's a very fine line between a groove and a rut; a fine line between eccentrics and people who are just plain nuts. — *Christine Lavin*

We do not have to visit a madhouse to find disordered minds; our planet is the mental institution of the universe. — *Johann von Goethe*

Some mornings it just doesn't seem worth it to gnaw through the leather straps. — *Emo Phillips*

Howard Hughes was able to afford the luxury of madness, like a man who not only thinks he is Napoleon but hires an army to prove it. — *Ted Morgan*

I'm not a paranoid deranged millionaire. Goddammit, I'm a billionaire. — *Howard Hughes*

The statistics on sanity are that one out of every four Americans is suffering from some form of mental illness. Think of your three best friends. If they're okay, then it's you.

— RITA MAE BROWN

Modern Life

The musings on the following pages cover all of the topics that the caveman never contemplated—work life, computers, celebrity, money, and more. Indeed, some were unheard-of a mere half-century ago.

Work

Genius is 1 percent inspiration, 99 percent perspiration.   — *Thomas Alva Edison*

Underpromise; overdeliver.   — *Tom Peters*

The key is not to prioritize what's on your schedule, but to schedule your priorities.   — *Stephen Covey*

Give me a stock clerk with a goal and I'll give you a man who will make history. Give me a man with no goals and I'll give you a stock clerk.   —*J. C. Penney*

Nothing is particularly hard if you divide it into small jobs.   — *Henry Ford*

The way to get started is to quit talking and begin doing.   — *Walt Disney*

Opportunity is missed by most people because it is dressed in overalls and looks like work.   — *Thomas Alva Edison*

Don't stay in bed, unless you can make money in bed.   — *George Burns*

It's a job that's never started that takes the longest to finish.   —*J.R.R. Tolkien*

The only place where success comes before work is in a dictionary.   — *Vidal Sassoon*

The more I want to get something done, the less I call it work.   — *Richard Bach*

Choose a job you love, and you will never have to work a day in your life.   — *Confucius*

The ability to focus attention on important things is a defining characteristic of intelligence.   — *Robert J. Shiller*

Being on a tightrope is living; everything else is waiting.   — *Karl Wallenda*

One thing life has taught me: If you are interested, you never have to look for new interests. They come to you. When you are genuinely interested in one thing, it will always lead to something else.   — *Eleanor Roosevelt*

I believe you are your work. Don't trade the stuff of your life, time, for nothing more than dollars. That's a rotten bargain.   — *Rita Mae Brown*

Work joyfully and peacefully, knowing that right thoughts and right efforts inevitably bring about right results.   —*James Allen*

Anyone can dabble, but once you've made that commitment, your blood has that particular thing in it, and it's very hard for people to stop you.   — *Bill Cosby*

Find a job you like and you add five days to every week.   — *H. Jackson Brown, Jr.*

Work as if you were to live a hundred years, Pray as if you were to die tomorrow.   — *Benjamin Franklin*

Some critics will write "Maya Angelou is a natural writer"—which is right after being a natural heart surgeon.   — *Maya Angelou*

What we really want to do is what we are really meant to do. When we do what we are meant to do, money comes to us, doors open for us, we feel useful, and the work we do feels like play to us.   —*Julia Cameron*

The key is to figure out what you want out of life, not what you want out of your career.
— *Goldie Hawn*

Nothing is really work unless you would rather be doing something else.
— *James M. Barrie*

Never continue in a job you don't enjoy. If you're happy in what you're doing, you'll like yourself, you'll have inner peace. And if you have that, along with physical health, you will have had more success than you could possibly have imagined.
— *Johnny Carson*

It's just a job. Grass grows, birds fly, waves pound the sand. I beat people up.
— *Muhammad Ali*

Creativity represents a miraculous coming together of the uninhibited energy of the child with its apparent opposite and enemy, the sense of order imposed on the disciplined adult intelligence.
— *Norman Podhoretz*

There is only one admirable form of the imagination: the imagination that is so intense that it creates a new reality, that it makes things happen.
— *Sean O'Faolain*

Of all the useless things a person can do, limerick writing is right up there with golf and fishing.
— *Garrison Keillor*

Creativity comes from trust. Trust your instincts. And never hope more than you work.
— *Rita Mae Brown*

Creativity is allowing yourself to make mistakes. Art is knowing which ones to keep.

— SCOTT ADAMS

A mule will labor 10 years willingly and patiently for you, for the privilege of kicking you once.
— *William Faulkner*

I do not pray for a lighter load, but for a stronger back.
— *Phillips Brooks*

Creative ideas flourish best in a shop which preserves some spirit of fun. Nobody is in business for fun, but that does not mean there cannot be fun in business.
— *Leo Burnett*

Creativity is a drug I cannot live without.
— *Cecil B. DeMille*

Keep on going and the chances are you will stumble on something, perhaps when you are least expecting it. I have never heard of anyone stumbling on something sitting down.
— *Charles F. Kettering*

You do things when the opportunities come along. I've had periods in my life when I've had a bundle of ideas come along, and I've had long dry spells. If I get an idea next week, I'll do something. If not, I won't do a damn thing.
— *Warren Buffett*

When inspiration does not come to me, I go halfway to meet it.
— *Sigmund Freud*

Creativity requires the courage to let go of certainties. — *Erich Fromm*

Punishing honest mistakes stifles creativity. I want people moving and shaking the earth and they're going to make mistakes. — *H. Ross Perot*

You live and learn. At any rate, you live. — *Douglas Adams*

Be nice to people on your way up because you meet them on your way down. — *Jimmy Durante*

If you haven't found something strange during the day, it hasn't been much of a day. — *John A. Wheeler*

A dead end can never be a one-way street; you can always turn around and take another road. — *Bo Bennett*

Those who do not want to imitate anything, produce nothing. — *Salvador Dalí*

If we keep doing what we're doing, we're going to keep getting what we're getting. — *Stephen Covey*

Don't worry about people stealing an idea. If it's original, you will have to ram it down their throats. — *Howard Aiken*

Originality is unexplored territory. You get there by carrying a canoe—you can't take a taxi. — *Alan Alda*

In order to be irreplaceable one must always be different. — *Coco Chanel*

Dressing up is inevitably a substitute for good ideas. It is no coincidence that technically inept business types are known as "suits." — *Paul Graham*

The secret to creativity is knowing how to hide your sources. — *Albert Einstein*

Precision is not reality. — *Henri Matisse*

Good questions outrank easy answers. — *Paul A. Samuelson*

Quality questions create a quality life. Successful people ask better questions, and as a result, they get better answers. — *Tony Robbins*

Creativity can solve almost any problem. The creative act, the defeat of habit by originality, overcomes everything. — *George Lois*

If everyone says you are wrong, you're one step ahead. If everyone laughs at you, you're two steps ahead. — *Charles "Chic" Thompson*

Curiosity about life in all of its aspects, I think, is still the secret of great creative people. — *Leo Burnett*

Intuition becomes increasingly valuable in the new information society precisely because there is so much data. — *John Naisbitt*

Progress isn't made by early risers. It's made by lazy men trying to find easier ways to do something. — *Robert A. Heinlein*

You can't build a reputation on what you are going to do. — *Henry Ford*

You've achieved success in your field when you don't know whether what you're doing is work or play. — *Warren Beatty*

Anyone can do any amount of work provided it isn't the work he is supposed to be doing at the moment. — *Robert Benchley*

Slump, and the world slumps with you.
Push, and you push alone.   — *Laurence J. Peter*

Work is much more fun than fun.
                    — *Noël Coward*

To be worn out is to be renewed.   — *Lao-tzu*

Get happiness out of your work or you may
never know what happiness is.
                    — *Elbert Hubbard*

You have freedom when you're easy in
your harness.   — *Robert Frost*

The harder you work, the luckier you get.
                    — *Gary Player*

Diamonds are nothing more than chunks
of coal that stuck to their jobs.
                    — *Malcolm Forbes*

There seems to be some perverse
human characteristic that likes to make
easy things difficult.   — *Warren Buffett*

I've only been doing this 54 years. With a
little experience, I might get better.
                    — *Harry Caray*

Whether you think you can or think you
can't, you're right.   — *Henry Ford*

If I had eight hours to chop down a tree,
I'd spend six hours sharpening my ax.
                    — *Abraham Lincoln*

I'm not a lawyer. I have many other faults
but that is not one of them.   — *Ed Broadbent*

I've always believed that if you put in the
work, the results will come. I don't do things
half-heartedly. Because I know if I do, then
I can expect half-hearted results.
                    — *Michael Jordan*

I don't wait for moods. You accomplish
nothing if you do that. Your mind must
know it has got to get down to work.
                    — *Pearl S. Buck*

The society which scorns excellence in
plumbing as a humble activity and tolerates
shoddiness in philosophy because it is an
exalted activity will have neither good
plumbing nor good philosophy: neither its
pipes nor its theories will hold water.
                    — *John W. Gardner*

There is no labor a person does that is
undignified—if they do it right.   — *Bill Cosby*

If a man is called to be a street sweeper, he
should sweep streets even as Michelangelo
painted, or Beethoven composed music, or
Shakespeare wrote poetry. He should sweep
streets so well that all the hosts of heaven
and earth will pause to say, Here lived a great
street sweeper who did his job well.
                    — *Martin Luther King, Jr.*

Don't rule out working with your hands.
It does not preclude using your head.
                    — *Andy Rooney*

You can't fake quality any more than you
can fake a good meal.   — *William S. Burroughs*

People forget how fast you did a job—
but they remember how well you did it.
                    — *Howard Newton*

Tradition is what you resort to when you don't have the time or the money to do it right. — *Kurt Herbert Alder*

Be true to your work, your word, and your friend. — *Henry David Thoreau*

You'll never prove you're too good for a job by not doing your best. — *Ethel Merman*

Labor disgraces no man; unfortunately, you occasionally find men who disgrace labor. — *Ulysses S. Grant*

Only those who want everything done for them are bored. — *Billy Graham*

You can't wait for inspiration. You have to go after it with a club. — *Jack London*

Getting ahead in a difficult profession requires avid faith in yourself. That is why some people with mediocre talent, but with great inner drive, go much further than people with vastly superior talent. — *Sophia Loren*

Formula for success: Rise early, work hard, strike oil. — *J. Paul Getty*

These days, the mind that's standing still is, in fact, slipping backwards down the competitive ladder. Fast. — *Tom Peters*

Careers, like rockets, don't always take off on time. The trick is to always keep the engine running. — *Gary Sinise*

A good way I know to find happiness, is to not bore a hole to fit the plug. — *Josh Billings*

Be miserable. Or motivate yourself. Whatever has to be done, it's always your choice. — *Wayne Dyer*

Make every thought, every fact, that comes into your mind pay you a profit. Make it work and produce for you. Think of things not as they are but as they might be. Don't merely dream—but create! — *Robert Collier*

A professional is someone who can do his best work when he doesn't feel like it. — *Alistair Cooke*

It is necessary to work, if not from inclination, at least from despair. Everything considered, work is less boring than amusing oneself. — *Charles Baudelaire*

The real man is one who always finds excuses for others, but never excuses himself. — *Henry Ward Beecher*

Hard work spotlights the character of people: Some turn up their sleeves, some turn up their noses, and some don't turn up at all. — *Sam Ewing*

The time to repair the roof is when the sun is shining. — *John F. Kennedy*

Work while you have the light. You are responsible for the talent that has been entrusted to you. — *Henri-Frédéric Amiel*

From each according to his abilities, to each according to his needs. — *Louis Blanc*

Do the hard jobs first. The easy jobs will take care of themselves. — *Dale Carnegie*

Everything comes to him who hustles while he waits. — *Thomas Alva Edison*

I'm impressed with the people from Chicago. Hollywood is hype, New York is talk, Chicago is work. — *Michael Douglas*

In the modern world of business, it is useless to be a creative original thinker unless you can also sell what you create. Management cannot be expected to recognize a good idea unless it is presented to them by a good salesman.

— DAVID M. OGILVY

Some people see things that are and ask, Why? Some people dream of things that never were and ask, Why not? Some people have to go to work and don't have time for all that. — *George Carlin*

Appealing workplaces are to be avoided. One wants a room with no view, so imagination can meet memory in the dark. — *Annie Dillard*

There is time for work. And time for love. That leaves no other time. — *Coco Chanel*

It has been my experience that one cannot, in any shape or form, depend on human relations for lasting reward. It is only work that truly satisfies. — *Bette Davis*

Success is a journey, not a destination. The doing is often more important than the outcome. — *Arthur Ashe*

Enthusiasm is *not* the same as just being excited. One gets excited about going on a roller coaster. One becomes enthusiastic about creating and building a roller coaster. — *Bo Bennett*

Promise is the capacity for letting people down. — *Cyril Connolly*

Try as hard as we may for perfection, the net result of our labors is an amazing variety of imperfectness. We are surprised at our own versatility in being able to fail in so many different ways. — *Samuel McChord Crothers*

Being busy does not always mean real work. The object of all work is production or accomplishment and to either of these ends there must be forethought, system, planning, intelligence, and honest purpose, as well as perspiration. Seeming to do is not doing. — *Thomas Alva Edison*

Hell, there are no rules here—we're trying to accomplish something. — *Thomas Alva Edison*

Rules are made for people who aren't willing to make up their own. — *Chuck Yeager*

I work for him despite his faults and he lets me work for him despite my deficiencies. — *Bill Moyers*

Few great men would have got past personnel. — *Paul Goodman*

My greatest strength as a consultant is to be ignorant and ask a few questions. — *Peter F. Drucker*

How lucky Adam was. He knew when he said a good thing, nobody had said it before. Adam was not alone in the Garden of Eden, however, and does not deserve all the credit; much is due to Eve, the first woman, and Satan, the first consultant. — *Mark Twain*

Consultants have credibility because they are not dumb enough to work at your company.
— *Scott Adams*

A desk is a dangerous place from which to watch the world. — *John le Carré*

Nothing interferes with my concentration. You could put on an orgy in my office and I wouldn't look up. Well, maybe once.
— *Isaac Asimov*

Moving fast is not the same as going somewhere. — *Robert Anthony*

If the only tool you have is a hammer, you tend to see every problem as a nail.
— *Abraham Maslow*

Farming looks mighty easy when your plow is a pencil, and you're a thousand miles from the corn field. — *Dwight D. Eisenhower*

When we ask for advice, we are usually looking for an accomplice. — *Saul Bellow*

It is easier to do a job right than to explain why you didn't. — *Martin Van Buren*

Anything not worth doing is worth not doing well. Think about it. — *Elias Schwartz*

I have not failed. I've just found 10,000 ways that won't work. — *Thomas Alva Edison*

A mistake is simply another way of doing things. — *Katharine Graham*

Experience is simply the name we give our mistakes. — *Oscar Wilde*

I have yet to see any problem, however complicated, which, when you looked at it in the right way, did not become still more complicated. — *Paul Anderson*

The problem is not that there are problems. The problem is expecting otherwise and thinking that having problems is a problem.
— *Theodore Rubin*

The best way to escape from a problem is to solve it. — *Alan Saporta*

Each success only buys an admission ticket to a more difficult problem. — *Henry Kissinger*

If you think your boss is stupid, remember: You wouldn't have a job if he was any smarter. — *John Gotti*

Carpe per diem—seize the check.
— *Robin Williams*

The two most beautiful words in the English language are "check enclosed."
— *Dorothy Parker*

I like work: it fascinates me. I can sit and look at it for hours. — *Jerome K. Jerome*

All I've ever wanted was an honest week's pay for an honest day's work.

— STEVE MARTIN

Work expands so as to fill the time available for its completion.   — C. Northcote Parkinson

I have long been of the opinion that if work were such a splendid thing the rich would have kept more of it for themselves.
— Bruce Grocott

Men think highly of those who rise rapidly in the world; whereas nothing rises quicker than dust, straw, and feathers.   — Lord Byron

I am a friend of the working man, and I would rather be his friend, than be one.
— Clarence Darrow

The only thing I was fit for was to be a writer, and this notion rested solely on my suspicion that I would never be fit for real work, and that writing didn't require any.
— Russell Baker

Spare no expense to save money on this one.
— Samuel Goldwyn

American business long ago gave up on demanding that prospective employees be honest and hardworking. It has even stopped hoping for employees who are educated enough that they can tell the difference between the men's room and the women's room without having little pictures on the doors.   — Dave Barry

A young man fills out an application for a job and does well until he gets to the last question, "Who should we notify in case of an accident?" He mulls it over and then writes, "Anybody in sight!"   — Milton Berle

Sometimes the best, and only effective, way to kill an idea is to put it into practice.
— Sydney J. Harris

I work until beer o'clock.   — Stephen King

***

Meetings

To get something done, a committee should consist of no more than three men, two of whom are absent.   — Robert Copeland

A committee is a group that keeps minutes and loses hours.   — Milton Berle

Meetings are indispensable when you don't want to do anything.   — John Kenneth Galbraith

The optimum committee has no members.
— Norman R. Augustine

There is no monument dedicated to the memory of a committee.   — Lester J. Pourciau

If you see a snake, just kill it—don't appoint a committee on snakes.   — H. Ross Perot

A conference is a gathering of important people who singly can do nothing, but together can decide that nothing can be done.   — Fred Allen

***

Bureaucracy Gone Berserk

Sorry, dear readers, but you won't be allowed to read this particular collection of quotations, on the subject of bureaucracy, until you have presented three forms of photo ID and have filled out the application form in triplicate. Why? Because that's the way it's always been done.

In a hierarchy, every employee tends to rise to his level of incompetence.
— LAURENCE J. PETER

It's a poor bureaucrat who can't stall a good idea until even its sponsor is relieved to see it dead and officially buried.
— ROBERT TOWNSEND

Bureaucracy is the epoxy that greases the wheels of progress.
— JIM BOREN

If we did not have such a thing as an airplane today, we would probably create something the size of NASA to make one.
— H. ROSS PEROT

A committee can make a decision that is dumber than any of its members. — DAVID COBLITZ

A committee is a cul-de-sac down which ideas are lured and then quietly strangled. — BARNETT COCKS

Any change is resisted because bureaucrats have a vested interest in the chaos in which they exist.
— RICHARD M. NIXON

The only thing that saves us from the bureaucracy is its inefficiency.
— EUGENE MCCARTHY

You will never understand bureaucracies until you understand that for bureaucrats procedure is everything and outcomes are nothing.

↳ THOMAS SOWELL

Every revolution evaporates and leaves behind only the slime of a new bureaucracy. ↳ FRANZ KAFKA

A civil servant doesn't make jokes. ↳ EUGENE IONESCO

A recent government publication on the marketing of cabbage contains, according to one report, 26,941 words. It is noteworthy in this regard that the Gettysburg Address contains a mere 279 words while the Lord's Prayer comprises but 67.

↳ NORMAN R. AUGUSTINE

Bureaucracy, the rule of no one, has become the modern form of despotism.

↳ MARY MCCARTHY

Too often I find that the volume of paper expands to fill the available briefcases.

↳ JERRY BROWN

Bureaucrats write memoranda both because they appear to be busy when they are writing and because the memos, once written, immediately become proof that they were busy.

↳ CHARLES PETERS

Bureaucracy defends the status quo long past the time when the quo has lost its status. ↳ LAURENCE J. PETER

If the copying machines that came along later had been here during the war, I'm not sure the Allies would have won. We'd all have drowned in paper. ↳ ALAN DICKEY

It seems to me that there must be an ecological limit to the number of paper pushers the earth can sustain, and that human civilization will collapse when the number of, say, tax lawyers exceeds the world's total population of farmers, weavers, fisherpersons, and pediatric nurses.

↳ BARBARA EHRENREICH

The perfect bureaucrat everywhere is the man who manages to make no decisions and escape all responsibility.

↳ BROOKS ATKINSON

Leadership

The question "Who ought to be boss?" is like asking, "Who ought to be the tenor in the quartet?" Obviously, the man who can sing tenor.

— *Henry Ford*

Good leaders make people feel that they're at the very heart of things, not at the periphery. Everyone feels that he or she makes a difference to the success of the organization. When that happens people feel centered and that gives their work meaning.

— *Warren Bennis*

The great leaders are like the best conductors—they reach beyond the notes to reach the magic in the players. — *Blaine Lee*

I believe managing is like holding a dove in your hand. If you hold it too tightly you kill it, but if you hold it too loosely, you lose it.

— *Tommy Lasorda*

The very essence of leadership is that you have to have vision. You can't blow an uncertain trumpet.

— *Theodore Hesburgh*

The most important quality in a leader is that of being acknowledged as such. All leaders whose fitness is questioned are clearly lacking in force.

— *André Maurois*

I am personally convinced that one person can be a change catalyst, a "transformer" in any situation, any organization. Such an individual is yeast that can leaven an entire loaf. It requires vision, initiative, patience, respect, persistence, courage, and faith to be a transforming leader.

— *Stephen Covey*

I like my players to be married and in debt. That's the way you motivate them.

— *Ernie Banks*

Executives are like joggers. If you stop a jogger, he goes on running on the spot. If you drag an executive away from his business, he goes on running on the spot, pawing the ground, talking business. He never stops hurtling onwards, making decisions and executing them.

— *Jean Baudrillard*

I am certainly not one of those who need to be prodded. In fact, if anything, I am the prod.

— *Winston Churchill*

I am looking for a lot of men who have an infinite capacity to not know what can't be done.

— *Henry Ford*

The ultimate leader is one who is willing to develop people to the point that they eventually surpass him or her in knowledge and ability.

— *Fred A. Manske, Jr.*

Leadership is a combination of strategy and character. If you must be without one, be without the strategy.

— *H. Norman Schwarzkopf*

The leadership instinct you are born with is the backbone. You develop the funny bone and the wishbone that go with it.

— *Elaine Agather*

One of the tests of leadership is the ability to recognize a problem before it becomes an emergency.

— *Arnold Glasgow*

It is very hard to be a female leader. While it is assumed that any man, no matter how tough, has a soft side . . . a female leader is assumed to be one-dimensional.

— *Billie Jean King*

The first responsibility of a leader is to define reality. The last is to say thank you. In between, the leader is a servant.

— *Max De Pree*

We still think of a powerful man as a born leader and a powerful woman as an anomaly.

— *Margaret Atwood*

Success in almost any field depends more on energy and drive than it does on intelligence. This explains why we have so many stupid leaders.

— *Sloan Wilson*

Motivation is everything. You can do the work of two people, but you can't be two people. Instead, you have to inspire the next guy down the line and get him to inspire his people.

— *Lee Iacocca*

The way to get things done is not to mind who gets the credit for doing them.

— *Benjamin Jowett*

Leadership is intangible, and therefore no weapon ever designed can replace it.

— *Omar N. Bradley*

Accept the fact that we have to treat almost anybody as a volunteer.

— *Peter F. Drucker*

Without initiative, leaders are simply workers in leadership positions.

— *Bo Bennett*

Fires can't be made with dead embers, nor can enthusiasm be stirred by spiritless men. Enthusiasm in our daily work lightens effort and turns even labor into pleasant tasks.

— *James Baldwin*

I don't want any yes-men around me. I want everybody to tell me the truth even if it costs them their jobs.

— SAMUEL GOLDWYN

Three billion people on the face of the earth go to bed hungry every night, but four billion people go to bed every night hungry for a simple word of encouragement and recognition.

— *Cavett Robert*

My grandfather once told me that there were two kinds of people: those who do the work and those who take the credit. He told me to try to be in the first group; there was much less competition.

— *Indira Gandhi*

No man will make a great leader who wants to do it all himself or get all the credit for doing it.

— *Andrew Carnegie*

Prosperity is a great teacher; adversity a greater.

— *William Hazlitt*

Show me a poorly uniformed troop and I'll show you a poorly uniformed leader.

— *Robert Baden-Powell*

You get the best out of others when you give the best of yourself.

— *Harry Firestone*

The most important thing in communication is hearing what isn't said.

— *Peter F. Drucker*

The employer generally gets the employees he deserves.

— *J. Paul Getty*

Example is not the main thing in influencing others. It is the only thing.
— *Albert Schweitzer*

Example has more followers than reason.
— *Christian Nestell Bovee*

Eagles don't flock—you have to find them one at a time.
— *H. Ross Perot*

If you pay peanuts, you get monkeys.
— *James Goldsmith*

We're overpaying him, but he's worth it.
— *Samuel Goldwyn*

The view only changes for the lead dog.
— *Norman O. Brown*

If you want creative workers, give them enough time to play.
—*John Cleese*

In fact, I wanted to be John Cleese and it took some time to realize the job was in fact taken.
— *Douglas Adams*

The only risk of failure is promotion.
— *Scott Adams*

By working faithfully 8 hours a day, you may get to be a boss and work 12 hours a day.
— *Robert Frost*

So much of what we call management consists in making it difficult for people to work.
— *Peter F. Drucker*

Make no little plans; they have no magic to stir men's blood and probably themselves will not be realized. Make big plans; aim high in hope and work, remembering that a noble, logical diagram once recorded will not die, but long after we are gone be a living thing, asserting itself with ever-growing insistence.
— *Daniel H. Burnham*

Don't tell people how to do things. Tell them what to do and let them surprise you with their results.
— *George S. Patton*

The question should be, Is it worth trying to do? not, Can it be done?
— *Allard Lowenstein*

No one has a greater asset for his business than a man's pride in his work.
— *Hosea Ballou*

Few things can help an individual more than to place responsibility on him, and to let him know that you trust him.
— *Booker T. Washington*

The people to fear are not those who disagree with you, but those who disagree with you and are too cowardly to let you know.
— *Napoleon Bonaparte*

A memorandum is written not to inform the reader but to protect the writer.
— *Dean Acheson*

Any task can be completed in only one-third more time than is currently estimated.
— *Norman R. Augustine*

Most projects start out slowly—and then sort of taper off.
— *Norman R. Augustine*

A small demerit extinguishes a long service.
— *Thomas Fuller*

A molehill man is a pseudo-busy executive who comes to work at 9 a.m. and finds a molehill on his desk. He has until 5 p.m. to make this molehill into a mountain. An accomplished molehill man will often have his mountain finished before lunch.
— *Fred Allen*

The longer the title, the less important the job.
— *George McGovern*

There is an enormous number of managers who have retired on the job.
— *Peter F. Drucker*

Habits are like supervisors that you don't notice.
— *Hannes Messemer*

There are two essential rules to management. One, the customer is always right; and two, they must be punished for their arrogance.
— *Scott Adams*

***

Media

A good newspaper, I suppose, is a nation talking to itself.
— *Arthur Miller*

When a dog bites a man, that is not news, because it happens so often. But if a man bites a dog, that is news.
— *John B. Bogart*

A newspaper is lumber made malleable. It is ink made into words and pictures. It is conceived, born, grows up and dies of old age in a day.
— *Jim Bishop*

Objective journalism and an opinion column are about as similar as the Bible and *Playboy* magazine.
— *Walter Cronkite*

Accuracy is to a newspaper what virtue is to a lady, but a newspaper can always print a retraction.
— *Adlai E. Stevenson*

With the newspaper strike on, I wouldn't consider dying.
— *Bette Davis*

I busted out of the place in a hurry and went to a saloon and drank beer and said that for the rest of my life I'd never take a job in a place where you couldn't throw cigarette butts on the floor. I was hooked on this writing for newspapers and magazines.
— *Jimmy Breslin*

I'm all in favor of keeping dangerous weapons out of the hands of fools. Let's start with typewriters.
— *Frank Lloyd Wright*

Rage is the only quality which has kept me, or anybody I have ever studied, writing columns for newspapers.
— *Jimmy Breslin*

We've uncovered some embarrassing ancestors in the not-too-distant past. Some horse thieves, and some people killed on Saturday nights. One of my relatives, unfortunately, was even in the newspaper business.
— *Jimmy Carter*

During a recent panel on the numerous failures of American journalism, I proposed that almost all stories about government should begin: "Look out! They're about to smack you around again!"

— MOLLY IVINS

Never pick a fight with people who buy ink by the barrel. — *Bill Clinton*

Hot lead can be almost as effective coming from a linotype as from a firearm.
— *John O'Hara*

The pen is mightier than the sword, and considerably easier to write with.
— *Marty Feldman*

Four hostile newspapers are more to be feared than a thousand bayonets.
— *Napoleon Bonaparte*

It's amazing that the amount of news that happens in the world every day always just exactly fits the newspaper. — *Jerry Seinfeld*

What one has not experienced, one will never understand in print. — *Isadora Duncan*

We tell the public which way the cat is jumping. The public will take care of the cat.
— *Arthur Hays Sulzberger*

A free press can, of course, be good or bad, but, most certainly without freedom, the press will never be anything but bad.
— *Albert Camus*

Freedom of the press is limited to those who own one. — *A. J. Liebling*

You can never get all the facts from just one newspaper, and unless you have all the facts, you cannot make proper judgments about what is going on. — *Harry S. Truman*

Editor: a person employed by a newspaper, whose business it is to separate the wheat from the chaff, and to see that the chaff is printed. — *Elbert Hubbard*

A journalist is a person who has mistaken his calling. — *Otto von Bismarck*

If one morning I walked on top of the water across the Potomac River, the headline that afternoon would read "President Can't Swim." — *Lyndon B. Johnson*

I could announce one morning that the world was going to blow up in three hours and people would be calling in about my hair. — *Katie Couric*

USA Today has come out with a new survey. Apparently, three out of every four people make up 75 percent of the population.
— *David Letterman*

Let blockheads read what blockheads wrote.
— *Warren Buffett*

The dirtiest book of all is the expurgated book. — *Walt Whitman*

Journalism largely consists of saying "Lord Jones is dead" to people who never knew that Lord Jones was alive.   — *G. K. Chesterton*

Trying to determine what is going on in the world by reading newspapers is like trying to tell the time by watching the second hand of a clock.   — *Ben Hecht*

For most folks, no news is good news; for the press, good news is not news.
— *Gloria Borger*

If I want to knock a story off the front page, I just change my hairstyle.   — *Hillary Clinton*

It is part of prudence to thank an author for his book before reading it so as to avoid the necessity of lying about it afterwards.
— *George Santayana*

Without words, without writing and without books there would be no history, there could be no concept of humanity.
— *Hermann Hesse*

Do not read beauty magazines. They only make you feel ugly.   — *Mary Schmich*

There's very little advice in men's magazines, because men don't think there's a lot they don't know. Women do. Women want to learn. Men think, "I know what I'm doing, just show me somebody naked."
— *Jerry Seinfeld*

Before I refuse to take your questions, I have an opening statement. — *Ronald Reagan*

I'm just preparing my impromptu remarks.
— *Winston Churchill*

Make sure you have finished speaking before your audience has finished listening.
— *Dorothy Sarnoff*

Tell the audience what you're going to say, say it; then tell them what you've said.
— *Dale Carnegie*

The public have an insatiable curiosity to know everything. Except what is worth knowing. Journalism, conscious of this, and having tradesman-like habits, supplies their demands.   — *Oscar Wilde*

What the mass media offers is not popular art, but entertainment which is intended to be consumed like food, forgotten, and replaced by a new dish.   — *W. H. Auden*

The television, that insidious beast, that Medusa which freezes a billion people to stone every night, staring fixedly, that Siren which called and sang and promised so much and gave, after all, so little.
— *Ray Bradbury*

The one function TV news performs very well is that when there is no news we give it to you with the same emphasis as if there were.   — *David Brinkley*

Television news is like a lightning flash. It makes a loud noise, lights up everything around it, leaves everything else in darkness and then is suddenly gone.   — *Hodding Carter*

When the politicians complain that TV turns the proceedings into a circus, it should be made clear that the circus was already there, and that TV has merely demonstrated that not all the performers are well trained.
— *Edward R. Murrow*

And that's the way it is.   — *Walter Cronkite*

Every time you think television has hit its lowest ebb, a new program comes along to make you wonder where you thought the ebb was.   — *Art Buchwald*

If I turn on the television, am I to believe that that is America? I'm sorry, I don't believe that's America. — *Karen Black*

When television came roaring in after the war they did a little school survey asking children which they preferred and why— television or radio. And there was this seven-year-old boy who said he preferred radio "because the pictures were better."
— *Alistair Cooke*

The new electronic independence re-creates the world in the image of a global village.
— *Marshall McLuhan*

Just because your voice reaches halfway around the world doesn't mean you are wiser than when it reached only to the end of the bar. — *Edward R. Murrow*

I have learned that any fool can write a bad ad, but that it takes a real genius to keep his hands off a good one. — *Leo Burnett*

Animation can explain whatever the mind of man can conceive. This facility makes it the most versatile and explicit means of communication yet devised for quick mass appreciation. — *Walt Disney*

God cannot alter the past, though historians can. — *Samuel Butler*

If we had 3 million exhibitionists and only one voyeur, nobody could make any money.
— *Albert Brooks*

Nobody believes the official spokesman . . . but everybody trusts an unidentified source.
— *Ron Nesen*

My advice to any diplomat who wants to have a good press is to have two or three kids and a dog. — *Carl Rowan*

A reporter is always concerned with tomorrow. There's nothing tangible of yesterday. All I can say I've done is agitate the air ten or fifteen minutes and then boom—it's gone. — *Edward R. Murrow*

I hate cameras. They are so much more sure than I am about everything. — *John Steinbeck*

A public-opinion poll is no substitute for thought. — *Warren Buffett*

Those who cannot remember the past are condemned to repeat it. — *George Santayana*

Never offend people with style when you can offend them with substance.
— *Sam Brown*

The function of the press in society is to inform, but its role in society is to make money. — *A. J. Liebling*

Asking a working writer what he thinks about critics is like asking a lamppost how it feels about dogs. — *Christopher Hampton*

A censor is a man who knows more than he thinks you ought to. — *Granville Hicks*

Have you ever observed that we pay much more attention to a wise passage when it is quoted than when we read it in the original author? — *Philip G. Hamerton*

When your work speaks for itself, don't interrupt. — *Henry J. Kaiser*

The word *meaningful* when used today is nearly always meaningless. — *Paul Johnson*

I take the view, and always have, that if you cannot say what you are going to say in 20 minutes you ought to go away and write a book about it. — *Lord Brabazon*

MODERN LIFE

News is history shot on the wing. The huntsmen from the Fourth Estate seek to bag only the peacock or the eagle of the swifting day.

— *Gene Fowler*

I feel that if a person has problems communicating the very least he can do is to shut up.

— *Tom Lehrer*

Drawing on my fine command of the English language, I said nothing.

— *Robert Benchley*

Facts and truth really don't have much to do with each other. — *William Faulkner*

Every improvement in communication makes the bore more terrible.

— *Frank Moore Colby*

Don't pay any attention to what they write about you. Just measure it in inches.

— *Andy Warhol*

***

Fame

I don't think anyone should write their autobiography until after they're dead.

— *Samuel Goldwyn*

Someday each of us will be famous for 15 minutes. — *Andy Warhol*

Now when I bore people at a party they think it's their fault. — *Henry Kissinger*

The celebrity is a person who is known for his well-knownness. — *Daniel J. Boorstin*

If you have to have a job in this world, a high-priced movie star is a pretty good gig.

— *Tom Hanks*

When Ginger Rogers danced with Astaire, it was the only time in the movies when you looked at the man, not the woman.

— *Gene Kelly*

Everyone wants to be Cary Grant. Even I want to be Cary Grant. — *Cary Grant*

Nobody can be exactly like me. Even I have trouble doing it. — *Tallulah Bankhead*

Glamour is what I sell. It's my stock in trade.

— *Marlene Dietrich*

A celebrity has just as much right to speak out as people who hold real jobs. This is America, after all, and you should not be precluded from voicing your opinions just because you sing songs, mouth other people's words on a sitcom or, for that matter, spin a giant multicolored wheel on a game show.

— *Pat Sajak*

If anyone asks you what kind of music you play, tell him "pop." Don't tell him "rock 'n' roll" or they won't even let you in the hotel.

— *Buddy Holly*

One thing about being successful is that I stopped being afraid of dying. Once you're a star you're dead already. You're embalmed.

— *Dustin Hoffman*

An actor's a guy who, if you ain't talking about him, ain't listening.   — *Marlon Brando*

You know, when I first went into the movies Lionel Barrymore played my grandfather. Later he played my father and finally he played my husband. If he had lived I'm sure I would have played his mother. That's the way it is in Hollywood. The men get younger and the women get older.
    — *Lillian Gish*

The only reason I'm in Hollywood is that I don't have the moral courage to refuse the money.   — *Marlon Brando*

I'm Chevy Chase and you're not.
    — *Chevy Chase*

Life is like a B-picture script! It is that corny. If I had my life story offered to me to film, I'd turn it down.   — *Kirk Douglas*

I have been very happy, very rich, very beautiful, much adulated, very famous and very unhappy.   — *Brigitte Bardot*

You're not a star until they can spell your name in Karachi.   — *Humphrey Bogart*

Give me a couple of years, and I'll make that actress an overnight success.
    — *Samuel Goldwyn*

Don't get me wrong, I'm very thankful for all the aliens I've met and loved.
    — *Jonathan Frakes*

I am a commentator, not a brain surgeon. I do not save people's lives. Knowing that I am not more important than anyone else, that I go on the air at 9 o'clock and then off again at 10 really puts things in perspective. This kind of awareness is important to any-one who has risen to prominence in their chosen career, for falling down can be much harder than rising up.   — *Larry King*

A celebrity is a person who works hard all his life to become well known, then wears dark glasses to avoid being recognized.
    — *Fred Allen*

Its better to be known by six people for something you're proud of than by 60 million for something you're not.
    — *Albert Brooks*

Actors have bodyguards and entourages not because anybody wants to hurt them—who would want to hurt an actor?—but because they want to get recognized. God forbid someone doesn't recognize them.
    — *James Caan*

If you want a place in the sun, you've got to expect a few blisters.   — *Abigail Van Buren*

Fame is a fickle food upon a shifting plate.
    — *Emily Dickinson*

I'm never going to be famous. I don't do anything, not one single thing. I used to bite my nails, but I don't even do that anymore.
    — *Dorothy Parker*

 My mother was against me being an actress— until I introduced her to Frank Sinatra.

— ANGIE DICKINSON

MODERN LIFE

Even though people may be well known, they hold in their hearts the emotions of a simple person for the moments that are the most important of those we know on earth: birth, marriage and death.

— *Jackie Kennedy Onassis*

I had pro offers from the Detroit Lions and Green Bay Packers, who were pretty hard up for linemen in those days. If I had gone into professional football the name Jerry Ford might have been a household word today.

— *Gerald R. Ford*

It wasn't until the Nobel Prize that they really thawed out. They couldn't understand my books, but they could understand $30,000.

— *William Faulkner*

To be great is to be misunderstood.

— *Ralph Waldo Emerson*

Fame—a few words upon a tombstone, and the truth of those not to be depended on.

— *Christian Nestell Bovee*

A celebrity is one who is known to many persons he is glad he doesn't know.

— *H. L. Mencken*

A sign of celebrity is that his name is often worth more than his services.

— *Daniel J. Boorstin*

Standing ovations have become far too commonplace. What we need are ovations where the audience members all punch and kick one another.

— *George Carlin*

I get a standing ovation just standing.

— *George Burns*

It took me fifteen years to discover that I had no talent for writing, but I couldn't give it up because by that time I was too famous.

— *Robert Benchley*

A celebrity is anyone who looks like he spends more than two hours working on his hair.

— *Steve Martin*

Fame is only good for one thing— they will cash your check in a small town.

— *Truman Capote*

Hollywood is a place where people from Iowa mistake each other for stars.

— *Fred Allen*

Hollywood is a place where a man can get stabbed in the back while climbing a ladder.

— *William Faulkner*

Fame is like a shaved pig with a greased tail, and it is only after it has slipped through the hands of some thousands, that some fellow, by mere chance, holds on to it!

— *Davy Crockett*

I regret the passing of the studio system. I was very appreciative of it because I had no talent.

— *Lucille Ball*

Celebrity was a long time in coming; it will go away. Everything goes away.

— *Carol Burnett*

I don't deserve this award, but I have arthritis and I don't deserve that either.

— *Jack Benny*

Fame usually comes to those who are thinking about something else.

— *Oliver Wendell Holmes*

Garrison Keillor

Homespun Humorist

It all began with the Grand Ole Opry.

A twenty-something, Minnesota-born writer for *The New Yorker* magazine was preparing an article about the renowned country music show when he had a fresh idea. Well, more appropriately, an old-fashioned idea: Why not stage a live, homespun variety show on the radio? Fill it with music, down-home Midwestern humor, and "commercials" for imaginary products ("Powdermilk Biscuits—heavens, they're tasty and expeditious!")

Garrison Keillor hosted his first live broadcast of *A Prairie Home Companion* in 1974 before an audience of 12. Today he is the patron saint of quiet and genteel people everywhere. More than 4 million listeners tune in each week to more than 550 public radio stations to hear the latest installment from the fictional Lake Wobegon—"where all the women are strong, all the men are good-looking, and all the children are above average."

Aside from broadcasting, Keillor is the author of several books for adults and children, writes poetry, and has made numerous recordings as a storyteller.

Beauty isn't worth thinking about; what's important is your mind.
You don't want a fifty-dollar haircut on a fifty-cent head.

A good newspaper is never nearly good enough,
but a lousy newspaper is a joy forever.

God writes a lot of comedy . . . the trouble is,
he's stuck with so many bad actors who don't know how to play funny.

It's a shallow life that doesn't give a person a few scars.

People will miss that it once meant something to be Southern or Midwestern.
It doesn't mean much now, except for the climate. The question
"Where are you from?" doesn't lead to anything odd or interesting.
They live somewhere near a Gap store, and what else do you need to know?

The funniest line in English is "Get it?" When you say that, everyone chortles.

Even in a time of elephantine vanity and greed,
one never has to look far to see the campfires of gentle people.

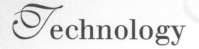Technology

Men have become the tools of their tools.
— *Henry David Thoreau*

Our Age of Anxiety is, in great part, the result of trying to do today's jobs with yesterday's tools.   — *Marshall McLuhan*

Humanity is acquiring all the right technology for all the wrong reasons.
— *R. Buckminster Fuller*

Is fuel efficiency really what we need most desperately? I say that what we really need is a car that can be shot when it breaks down.
— *Russell Baker*

The best car safety device is a rearview mirror with a cop in it.   — *Dudley Moore*

People can have the Model T in any color— so long as it's black.   — *Henry Ford*

I know a lot about cars. I can look at a car's headlights and tell you exactly which way it's coming.   — *Mitch Hedberg*

To invent, you need a good imagination and a pile of junk.   — *Thomas Alva Edison*

A specification that will not fit on one page of 8.5 x 11-inch paper cannot be understood.
— *Mark Ardis*

Inanimate objects can be classified scientifically into three major categories; those that don't work, those that break down and those that get lost.   — *Russell Baker*

The shortest distance between two points is under construction.   — *Noelie Altito*

It is no coincidence that in no known language does the phrase "as pretty as an airport" appear.   — *Douglas Adams*

Our scientific power has outrun our spiritual power. We have guided missiles and misguided men.   — *Martin Luther King, Jr.*

The first rule of any technology used in a business is that automation applied to an efficient operation will magnify the efficiency. The second is that automation applied to an inefficient operation will magnify the inefficiency.   — *Bill Gates*

Bill Gates is a very rich man today . . . and do you want to know why? The answer is one word: versions.   — *Dave Barry*

At the present rate of progress, it is almost impossible to imagine any technical feat that cannot be achieved—if it can be achieved at all—within the next few hundred years.
— *Arthur C. Clarke*

The robot is going to lose. Not by much. But when the final score is tallied, flesh and blood is going to beat the damn monster.
— *Adam Smith*

I do not fear computers. I fear lack of them.
— *Isaac Asimov*

The most likely way for the world to be destroyed, most experts agree, is by accident. That's where we come in; we're computer professionals. We cause accidents.
— *Nathaniel Borenstein*

To err is human—and to blame it on a computer is even more so.   — *Robert Orben*

The future is here. It's just not widely distributed yet. — *William Gibson*

I want to put a ding in the universe. — *Steve Jobs*

Never trust a computer you can't throw out a window. — *Steve Wozniak*

I think computer viruses should count as life. I think it says something about human nature that the only form of life we have created so far is purely destructive. We've created life in our own image. — *Stephen Hawking*

The first rule of intelligent tinkering is to save all the parts. — *Paul Ehrlich*

Oh, I never look under the hood. — *E. B. White*

Programming is like sex: one mistake and you have to support it for the rest of your life. — *Michael Sinz*

A computer lets you make more mistakes faster than any invention in human history—with the possible exceptions of handguns and tequila. — *Mitch Ratliffe*

My favorite thing about the Internet is that you get to go into the private world of real creeps without having to smell them. — *Penn Jillette*

I used to think that cyberspace was 50 years away. What I thought was 50 years away, was only 10 years away. And what I thought was 10 years away . . . it was already here. I just wasn't aware of it yet. — *Bruce Sterling*

The real problem is not whether machines think but whether men do. — *B. F. Skinner*

Programming today is a race between software engineers striving to build bigger and better idiot-proof programs, and the Universe trying to produce bigger and better idiots. So far, the Universe is winning. — *Rich Cook*

If it keeps up, man will atrophy all his limbs but the push-button finger.

— FRANK LLOYD WRIGHT

The danger from computers is not that they will eventually get as smart as men, but we will meanwhile agree to meet them halfway. — *Bernard Avishai*

To err is human, but to really foul things up you need a computer. — *Paul Ehrlich*

The great thing about a computer notebook is that no matter how much you stuff into it, it doesn't get bigger or heavier. — *Bill Gates*

In all large corporations, there is a pervasive fear that someone, somewhere is having fun with a computer on company time. Networks help alleviate that fear. — *John C. Dvorak*

We've heard that a million monkeys at a million keyboards could produce the complete works of Shakespeare. Now, thanks to the Internet, we know that is not true. — *Robert Wilensky*

Looking at the proliferation of personal Web pages on the Net, it looks like very soon everyone on earth will have 15 megabytes of fame. — *M. G. Siriam*

Ours is the age that is proud of machines that think and suspicious of men who try to. — *H. Mumford Jones*

It can take quite a while for a Web page to appear on your screen. The reason for the delay is that, when you type in a Web address, your computer passes it along to another computer, which in turn passes it along to another computer, and so on through as many as five computers before it finally reaches the work station of a disgruntled U.S. Postal Service employee, who throws it in the trash. — *Dave Barry*

A common mistake that people make when trying to design something completely foolproof is to underestimate the ingenuity of complete fools. — *Douglas Adams*

Never worry about theory as long as the machinery does what it's supposed to do. — *Robert A. Heinlein*

Technology is the knack of so arranging the world that we don't have to experience it. — *Max Frisch*

I have always hated machinery, and the only machine I ever understood was a wheelbarrow, and that but imperfectly. — *E. T. Bell*

The nice thing about standards is that there are so many of them to choose from. — *Andrew S. Tanenbaum*

The days of the digital watch are numbered. — *Tom Stoppard*

Aircraft flight in the 21st century will always be in a westerly direction, preferably supersonic, crossing time zones to provide the additional hours needed to fix the broken electronics. — *Norman R. Augustine*

If we had a reliable way to label our toys good and bad, it would be easy to regulate technology wisely. But we can rarely see far enough ahead to know which road leads to damnation. — *Freeman Dyson*

People are broad-minded. They'll accept the fact that a person can be an alcoholic, a dope fiend, a wife beater and even a newspaperman, but if a man doesn't drive, there's something wrong with him. — *Art Buchwald*

The best way to predict the future is to invent it. — *Alan Kay*

In the information age, you don't teach philosophy as they did after feudalism. You perform it. If Aristotle were alive today he'd have a talk show. — *Timothy Leary*

For a successful technology, reality must take precedence over public relations, for Nature cannot be fooled. — *Richard Feynman*

One machine can do the work of 50 ordinary men. No machine can do the work of one extraordinary man. — *Elbert Hubbard*

We are more ready to try the untried when what we do is inconsequential. Hence the fact that many inventions had their birth as toys. — *Eric Hoffer*

Engineers like to solve problems. If there are no problems handily available, they will create their own problems. — *Scott Adams*

Stress

A woman is like a tea bag—you never know how strong she is until she gets in hot water.
— *Eleanor Roosevelt*

Accomplishing the impossible means only that the boss will add it to your regular duties.
— *Doug Larson*

I don't know the key to success, but the key to failure is trying to please everybody.
— *Bill Cosby*

Plan your work, work your plan. Lack of system produces that "I'm swamped" feeling.
— *Norman Vincent Peale*

There cannot be a crisis next week. My schedule is already full.   — *Henry Kissinger*

There is a vast world of work out there in this country, where at least 111 million people are employed in this country alone—many of whom are bored out of their minds. All day long. Not for nothing is their motto TGIF—"Thank God It's Friday." They live for the weekends, when they can go do what they really want to do.
— *Richard Nelson Bolles*

All paid jobs absorb and degrade the mind.
— *Aristotle*

Half the battle in alleviating stress involves knowing how to handle new information that crosses your desk.   — *Jeff Davidson*

Anyone who says he won't resign four times, will.   — *John Kenneth Galbraith*

The way to get five weeks of vacation is to have open-heart surgery. It is the perfect cover. Bipolar depression is a downer and TB makes your friends nervous and a hip replacement is terribly inconvenient, but cardiac surgery poses few risks, is mostly painless, and has a grandeur about it that erases all obligations, social and professional. It is the Get Out of Work card.
— *Garrison Keillor*

Everyone rises to their level of incompetence.
— *Laurence J. Peter*

Getting fired is nature's way of telling you that you had the wrong job in the first place.
— *Hal Lancaster*

No man ever listened himself out of a job.
— *Calvin Coolidge*

If you want to gather honey, don't kick over the beehive.   — *Dale Carnegie*

If you aren't fired with enthusiasm, you will be fired with enthusiasm.   — *Vince Lombardi*

Gain a modest reputation for being unreliable and you will never be asked to do a thing.
— *Paul Theroux*

One of the symptoms of an approaching nervous breakdown is the belief that one's work is terribly important.   — *Bertrand Russell*

It is difficult to get a man to understand something when his job depends on not understanding it.   — *Upton Sinclair*

You don't get anything clean without getting something else dirty.   — *Cecil Baxter*

My second favorite household chore is ironing. My first being hitting my head on the top bunk bed until I faint.   — *Erma Bombeck*

A psychiatrist is a fellow who asks you a lot of expensive questions your wife asks for nothing.

— JOEY ADAMS

You make the beds, you wash the dishes, and six months later you have to start all over again. *—Joan Rivers*

What the world really needs is more love and less paperwork. *— Pearl Bailey*

Open your mail over the wastebasket. *—Jeff Davidson*

You moon the wrong person at an office party and suddenly you're not "professional" anymore. *—Jeff Foxworthy*

Informed decision-making comes from a long tradition of guessing and then blaming others for inadequate results. *— Scott Adams*

Advice is like castor oil, easy enough to give but dreadful uneasy to take. *—Josh Billings*

The price one pays for pursuing any profession or calling is an intimate knowledge of its ugly side. *—James Baldwin*

Turbulence is life force. It is opportunity. Let's love turbulence and use it for change. *— Ramsey Clark*

Habit is the denial of creativity and the negation of freedom; a self-imposed straitjacket of which the wearer is unaware. *— Arthur Koestler*

Are we having fun yet? *— Carol Burnett*

The human brain starts working the moment you are born and never stops until you stand up to speak in public. *— George Jessel*

An objection is not a rejection; it is simply a request for more information. *— Bo Bennett*

America is the country where you buy a lifetime supply of aspirin for one dollar and use it up in two weeks. *—John Barrymore*

When you are not physically starving, you have the luxury to realize psychic and emotional starvation. *— Cherrie Moraga*

When Solomon said there was a time and a place for everything he had not encountered the problem of parking his automobile. *— Bob Edwards*

Believe, when you are most unhappy, that there is something for you to do in the world. So long as you can sweeten another's pain, life is not in vain. *— Helen Keller*

The most difficult thing in the world is to know how to do a thing and to watch someone else do it wrong, without comment. *— T. H. White*

Each man is afraid of his neighbor's disapproval—a thing which, to the general run of the human race, is more dreaded than wolves and death. *— Mark Twain*

If you're going through hell, keep going.
— *Walt Disney*

I believe in trusting. Trust begets trust. Suspicion is fetid and only stinks. He who trusts has never yet lost in the world.
— *Mahatma Gandhi*

Have you ever noticed? Anybody going slower than you is an idiot, and anyone going faster than you is a moron.
— *George Carlin*

Three o'clock is always too late or too early for anything you want to do.
— *Jean-Paul Sartre*

If we were all given by magic the power to read each other's thoughts, I suppose the first effect would be to dissolve all friendships.
— *Bertrand Russell*

Happiness is having a large, loving, caring, close-knit family in another city.
— *George Burns*

Man does not live by words alone, despite the fact that sometimes he has to eat them.
— *Adlai E. Stevenson*

***

$\mathscr{S}$tyle

Fashion can be bought.
Style one must possess. — *Edna Woolman Chase*

I base my fashion taste on what doesn't itch.
— *Gilda Radner*

Where lipstick is concerned, the important thing is not color, but to accept God's final word on where your lips end.
— *Jerry Seinfeld*

I can't take a well-tanned person seriously.
— *Cleveland Amory*

She got her looks from her father. He's a plastic surgeon. — *Groucho Marx*

Every generation laughs at the old fashions but religiously follows the new.
— *Henry David Thoreau*

I've exercised with women so thin that buzzards followed them to their cars.
— *Erma Bombeck*

Luxury must be comfortable, otherwise it is not luxury. — *Coco Chanel*

If you stay in Beverly Hills too long you become a Mercedes. — *Robert Redford*

Comedians Gone Wise

Offstage, comedians pay bills, tie their shoes, and hunt for parking spaces just like the rest of us. They're good at what they do because they're keen observers of humankind and because they're good communicators. Here are some of their serious thoughts— more wise than wisecracking.

Laughter is the closest distance between two people.
⮑ VICTOR BORGE

A bookstore is one of the only pieces of evidence we have that people are still thinking. ⮑ JERRY SEINFELD

Talent alone won't make you a success. Neither will being in the right place at the right time, unless you are ready. The most important question is: "Are you ready?"
⮑ JOHNNY CARSON

Look, I don't want to wax philosophic, but I will say that if you're alive you've got to flap your arms and legs, you've got to jump around a lot, for life is the very opposite of death, and therefore you must at very least think noisy and colorfully, or you're not alive. ⮑ MEL BROOKS

If you want something done, ask a busy person to do it. The more things you do, the more you can do.
⮑ LUCILLE BALL

You're only given a little spark of madness. You mustn't lose it.
⮑ ROBIN WILLIAMS

If your ship doesn't come in, swim out to it!
⮑ JONATHAN WINTERS

The heart of marriage is memories; and if the two of you happen to have the same ones and can savor your reruns, then your marriage is a gift from the gods.

— BILL COSBY

If you have it and you know you have it, then you have it. If you have it and don't know you have it, you don't have it. If you don't have it but you think you have it, then you have it.

— JACKIE GLEASON

I've had a few arguments with people, but I never carry a grudge. You know why? While you're carrying a grudge, they're out dancing.

— BUDDY HACKETT

Throughout life people will make you mad, disrespect you and treat you bad. Let God deal with the things they do, 'cause hate in your heart will consume you too.

— WILL SMITH

Failure seldom stops you. What stops you is the fear of failure.

— JACK LEMMON

The greatest thing you can do is surprise yourself.

— STEVE MARTIN

Laughter gives us distance. It allows us to step back from an event, deal with it and then move on. — BOB NEWHART

Armageddon is not around the corner. This is only what the people of violence want us to believe. The complexity and diversity of the world is the hope for the future.

— MICHAEL PALIN

If you send out good people into the world, you know you've done something good. — CARL REINER

Anger is a symptom, a way of cloaking and expressing feelings too awful to experience directly—hurt, bitterness, grief and, most of all, fear. — JOAN RIVERS

Live by this credo: Have a little laugh at life and look around you for happiness instead of sadness. Laughter has always brought me out of unhappy situations.

— RED SKELTON

These are my new shoes.
They're good shoes.
They won't make you rich like me,
they won't make you rebound like me,
they definitely won't make you handsome like me.
They'll only make you have shoes like me.
That's it.

— CHARLES BARKLEY

I will buy any creme, cosmetic, or elixir
from a woman with a European accent.
— *Erma Bombeck*

She was what we used to call a suicide
blond—dyed by her own hand.
— *Saul Bellow*

Fashion is what you adopt when you don't
know who you are.   — *Quentin Crisp*

I think that the most important thing a
woman can have—next to talent, of
course—is her hairdresser.   — *Joan Crawford*

Darling, the legs aren't so beautiful. I just
know what to do with them.
— *Marlene Dietrich*

Plain women know more about men than
beautiful women do.   — *Katharine Hepburn*

I always say shopping is cheaper than
a psychiatrist.   — *Tammy Faye Bakker*

I buy expensive suits. They just look cheap
on me.   — *Warren Buffett*

It is amazing how complete is the delusion
that beauty is goodness.   — *Leo Tolstoy*

Put even the plainest woman into a beautiful
dress and unconsciously she will try to live
up to it.   — *Lucie Duff-Gordon*

Beauty is mysterious as well as terrible.
God and devil are fighting there, and the
battlefield is the heart of man.
— *Fyodor Dostoyevsky*

I always say that beauty is only sin deep.
— *Saki*

A thing of beauty is a joy forever.
— *John Keats*

I never go out unless I look like Joan
Crawford the movie star. If you want to see
the girl next door, go next door.
— *Joan Crawford*

Women are most fascinating between the
ages of 35 and 40 after they have won a few
races and know how to pace themselves.
Since few women ever pass 40, maximum
fascination can continue indefinitely.
— *Christian Dior*

My religious background is that my
mother is a Christian Dior Scientist.
— *Robin Williams*

A man of 80 has outlived probably three new schools of painting, two of architecture and poetry and a hundred in dress.

— *Lord Byron*

Art produces ugly things which frequently become more beautiful with time. Fashion, on the other hand, produces beautiful things which always become ugly with time.

— *Jean Cocteau*

Fallacies do not cease to be fallacies because they become fashions. — *G. K. Chesterton*

Women thrive on novelty and are easy meat for the commerce of fashion. Men prefer old pipes and torn jackets. — *Anthony Burgess*

It is easy to be beautiful; it is difficult to appear so. — *Hosea Ballou*

I think I'm vaguely blonde. To be perfectly frank, I don't know. — *Cate Blanchett*

Going hungry never bothered me— it was having no clothes. — *Cher*

No matter what a woman looks like, if she's confident, she's sexy. — *Paris Hilton*

The fashion wears out more apparel than the man. — *William Shakespeare*

If men can run the world, why can't they stop wearing neckties? How intelligent is it to start the day by tying a little noose around your neck? — *Linda Ellerbee*

We seem to believe it is possible to ward off death by following rules of good grooming.

— *Don DeLillo*

In Cleveland there is legislation moving forward to ban people from wearing pants that fit too low. However, there is lots of opposition from the plumbers union.

— *Conan O'Brien*

A little bad taste is like a nice dash of paprika.

— *Dorothy Parker*

***

Money

The trouble with the rat race is that even if you win, you're still a rat. — *Lily Tomlin*

The only thing money gives you is the freedom of not worrying about money.

— *Johnny Carson*

Whoever said money can't buy happiness simply didn't know where to go shopping.

— *Bo Derek*

Retirement at sixty-five is ridiculous. When I was sixty-five I still had pimples.

— *George Burns*

Admit it, sport-utility-vehicle owners! It's shaped a little differently, but it's a station wagon! And you do not drive it across rivers! You drive it across the Wal-Mart parking lot!

— *Dave Barry*

Don't simply retire from something;
have something to retire to.

— *Harry Emerson Fosdick*

A lawyer starts life giving $500 worth of law
for $5 and ends giving $5 worth for $500.

— *Benjamin H. Brewster*

Normal is getting dressed in clothes that you
buy for work, driving through traffic in a car
that you are still paying for, in order to get
to a job that you need so you can pay for
the clothes, car and the house that you leave
empty all day in order to afford to live in it.

— *Ellen Goodman*

It's diamonds in your pockets one week,
macaroni and cheese the next.

— *Jolene Blalock*

If it isn't the sheriff, it's the finance
company; I've got more attachments on
me than a vacuum cleaner. — *John Barrymore*

Although most products will soon be
too costly to purchase, there will be a
thriving market in the sale of books on
how to fix them. — *Norman R. Augustine*

Inflation is bringing us true democracy.
For the first time in history, luxuries and
necessities are selling at the same price.

— *Robert Orben*

Why grab possessions like thieves, or divide
them like socialists when you can ignore
them like wise men? — *Natalie Clifford Barney*

I bought some batteries, but they weren't
included. — *Steven Wright*

In spite of the cost of living, it's still popular.

— *Laurence J. Peter*

There are plenty of good five-cent cigars
in the country. The trouble is they cost a
quarter. What this country needs is a good
five-cent nickel. — *Franklin P. Adams*

Why is there so much month left at the end
of the money? — *John Barrymore*

No one goes there nowadays.
It's too crowded. — *Yogi Berra*

I'm spending a year dead for tax reasons.

— *Douglas Adams*

Big business never pays a nickel in taxes,
according to Ralph Nader, who represents
a big consumer organization that never pays
a nickel in taxes. — *Dave Barry*

The hardest thing in the world to understand is income tax. — *Albert Einstein*

The income tax has made more liars out of
the American people than golf has.

— *Will Rogers*

Every crowd has a silver lining.

— *P. T. Barnum*

People will buy anything that is one to
a customer. — *Sinclair Lewis*

Take all the fools out of this world and there
wouldn't be any fun living in it, or profit.

— *Josh Billings*

MODERN LIFE

There is only one boss: the customer. And he can fire everybody in the company, from the chairman on down, simply by spending his money somewhere else.   — *Sam Walton*

Your most unhappy customers are your greatest source of learning.   — *Bill Gates*

The safest way to double your money is to fold it over and put it in your pocket.
    — *Kin Hubbard*

Free advice is worth the price.   — *Robert Half*

If your imagination leads you to understand how quickly people grant your requests when those requests appeal to their self-interest, you can have practically anything you go after.   — *Napoleon Hill*

Advertising may be described as the science of arresting human intelligence long enough to get money from it.   — *Stephen Leacock*

Every time you spend money, you're casting a vote for the kind of world you want.

— ANNA LAPPE

Money is the most egalitarian force in society. It confers power on whoever holds it.
    — *Roger Starr*

People who work sitting down get paid more than people who work standing up.
    — *Ogden Nash*

All work and no play makes Jack a dull boy—and Jill a wealthy widow.   — *Evan Esar*

The only really good place to buy lumber is at a store where the lumber has already been cut and attached together in the form of furniture, finished, and put inside boxes.
    — *Dave Barry*

Why pay a dollar for a bookmark? Why not use the dollar for a bookmark?
    — *Steven Spielberg*

If we could sell our experiences for what they cost us, we'd all be millionaires.
    — *Abigail Van Buren*

What is the difference between unethical and ethical advertising? Unethical advertising uses falsehoods to deceive the public; ethical advertising uses truth to deceive the public.
    — *Vilhjalmur Stefansson*

A great ad campaign will make a bad product fail faster. It will get more people to know it's bad.   — *William Bernbach*

Half the money I spend on advertising is wasted; the trouble is I don't know which half.   — *John Wanamaker*

Few people at the beginning of the nineteenth century needed an adman to tell them what they wanted.
    — *John Kenneth Galbraith*

We grew up founding our dreams on the infinite promise of American advertising. I still believe that one can learn to play the piano by mail and that mud will give you a perfect complexion.   — *Zelda Fitzgerald*

Advertising is a valuable economic factor because it is the cheapest way of selling goods, particularly if the goods are worthless.

— *Sinclair Lewis*

The philosophy behind much advertising is based on the old observation that every man is really two men—the man he is and the man he wants to be. — *William Feather*

Too many of us look upon Americans as dollar chasers. This is a cruel libel, even if it is reiterated thoughtlessly by the Americans themselves. — *Albert Einstein*

He who will not economize will have to agonize. — *Confucius*

Finance is the art of passing currency from hand to hand until it finally disappears.

— *Robert W. Sarnoff*

Money, it turned out, was exactly like sex. You thought of nothing else if you didn't have it and thought of other things if you did.

— *James Baldwin*

Money is a singular thing. It ranks with love as man's greatest source of joy. And with death as his greatest source of anxiety. Over all history it has oppressed nearly all people in one of two ways: either it has been abundant and very unreliable, or reliable and very scarce.

— *John Kenneth Galbraith*

Advertising is the modern substitute for argument; its function is to make the worse appear the better. — *George Santayana*

A bank is a place where they lend you an umbrella in fair weather and ask for it back when it begins to rain. — *Robert Frost*

I hate banks. They do nothing positive for anybody except take care of themselves. They're first in with their fees and first out when there's trouble. — *Earl Warren*

If you owe the bank $100, that's your problem. If you owe the bank $100 million, that's the bank's problem. — *J. Paul Getty*

A bank is a place that will lend you money if you can prove that you don't need it.

— *Bob Hope*

Banking establishments are more dangerous than standing armies. — *Thomas Jefferson*

Drive-in banks were established so most of the cars today could see their real owners.

— *E. Joseph Crossman*

An economist is a man who states the obvious in terms of the incomprehensible.

— *Alfred A. Knopf*

I guess I should warn you, if I turn out to be particularly clear, you've probably misunderstood what I've said. — *Alan Greenspan*

Never invest in a business you cannot understand.

— WARREN BUFFETT

MODERN LIFE

An economist is an expert who will know tomorrow why the things he predicted yesterday didn't happen today.
— *Laurence J. Peter*

A study of economics usually reveals that the best time to buy anything is last year.
— *Marty Allen*

If all economists were laid end to end, they would not reach a conclusion.
— *George Bernard Shaw*

Economics is extremely useful as a form of employment for economists.
— *John Kenneth Galbraith*

Risk comes from not knowing what you're doing.
— *Warren Buffett*

If stock market experts were so expert, they would be buying stock, not selling advice.
— *Norman R. Augustine*

A speculator is a man who observes the future, and acts before it occurs.
— *Bernard Baruch*

Emotions are your worst enemy in the stock market.
— *Don Hays*

Don't try to buy at the bottom and sell at the top. It can't be done except by liars.
— *Bernard Baruch*

The business of America is business.
— *Calvin Coolidge*

You can close more business in two months by becoming interested in other people than you can in two years by trying to get people interested in you.
— *Dale Carnegie*

Small opportunities are often the beginning of great enterprises.
— *Demosthenes*

I have probably purchased 50 "hot tips" in my career, maybe even more. When I put them all together, I know I am a net loser.
— *Charles Schwab*

That which costs little is less valued.
— *Miguel de Cervantes*

People want economy and they will pay any price to get it.
— *Lee Iacocca*

A billion saved is a billion earned.
— *Norman R. Augustine*

The only reason I made a commercial for American Express was to pay for my American Express bill.
— *Peter Ustinov*

I don't think meals have any business being deductible. I'm for separation of calories and corporations.
— *Ralph Nader*

If past history was all there was to the game, the richest people would be librarians.
— *Warren Buffett*

Always listen to experts. They'll tell you what can't be done and why. Then do it.
— *Robert A. Heinlein*

An expert is a person who has made all the mistakes that can be made in a very narrow field.
— *Niels Bohr*

Much ingenuity with a little money is vastly more profitable and amusing than much money without ingenuity.
— *Arnold Bennett*

Anyone who says businessmen deal in facts, not fiction, has never read old five-year projections.
— *Malcolm Forbes*

The best minds are not in government. If any were, business would steal them away.
— *Ronald Reagan*

There are many highly successful businesses in the United States. There are also many highly paid executives. The policy is not to intermingle the two. — *Norman R. Augustine*

Capital isn't so important in business. Experience isn't so important. You can get both these things. What is important is ideas. If you have ideas, you have the main asset you need, and there isn't any limit to what you can do with your business and your life. — *Harvey S. Firestone*

Capitalism needs to function like a game of tug-of-war. Two opposing sides need to continually struggle for dominance, but at no time can either side be permitted to walk away with the rope. — *Pete Holiday*

I don't want to do business with those who don't make a profit, because they can't give the best service. — *Richard Bach*

Every economy is uncertain. Referring to this or any economy as "uncertain" is an unnecessary and pessimistic redundancy. — *Bo Bennett*

Business, that's easily defined— it's other people's money. — *Peter F. Drucker*

If you work just for money, you'll never make it, but if you love what you're doing and you always put the customer first, success will be yours. — *Ray Kroc*

Corporation: An ingenious device for obtaining profit without individual responsibility. — *Ambrose Bierce*

The use of solar energy has not been opened up because the oil industry does not own the sun. — *Ralph Nader*

Business opportunities are like buses, there's always another one coming. — *Richard Branson*

It puzzles me how they know what corners are good for filling stations. Just how did they know gas and oil was under there? — *Dizzy Dean*

I think it's wrong that only one company makes the game Monopoly. — *Steven Wright*

A verbal contract isn't worth the paper it's written on. — *Samuel Goldwyn*

When buying and selling are controlled by legislation, the first things to be bought and sold are legislators. — *P. J. O'Rourke*

I find it rather easy to portray a businessman. Being bland, rather cruel and incompetent comes naturally to me. — *John Cleese*

It costs a lot to build bad products. — *Norman R. Augustine*

Growth for the sake of growth is the ideology of the cancer cell. — *Edward Abbey*

MODERN LIFE

Oil prices have fallen lately.
We include this news for the benefit of gas stations,
which otherwise wouldn't learn of it for six months.

— BILL TAMMEUS

War, **Peace**, and Politics

This selection of quotations covers what politicians are best at—
pontification—as well as such really important matters as laws
and liberty, states and statesmen, power and presidents, war and
peace. Perhaps we should have called it "Your Tax Dollars
at Work."

Nations

And so my fellow Americans, ask not what your country can do for you; ask what you can do for your country. — *John F. Kennedy*

A strong nation, like a strong person, can afford to be gentle, firm, thoughtful, and restrained. It can afford to extend a helping hand to others. It's a weak nation, like a weak person, that must behave with bluster and boasting and rashness and other signs of insecurity. — *Jimmy Carter*

We must learn to live together as brothers or perish together as fools. — *Martin Luther King, Jr.*

United we stand, divided we fall. — *Aesop*

Unlike any other nation, here the people rule, and their will is the supreme law. It is sometimes sneeringly said by those who do not like free government, that here we count heads. True, heads are counted, but brains also. — *William McKinley*

Civilization is a method of living, an attitude of equal respect for all men. — *Jane Addams*

Civilization had too many rules for me, so I did my best to rewrite them. — *Bill Cosby*

Our country, right or wrong. When right, to be kept right, when wrong, to be put right. — *Carl Schurz*

Everyone who receives the protection of society owes a return for the benefit. — *John Stuart Mill*

By gnawing through a dike, even a rat may drown a nation. — *Edmund Burke*

If I had to choose between betraying my country and betraying my friend, I hope I should have the guts to betray my country. — *E. M. Forster*

When I am abroad, I always make it a rule never to criticize or attack the government of my own country. I make up for lost time when I come home. — *Winston Churchill*

Immigration is the sincerest form of flattery. — *Jack Paar*

The most important lesson of American history is the promise of the unexpected. None of our ancestors would have imagined settling way over here on this unknown continent. So we must continue to have society that is hospitable to the unexpected, which allows possibilities to develop beyond our own imaginings. — *Daniel J. Boorstin*

I am a firm believer in the people. If given the truth, they can be depended upon to meet any national crises. The great point is to bring them the real facts. — *Abraham Lincoln*

I see America, not in the setting sun of a black night of despair ahead of us, I see America in the crimson light of a rising sun fresh from the burning, creative hand of God. I see great days ahead, great days possible to men and women of will and vision. — *Carl Sandburg*

The strength of the United States is not the gold at Fort Knox or the weapons of mass destruction that we have, but the sum total of the education and the character of our people. — *Claiborne Pell*

This is a great country, and it wasn't made so by angry people. We have a sacred duty to bequeath it to our grandchildren in better shape than however we found it. We have a long way to go and we're not getting any younger. Dante said that the hottest place in hell is reserved for those who in time of crisis remain neutral, so I have spoken my piece, and thank you, dear reader. It's a beautiful world, rain or shine, and there is more to life than winning.

— *Garrison Keillor*

I was born an American; I will live an American; I shall die an American.

— *Daniel Webster*

America is a vast conspiracy to make you happy.

—*John Updike*

Intellectually, I know that America is no better than any other country; emotionally I know she is better than every other country.

— *Sinclair Lewis*

America is not only big and rich, it is mysterious; and its capacity for the humorous or ironical concealment of its interests matches that of the legendary inscrutable Chinese.

— *David Riesman*

For a nation which has an almost evil reputation for bustle, bustle, bustle, and rush, rush, rush, we spend an enormous amount of time standing around in line in front of windows, just waiting.

— *Robert Benchley*

I want a kinder, gentler nation.

— *George H. W. Bush*

Give me your tired, your poor,
Your huddled masses yearning to breathe free,
The wretched refuse of your teeming shore.
Send these, the homeless, tempest-tossed to me,
I lift my lamp beside the golden door.

— EMMA LAZARUS

In America only the successful writer is important, in France all writers are important, in England no writer is important, and in Australia you have to explain what a writer is.

— *Geoffrey Cottrell*

America is not merely a nation but a nation of nations.

— *Lyndon B. Johnson*

America had often been discovered before Columbus, but it had always been hushed up.

— *Oscar Wilde*

A people that values its privileges above its principles soon loses both.

— *Dwight D. Eisenhower*

I love America more than any other country in this world, and, exactly for this reason, I insist on the right to criticize her perpetually.

—*James Baldwin*

America did not invent human rights. In a very real sense ... human rights invented America.

—*Jimmy Carter*

Nelson Mandela

From Prisoner to President

"The struggle is my life," said Nelson Mandela, and so it was.

Born in 1918 in oppressive, white-dominated South Africa, Mandela decided early in life to become a lawyer and to fight for freedom and equality for the black majority. He opened a law practice; he moved up the ranks of the activist African National Congress; he helped to topple the apartheid system; he was awarded the Nobel Peace Prize; and he was elected president of South Africa. The obstacles along the way, however, were grueling and relentless—including nearly 30 years spent in prison.

During Mandela's confinement, the world got heroic glimpses of the man. Facing a probable death sentence, Mandela made a statement to the court that resounded across the globe: "During my lifetime I have dedicated myself to the struggle of the African people. I have fought against white domination, and I have fought against black domination. I have cherished the ideal of a democratic and free society in which all persons live together in harmony and with equal opportunities. It is an ideal which I hope to live for and to achieve. But, if needs be, it is an ideal for which I am prepared to die."

Years later, Mandela would repeatedly refuse to compromise his political positions in exchange for less time behind bars, further enhancing the reputation of the world's most famous political prisoner.

*

In my country we go to prison first and then become president.

*

*No one is born hating another person because of the color of his skin,
or his background, or his religion. People must learn to hate,
and if they can learn to hate, they can be taught to love,
for love comes more naturally to the human heart than its opposite.*

*

Any man or institution that tries to rob me of my dignity will lose.

*

A good head and a good heart are always a formidable combination.

*

*I have walked that long road to freedom. I have tried not to falter;
I have made missteps along the way. But I have discovered the secret
that after climbing a great hill, one only finds that there are many more hills to climb.
I have taken a moment here to rest, to steal a view of the glorious vista
that surrounds me, to look back on the distance I have come.
But I can only rest for a moment, for with freedom comes responsibilities,
and I dare not linger, for my long walk is not ended.*

*

*I learned that courage was not the absence of fear, but the triumph over it.
The brave man is not he who does not feel afraid, but he who conquers that fear.*

*

*If you talk to a man in a language he understands, that goes to his head.
If you talk to him in his language, that goes to his heart.*

*

*Why is it that in this courtroom I am facing a white magistrate,
confronted by a white prosecutor, escorted by white orderlies?
Can anybody honestly and seriously suggest that in this type of atmosphere
the scales of justice are evenly balanced? Why is it that no African
in the history of this country has ever had the honor of being tried
by his own kind, by his own flesh and blood?*

If anyone tells you that America's best days are behind her, they're looking the wrong way.
— *George H. W. Bush*

A man's feet should be planted in his country, but his eyes should survey the world.
— *George Santayana*

History teaches us that men and nations behave wisely once they have exhausted all other alternatives.
— *Abba Eban*

A patriot must always be ready to defend his country against his government.
— *Edward Abbey*

I hear that melting-pot stuff a lot, and all I can say is that we haven't melted.
— *Jesse Jackson*

Governments never learn. Only people learn.
— *Milton Friedman*

My lands are where my dead lie buried.
— *Crazy Horse*

There is a tendency for the world to say to America, "The big problems of the world are yours—you go and sort them out," and then to worry when America wants to sort them out.
— *Tony Blair*

England and America are two countries separated by a common language.
— *George Bernard Shaw*

Europe was created by history. America was created by philosophy.
— *Margaret Thatcher*

To understand Europe, you have to be a genius—or French.
— *Madeleine Albright*

History is a vast early warning system.
— *Norman Cousins*

America is a large, friendly dog in a very small room. Every time it wags its tail, it knocks over a chair.
— *Arnold Toynbee*

Americans are benevolently ignorant about Canada, while Canadians are malevolently well informed about the United States.
— *J. Bartlett Brebner*

It has been said that arguing against globalization is like arguing against the laws of gravity.
— *Kofi Annan*

I dream of the realization of the unity of Africa, whereby its leaders combine in their efforts to solve the problems of this continent. I dream of our vast deserts, of our forests, of all our great wildernesses.
— *Nelson Mandela*

Russia is a riddle wrapped in a mystery inside an enigma.
— *Winston Churchill*

If the people of New Zealand want to be part of our world, I believe they should hop off their islands, and push 'em closer.
— *Lewis Black*

There can be hope only for a society which acts as one big family, not as many separate ones.
— *Anwar Sadat*

You cannot shake hands with a clenched fist.
— *Indira Gandhi*

This is the devilish thing about foreign affairs: they are foreign and will not always conform to our whim.
— *James Reston*

The great nations have always acted like gangsters, and the small nations like prostitutes.
— *Stanley Kubrick*

WAR, PEACE, AND POLITICS

Cultures

If man is to survive, he will have learned to take a delight in the essential differences between men and between cultures. He will learn that differences in ideas and attitudes are a delight, part of life's exciting variety, not something to fear.　*— Gene Roddenberry*

Other nations of different habits are not enemies: they are godsends. Men require of their neighbors something sufficiently akin to be understood, something sufficiently different to provoke attention, and something great enough to command admiration. We must not expect, however, all the virtues.
— Alfred North Whitehead

No race can prosper till it learns that there is as much dignity in tilling a field as in writing a poem.　*— Booker T. Washington*

The truly civilized man is always skeptical and tolerant. . . . His culture is based on "I am not too sure."　*— H. L. Mencken*

The Romans would never have found time to conquer the world if they had been obliged first to learn Latin.　*— Heinrich Heine*

In the future we'll all have 15 minutes of fame and 15 minutes of health care.
— Nicole Hollander

Much of the social history of the Western world over the past three decades has involved replacing what worked with what sounded good.　*— Thomas Sowell*

History does not always repeat itself. Sometimes it just yells, "Can't you remember anything I told you?" and lets fly with a club.
— John W. Campbell

All over the place, from the popular culture to the propaganda system, there is constant pressure to make people feel that they are helpless, that the only role they can have is to ratify decisions and to consume.
— Noam Chomsky

Simplicity is the peak of civilization.
— Jessie Sampter

You can tell the ideals of a nation by its advertisements.　*— Norman Douglas*

The public is wiser than the wisest critic.
— George Bancroft

Human beings are perhaps never more frightening than when they are convinced beyond doubt that they are right.
— Laurens van der Post

Upper classes are a nation's past; the middle class is its future.　*— Ayn Rand*

Nothing travels faster than the speed of light with the possible exception of bad news, which obeys its own special laws.
— Douglas Adams

Americans will put up with anything provided it doesn't block traffic.

— DAN RATHER

There are three social classes in America: upper middle class, middle class, and lower middle class. — *Judith Martin*

How can you govern a country which has 246 varieties of cheese? — *Charles de Gaulle*

Boy, those French: They have a different word for everything! — *Steve Martin*

We have too many high-sounding words, and too few actions that correspond with them. — *Abigail Adams*

Every man is surrounded by a neighborhood of voluntary spies. — *Jane Austen*

The best way to keep one's word is not to give it. — *Napoleon Bonaparte*

The only normal people are the ones you don't know very well. — *Joe Ancis*

There's a difference between a philosophy and a bumper sticker. — *Charles M. Schulz*

***

 Freedom

I know not what course others may take, but as for me, give me liberty, or give me death. — *Patrick Henry*

Those who want to give up essential liberty to purchase a little temporary safety, deserve neither liberty nor safety. — *Benjamin Franklin*

For to be free is not merely to cast off one's chains, but to live in a way that respects and enhances the freedom of others. — *Nelson Mandela*

The more freedom we enjoy, the greater the responsibility we bear, toward others as well as ourselves. — *Oscar Arias Sanchez*

An oppressed people are authorized whenever they can to rise and break their fetters. — *Henry Clay*

The most certain test by which we judge whether a country is really free is the amount of security enjoyed by minorities. — *Lord Acton*

A man does not become a freedom fighter in the hope of winning awards, but when I was notified that I had won the 1993 Nobel Peace Prize jointly with [President F. W.] de Klerk, I was deeply moved. The Nobel Peace Prize had a special meaning to me because of its involvement with South African history. . . . The award was a tribute to all South Africans and especially to those who fought in the struggle; I would accept it on their behalf. — *Nelson Mandela*

Oppression can only survive through silence. — *Carmen de Monteflores*

People demand freedom of speech as a compensation for the freedom of thought which they seldom use. — *Soren Kierkegaard*

The right to be heard does not automatically include the right to be taken seriously. — *Hubert H. Humphrey*

WAR, PEACE, AND POLITICS

The oppression of any people for opinion's sake has rarely had any other effect than to fix those opinions deeper, and render them more important.
— Hosea Ballou

It's ironical that the first people to demand free speech are the first people to deny it to others.
— Claude T. Bissell

The only real prison is fear, and the only real freedom is freedom from fear.
— Aung San Suu Kyi

Liberty without learning is always in peril; learning without liberty is always in vain.
— John F. Kennedy

Liberty means responsibility. That is why most men dread it.
— George Bernard Shaw

Liberty for wolves is death to the lambs.
— Isaiah Berlin

The best way to enhance freedom in other lands is to demonstrate here that our democratic system is worthy of emulation.
—Jimmy Carter

I think people should be allowed to do anything they want. We haven't tried that for a while. Maybe this time it'll work.
— George Carlin

We who lived in concentration camps can remember the men who walked through the huts comforting others, giving away their last piece of bread. They may have been few in number, but they offer sufficient proof that everything can be taken from a man but one thing: the last of human freedoms—to choose one's attitude in any given set of circumstances—to choose one's own way.
— Viktor E. Frankl

If society fits you comfortably enough, you call it freedom.
— Robert Frost

Freedom is nothing but a chance to be better.
— Albert Camus

You can have peace. Or you can have freedom. Don't ever count on having both at once.
— Robert A. Heinlein

Freedom is not worth having if it does not include the freedom to make mistakes.
— Mahatma Gandhi

The truth that makes men free is for the most part the truth which men prefer not to hear.
— Herbert Agar

Underlying most arguments against the free market is a lack of belief in freedom itself.
— Milton Friedman

One should never put on one's best trousers to go out to battle for freedom and truth.
— Henrik Ibsen

It is easier to fight for one's principles than to live up to them.
— Alfred Adler

Whenever I hear anyone arguing for slavery, I feel a strong impulse to see it tried on him personally. *— Abraham Lincoln*

There is no king who has not had a slave among his ancestors, and no slave who has not had a king among his. *— Helen Keller*

My definition of a free society is a society where it is safe to be unpopular.
— Adlai E. Stevenson

Do not fear to be eccentric in opinion, for every opinion now accepted was once eccentric. *— Bertrand Russell*

Politics

The most important political office is that of the private citizen. — *Louis D. Brandeis*

The job of a citizen is to keep his mouth open. — *Günter Grass*

The one thing that doesn't abide by majority rule is a person's conscience. — *Harper Lee*

Vote for the man who promises least; he'll be the least disappointing. — *Bernard Baruch*

This is the first convention of the space age—where a candidate can promise the moon and mean it. — *David Brinkley*

Never believe anything until it has been officially denied. — *Claud Cockburn*

Democracy is a process by which the people are free to choose the man who will get the blame. — *Laurence J. Peter*

It's not the voting that's democracy, it's the counting. — *Tom Stoppard*

What's a cult? It just means not enough people to make a minority. — *Robert Altman*

The great thing about democracy is that it gives every voter a chance to do something stupid. — *Art Spander*

A straw vote only shows which way the hot air blows. — *O. Henry*

A citizen of America will cross the ocean to fight for democracy, but won't cross the street to vote in a national election. — *Bill Vaughan*

The ballot is stronger than bullets. — *Joseph A. Schumpeter*

Apparently, a democracy is a place where numerous elections are held at great cost without issues and with interchangeable candidates. — *Gore Vidal*

Democracy is a device that ensures we shall be governed no better than we deserve. — *George Bernard Shaw*

Since a politician never believes what he says, he is quite surprised to be taken at his word. — *Charles de Gaulle*

It does not require a majority to prevail, but rather an irate, tireless minority keen to set brush fires in people's minds. — *Samuel Adams*

People who want to understand democracy should spend less time in the library with Aristotle and more time on the buses and in the subway. — *Simeon Strunsky*

Politics is not a bad profession.
If you succeed there are many rewards,
if you disgrace yourself you can always write a book.

— RONALD REAGAN

One of the lessons of history is that nothing is often a good thing to do and always a clever thing to say. — *Will Durant*

In order to become the master, the politician poses as the servant. — *Charles de Gaulle*

Contrary to what the politicians and religious leaders would like us to believe, the world won't be made safer by creating barriers between people. — *Michael Palin*

Politics is not the art of the possible. It consists in choosing between the disastrous and the unpalatable. — *John Kenneth Galbraith*

It is not worth an intelligent man's time to be in the majority. By definition, there are already enough people to do that. — *G. H. Hardy*

A politician needs the ability to foretell what is going to happen tomorrow, next week, next month, and next year. And to have the ability afterwards to explain why it didn't happen. — *Winston Churchill*

The danger is not that a particular class is unfit to govern. Every class is unfit to govern. — *Lord Acton*

Politicians are the same all over. They promise to build a bridge even where there is no river. — *Nikita Khrushchev*

Folk who don't know why America is the Land of Promise should be here during an election campaign. — *Milton Berle*

In politics, a lie unanswered becomes truth within 24 hours. — *Willie Brown*

Four-fifths of all our troubles would disappear, if we would only sit down and keep still. — *Calvin Coolidge*

What troubles me is not that movie stars run for office, but that they find it easy to get elected. It should be difficult. It should be difficult for millionaires, too. — *Shana Alexander*

Numerous politicians have seized absolute power and muzzled the press. Never in history has the press seized absolute power and muzzled the politicians. — *David Brinkley*

It is inaccurate to say that I hate everything. I am strongly in favor of common sense, common honesty, and common decency. This makes me forever ineligible for public office. — *H. L. Mencken*

Politics, as a practice, whatever its professions, has always been the systematic organization of hatreds. — *Henry B. Adams*

Ninety percent of the politicians give the other ten percent a bad reputation. — *Henry Kissinger*

My brother Bob doesn't want to be in government—he promised Dad he'd go straight. — *John F. Kennedy*

Politicians should read science fiction, not westerns and detective stories. — *Arthur C. Clarke*

In politics, madame, you need two things: friends, but above all an enemy. — *Brian Mulroney*

If you want to know who is going to change this country, go home and look in the mirror. — *Maude Barlow*

We used to say that if there were two Greeks left in the world they would form three political parties. — *John Turner*

Vote early and vote often. *— Al Capone*

Politics, when I am in it, makes me sick.
— William Howard Taft

The greatest mistake I made was not to die in office. *— Dean Acheson*

When all men think alike, no one thinks very much. *— Walter Lippmann*

A foolish consistency is the hobgoblin of little minds, adored by little statesmen and philosophers and divines.
— Ralph Waldo Emerson

The middle of the road is where the white line is—and that's the worst place to drive.
— Robert Frost

We know what happens to people who stay in the middle of the road. They get run over.
— Ambrose Bierce

I am a man of fixed and unbending principles, the first of which is to be flexible at all times. *— Everett Dirksen*

In politics, absurdity is not a handicap.
— Napoleon Bonaparte

Trying to take money out of politics is like trying to take jumping out of basketball.
— Bill Bradley

People expect Byzantine, Machiavellian logic from politicians. But the truth is simple. Trial lawyers learn a good rule: "Don't decide what you don't have to decide." That's not evasion, it's wisdom.
— Mario Cuomo

The ultimate measure of a man is not where he stands in moments of comfort and convenience, but where he stands at times of challenge and controversy.
— Martin Luther King, Jr.

What counts is not necessarily the size of the dog in the fight—it's the size of the fight in the dog. *— Dwight D. Eisenhower*

Politics is the art of looking for trouble, finding it whether it exists or not, diagnosing it incorrectly, and applying the wrong remedy.
— Ernest Benn

Being in politics is like being a football coach. You have to be smart enough to understand the game, and dumb enough to think it's important. *— Eugene McCarthy*

The oil can is mightier than the sword.
— Everett Dirksen

You never change things by fighting the existing reality. To change something, build a new model that makes the existing model obsolete. *— R. Buckminster Fuller*

Whenever a fellow tells me he's bipartisan, I know he's going to vote against me.
— Harry S. Truman

What this country needs is more unemployed politicians. *— Angela Davis*

Now I know what a statesman is; he's a dead politician. We need more statesmen.
— Bob Edwards

WAR, PEACE, AND POLITICS

A statesman is a successful politician who is dead.   — *Thomas B. Reed*

A liberal is a man too broadminded to take his own side in a quarrel.   — *Robert Frost*

A conservative is a man who believes that nothing should be done for the first time.   — *Alfred E. Wiggam*

You can't teach an old dogma new tricks.   — *Dorothy Parker*

Be wary of the man who urges an action in which he himself incurs no risk.   —*Joaquin Setanti*

Idealism is fine, but as it approaches reality, the costs become prohibitive.   — *William F. Buckley, Jr.*

You can't make up anything anymore. The world itself is a satire. All you're doing is recording it.   — *Art Buchwald*

The only courage that matters is the kind that gets you from one moment to the next.   — *Mignon McLaughlin*

The art of politics consists in knowing precisely when it is necessary to hit an opponent slightly below the belt.   — *Konrad Adenauer*

 Good thing we've still got politics in Texas— finest form of free entertainment ever invented.

— MOLLY IVINS

Politics: *Poli,* a Latin word meaning "many"; and *tics,* meaning "bloodsucking creatures."   — *Robin Williams*

Don't ever take a fence down until you know the reason it was put up.   — *G. K. Chesterton*

Ten people who speak make more noise than ten thousand who are silent.   — *Napoleon Bonaparte*

You've got to know where the machinery is and how it works before you can throw a monkey-wrench into it.   — *Michael H. Brown*

Sacred cows make the tastiest hamburger.   — *Abbie Hoffman*

It's the opinion of some that crops could be grown on the moon. Which raises the fear that it may not be long before we're paying somebody not to.   — *Franklin P. Jones*

I have acted fearless and independent and I never will regret my course. I would rather be politically buried that to be hypocritically immortalized.   — *Davy Crockett*

The most dangerous strategy is to jump a chasm in two leaps.   — *Benjamin Disraeli*

You campaign in poetry. You govern in prose.   — *Mario Cuomo*

Do not let us mistake necessary evils for good.   — *C. S. Lewis*

In any moment of decision
the best thing you can do is the right thing,
the next best thing is the wrong thing,
and the worst thing you can do is nothing.

— THEODORE ROOSEVELT

Nothing is so admirable in politics as a
short memory.   *— John Kenneth Galbraith*

An appeaser is one who feeds a crocodile—
hoping it will eat him last.
    — Winston Churchill

Diplomacy is the art of saying "Nice doggie"
until you can find a rock.   *— Will Rogers*

From each, according to his ability; to each,
according to his need.   *— Karl Marx*

Communism is the corruption of a dream
of justice.   *— Adlai E. Stevenson*

Capitalism, it is said, is a system wherein
man exploits man. And communism—
is vice versa.   *— Daniel Bell*

Somebody has to do something, and it's just
incredibly pathetic that it has to be us.
    — Jerry Garcia

The main dangers in this life are the
people who want to change everything—
or nothing.   *— Nancy Astor*

Politics is supposed to be the second oldest
profession. I have come to realize that it
bears a very close resemblance to the first.
    — Ronald Reagan

Politicians are interested in people. Not that it
is always a virtue. Fleas are interested in dogs.
    — P. J. O'Rourke

The incestuous relationship between government and big business thrives in the dark.
    — Jack Anderson

Have you ever seen a candidate talking to a
rich person on television?   *— Art Buchwald*

Get all the fools on your side and you can
be elected to anything.   *— Frank Dane*

Even Napoleon had his Watergate.
    — Yogi Berra

We need anything politically important
rationed out like Pez: small, sweet, and
coming out of a funny, plastic head.
    — Dennis Miller

The world needs anger. The world often
continues to allow evil because it isn't
angry enough.   *— Bede Jarrett*

In politics stupidity is not a handicap.
    — Napoleon Bonaparte

CNN said that after the war, there is a
plan to divide Iraq into three parts: regular,
premium and unleaded.   *—Jay Leno*

A compromise is the art of dividing a cake
in such a way that everyone believes he has
the biggest piece.   — *Ludwig Erhard*

I don't like to hurt people, I really don't
like it at all. But in order to get a red light
at the intersection, you sometimes have to
have an accident.   — *Jack Anderson*

We hang the petty thieves and appoint the
great ones to public office.   — *Aesop*

Too bad that all the people who really know
how to run the country are busy driving
taxi cabs and cutting hair.   — *George Burns*

The reason there are so few female politicians
is that it is too much trouble to put makeup
on two faces.   — *Maureen Murphy*

I usually make up my mind about a man in
ten seconds; and I very rarely change it.
        — *Margaret Thatcher*

People who fight fire with fire usually end
up with ashes.   — *Abigail Van Buren*

What is a rebel? A man who says no.
        — *Albert Camus*

It's a sad and stupid thing to have to
proclaim yourself a revolutionary just
to be a decent man.   — *David Harris*

The first duty of a revolutionary is to get
away with it.   — *Abbie Hoffman*

All successful revolutions
are the kicking in of a rotten door.
        — *John Kenneth Galbraith*

The most radical revolutionary will become
a conservative the day after the revolution.
        — *Hannah Arendt*

Those who make peaceful
revolution impossible will make
violent revolution inevitable.
        — *John F. Kennedy*

If you want a symbolic gesture, don't burn
the flag; wash it.   — *Norman Thomas*

If you want a friend in Washington, get a dog.
        — *Harry S. Truman*

A diplomat's life is made up of three
ingredients: protocol, Geritol and alcohol.
        — *Adlai E. Stevenson*

A diplomat ... is a person who can tell you
to go to hell in such a way that you actually
look forward to the trip.   — *Caskie Stinnett*

I want to find a voracious, small-minded
predator and name it after the IRS.
        — *Robert Bakker*

When the political columnists say
"Every thinking man" they mean
themselves, and when candidates
appeal to "Every intelligent voter"
they mean everybody who is going
to vote for them.   — *Franklin P. Adams*

An honest politician is one who, when he
is bought, will stay bought.   — *Simon Cameron*

Instead of giving a politician the keys to the
city, it might be better to change the locks.
        — *Doug Larson*

Ninety-eight percent of the adults in this
country are decent, hard-working, honest
Americans. It's the other lousy two percent
that get all the publicity. But then, we
elected them.   — *Lily Tomlin*

Ronald Reagan

Winning Personality

He was the Gipper, all right, determined to renew America's winning spirit.

Ronald Reagan was born in Tampico, Illinois, in 1911. At Eureka College, he studied sociology and economics, acted in school plays, and was a member of the football team. After college, he found work as a radio sportscaster. Then a screen test for Warner Bros. launched his 53-film career, and he later hosted television's popular *General Electric Theater*.

As president of the Screen Actors Guild, Reagan became embroiled in the politics of the time. He shifted his political leanings from liberal to conservative and switched to the Republican Party in 1962. In 1966 he was elected governor of California, and in 1980 he was elected President of the United States, the oldest man to become the nation's chief executive.

While Reagan was known politically for guiding America through the end of the Cold War and downsizing big government, he was known personally for his warmth and wit. He was dubbed "the Great Communicator" in recognition of his ability to pack a lot of meaning into just a few words—for instance, his election line "Are you better off than you were four years ago?" Or his simple condemnation of Soviet oppression: "Mr. Gorbachev, tear down this wall!"

Reagan died of Alzheimer's disease in 2004.

How do you tell a Communist? Well, it's someone who reads Marx and Lenin.
And how do you tell an anti-Communist? It's someone who understands
Marx and Lenin.

✳

I will not make age an issue of this campaign. I am not going to exploit,
for political purposes, my opponent's youth and inexperience.

✳

The nine most terrifying words in the English language are,
"I'm from the government and I'm here to help."

✳

I have wondered at times what the Ten Commandments would have looked like if
Moses had run them through the U.S. Congress.

✳

Freedom is never more than one generation away from extinction.
We didn't pass it to our children in the bloodstream. It must be fought for, protected,
and handed on for them to do the same, or one day we will spend our sunset years
telling our children and our children's children what it was once like in the
United States where men were free.

✳

I have left orders to be awakened at any time in case of national emergency,
even if I'm in a cabinet meeting.

✳

Government is like a baby: An alimentary canal with a big appetite at one end
and no sense of responsibility at the other.

✳

In closing, let me thank you, the American people, for giving me the great honor
of allowing me to serve as your President. When the Lord calls me home, whenever
that day may be, I will leave with the greatest love for this country of ours and eternal
optimism for its future. I now begin the journey that will lead me into the sunset of
my life. I know that for America there will always be a bright dawn ahead.

Presidency

Anyone who is capable of getting themselves made President should on no account be allowed to do the job. — *Douglas Adams*

When I was a boy I was told that anybody could become President; I'm beginning to believe it. — *Clarence Darrow*

We need a president who's fluent in at least one language. — *Buck Henry*

All the president is, is a glorified public relations man who spends his time flattering, kissing, and kicking people to get them to do what they are supposed to do anyway. — *Harry S. Truman*

Harry Truman is the last president who did not go to college. Consider all the presidents since Harry Truman and tell me that college has improved anything. — *Roger Simon*

And who knows? Somewhere out there in this audience may even be someone who will one day follow my footsteps, and preside over the White House as the president's spouse. I wish him well! — *Barbara Bush*

I have the consolation of having added nothing to my private fortune during my public service, and of retiring with hands clean as they are empty. — *Thomas Jefferson*

My God, this is a hell of a job!
I have no trouble with my enemies ... but my damn friends, they're the ones that keep me walking the floor nights. — *Warren G. Harding*

A lot of presidential memoirs, they say, are dull and self-serving. I hope mine is interesting and self-serving. — *Bill Clinton*

I am not worried about the deficit. It is big enough to take care of itself. — *Ronald Reagan*

Being president is like being a jackass in a hailstorm. There's nothing to do but to stand there and take it. — *Lyndon B. Johnson*

Democracy means that anyone can grow up to be president, and anyone who doesn't grow up can be vice president. — *Johnny Carson*

Mothers all want their sons to grow up to be president, but they don't want them to become politicians in the process. — *John F. Kennedy*

You really have to experience the feeling of being with the president in the oval office. ... It's a disease I came to call Ovalitis. — *John Dean*

When we got into office, the thing that surprised me the most was that things were as bad as we'd been saying they were. — *John F. Kennedy*

I'd rather be right than President. — *Henry Clay*

Half of the American people have never read a newspaper. Half never voted for President. One hopes it is the same half. — *Gore Vidal*

Take our politicians: they're a bunch of yo-yos. The presidency is now a cross between a popularity contest and a high school debate, with an encyclopedia of clichés the first prize. — *Saul Bellow*

Government

For every action there is an equal and opposite government program. — *Bob Wells*

You will find that the State is the kind of organization which, though it does big things badly, does small things badly, too.
— *John Kenneth Galbraith*

A union of government and religion tends to destroy government and degrade religion.
— *Hugo Black*

Now and then an innocent man is sent to the legislature. — *Kin Hubbard*

The worst thing in this world, next to anarchy, is government.
— *Henry Ward Beecher*

Government always finds a need for whatever money it gets. — *Ronald Reagan*

Many people want the government to protect the consumer. A much more urgent problem is to protect the consumer from the government. — *Milton Friedman*

No man's life, liberty or property are safe while the legislature is in session.
— *Gideon J. Tucker*

A government big enough to give you everything you want is a government big enough to take from you everything you have. — *Gerald R. Ford*

Be thankful we're not getting all the government we're paying for. — *Will Rogers*

I just filled out my income tax forms. Who says you can't get killed by a blank?
— *Milton Berle*

The taxpayer—that's someone who works for the federal government but doesn't have to take the civil service examination.
— *Ronald Reagan*

A billion here, a billion there— pretty soon it adds up to real money.
— *Everett Dirksen*

There is just one thing I can promise you about the outer-space program—your tax dollar will go further. — *Wernher von Braun*

The intermediate stage between socialism and capitalism is alcoholism.
— *Norman Brenner*

I don't make jokes.
I just watch the government
and report the facts.

—WILL ROGERS

Congress: Bingo with billions.   — *Red Skelton*

In my many years I have come to a conclusion that one useless man is a shame, two is a law firm, and three or more is a Congress.   —*John Adams*

A little government and a little luck are necessary in life; but only a fool trusts either of them.   — *P. J. O'Rourke*

Disbelief in magic can force a poor soul into believing in government and business.

— *Tom Robbins*

The important work of moving the world forward does not wait to be done by perfect men.   — *George Eliot*

Congress is so strange. A man gets up to speak and says nothing. Nobody listens— and then everybody disagrees.

— *Boris Marshalov*

We may not imagine how our lives could be more frustrating and complex— but Congress can.   — *Cullen Hightower*

Congress shall also create a tax code weighing more than the combined poundage of the largest member of the House and the largest member of the Senate, plus a standard musk ox.

— *Dave Barry*

I wouldn't mind paying taxes—if I knew they were going to a friendly country.

— *Dick Gregory*

The House looks like more fun. It's like the Donahue show. The Senate is like one of those Sunday morning public service programs.   — *Phil Donahue*

I don't know what people have got against the government; they've done nothing.

— *Bob Hope*

Washington is a city of Southern efficiency and Northern charm.   —*John F. Kennedy*

Washington, D.C., is a city filled with people who believe they are important.

— *David Brinkley*

The reason there are two senators for each state is so that one can be the designated driver.   —*Jay Leno*

You can lead a man to Congress, but you can't make him think.   — *Milton Berle*

Congress seems drugged and inert most of the time. ... Its idea of meeting a problem is to hold hearings or, in extreme cases, to appoint a commission.   — *Shirley Chisholm*

What stuns me most about contemporary politics is not even that the system has been so badly corrupted by money. It is that so few people get the connection between their lives and what the bozos do in Washington and our state capitols.

— *Molly Ivins*

The thickness of the proposal required to win a multimillion-dollar contract is about one millimeter per million dollars. If all the proposals conforming to this standard were piled on top of each other at the bottom of the Grand Canyon, it would probably be a good idea.

— *Norman R. Augustine*

The mystery of government is not how Washington works but how to make it stop.

— *P. J. O'Rourke*

WAR, PEACE, AND POLITICS

If everybody in this town connected with politics had to leave town because of chasing women and drinking, you would have no government. — *Barry M. Goldwater*

A government is the only known vessel that leaks from the top. — *James Reston*

I believe there is something out there watching us. Unfortunately, it's the government. — *Woody Allen*

If "pro" is the opposite of "con" what is the opposite of "progress"? — *Paul Harvey*

***

$\mathcal{D}$ebate

I have never in my life learned anything from any man who agreed with me. — *Dudley Field Malone*

Fight for your opinions, but do not believe that they contain the whole truth, or the only truth. — *Charles A. Dana*

To think is to differ. — *Clarence Darrow*

If you can find something everyone agrees on, it's wrong. — *Morris K. Udall*

The most important thing in an argument, next to being right, is to leave an escape hatch for your opponent, so that he can gracefully swing over to your side without too much apparent loss of face. — *Sydney J. Harris*

It's a rare person who wants to hear what he doesn't want to hear. — *Dick Cavett*

A good listener tries to understand thoroughly what the other person is saying. In the end he may disagree sharply, but before he disagrees, he wants to know exactly what it is he is disagreeing with. — *Kenneth A. Wells*

A technical objection is the first refuge of a scoundrel. — *Heywood Broun*

There is no such thing as conversation. It is an illusion. There are intersecting monologues. That is all. — *Rebecca West*

It is impossible to defeat an ignorant man in argument. — *William G. McAdoo*

The highest honor that my friends can do me is to enforce in their own lives the program that I stand for or to resist me to their utmost if they do not believe in it. — *Mahatma Gandhi*

I argue very well. Ask any of my remaining friends. I can win an argument on any topic, against any opponent. People know this, and steer clear of me at parties. Often, as a sign of their great respect, they don't even invite me. — *Dave Barry*

Every man has a right to his opinion, but no man has a right to be wrong in his facts.

— *Bernard Baruch*

It is better to debate a question without settling it than to settle a question without debating it.

— *Joseph Joubert*

The people who oppose your ideas are inevitably those who represent the established order that your ideas will upset.

— *Anthony J. D'Angelo*

Opinion is that exercise of the human will which helps us to make a decision without information.

— *John Erskine*

Democracy means government by discussion, but it is only effective if you can stop people talking.

— *Clement Attlee*

If our democracy is to flourish, it must have criticism; if our government is to function it must have dissent.

— *Henry Steele Commager*

If we cannot end now our differences, at least we can help make the world safe for diversity.

— JOHN F. KENNEDY

It is by universal misunderstanding that all agree. For if, by ill luck, people understood each other, they would never agree.

— *Charles Baudelaire*

I've never had a humble opinion. If you've got an opinion, why be humble about it?

— *Joan Baez*

Why prove to a man he is wrong? Is that going to make him like you? Why not let him save face? He didn't ask for your opinion. He didn't want it. Why argue with him? You can't win an argument, because if you lose, you lose it; and if you win it, you lose it. Why? You will feel fine. But what about him? You have made him feel inferior, you hurt his pride, insult his intelligence, his judgment, and his self-respect, and he'll resent your triumph. That will make him strike back, but it will never make him want to change his mind.

— *Dale Carnegie*

Civilization began the first time an angry person cast a word instead of a rock.

— *Sigmund Freud*

When we are young we generally estimate an opinion by the size of the person that holds it, but later we find that is an uncertain rule, for we realize that there are times when a hornet's opinion disturbs us more than an emperor's.

— *Mark Twain*

Courage is what it takes to stand up and speak; courage is also what it takes to sit down and listen.

— *Winston Churchill*

Each time someone stands up for an ideal, or acts to improve the lot of others, or strikes out against injustice, he sends forth a tiny ripple of hope.

— *Robert F. Kennedy*

Before you speak, it is necessary for you to listen, for God speaks in the silence of the heart.

— *Mother Teresa*

WAR, PEACE, AND POLITICS

Those who agree with us may not be right, but we admire their astuteness.

— *Cullen Hightower*

I don't give them hell. I just tell the truth and they think it is hell.   — *Harry S. Truman*

When everyone is against you,
it means that you are absolutely wrong—
or absolutely right.   — *Albert Guinon*

Do not think of knocking out another person's brains because he differs in opinion from you. It would be as rational to knock yourself on the head because you differ from yourself ten years ago.   — *Horace Mann*

I'm sorry, if you were right,
I'd agree with you.   — *Robin Williams*

The opposite of a correct statement is a false statement. But the opposite of a profound truth may well be another profound truth.

— *Niels Bohr*

Most quarrels amplify a misunderstanding.

— *André Gide*

A fanatic is one who can't change his mind and won't change the subject.

— *Winston Churchill*

As we must account for every idle word, so we must for every idle silence.

— *Benjamin Franklin*

At times one remains faithful to a cause only because its opponents do not cease to be insipid.   — *Friedrich Nietzsche*

Most of us are about as eager to be changed as we were to be born, and go through our changes in a similar state of shock.

— *James Baldwin*

There is only one thing a philosopher can be relied upon to do, and that is to contradict other philosophers.   — *William James*

***

Power

Knowledge is power.   — *Francis Bacon*

Govern a great nation as you would cook a small fish. Do not overdo it.   — *Lao-tzu*

I have always been fond of the West African proverb: "Speak softly and carry a big stick; you will go far."   — *Theodore Roosevelt*

Being powerful is like being a lady. If you have to tell people you are—you aren't.

— *Margaret Thatcher*

Power doesn't have to show off. Power is confident, self-assuring, self-starting and self-stopping, self-warming and self-justifying. When you have it, you know it.

— *Ralph Ellison*

Knowing others is intelligence; knowing yourself is true wisdom. Mastering others is strength, mastering yourself is true power.

— *Lao-tzu*

Influence is like a savings account. The less you use it, the more you've got.

— *Andrew Young*

A good leader can't get too far ahead of his followers. — *Franklin D. Roosevelt*

The job of mayor and governor is becoming more and more like the job of university president, which I used to be; it looks like you are in charge, but you are not.

— *Lamar Alexander*

If I only had a little humility, I'd be perfect.

— *Ted Turner*

CNN is one of the participants in the war. I have a fantasy where Ted Turner is elected president but refuses because he doesn't want to give up power. — *Arthur C. Clarke*

If you want anything said, ask a man. If you want something done, ask a woman.

— *Margaret Thatcher*

If you are the master be sometimes blind, if you are the servant be sometimes deaf.

— *R. Buckminster Fuller*

Power is not only what you have but what the enemy thinks you have. — *Saul Alinsky*

An armed society is a polite society. Manners are good when one may have to back up his acts with his life.

— *Robert A. Heinlein*

Power is poison. Its effect on Presidents had always been tragic. — *Henry B. Adams*

I have found some of the best reasons I ever had for remaining at the bottom simply by looking at the men at the top.

— *Frank Moore Colby*

History will be kind to me for I intend to write it. — *Winston Churchill*

Courage is fire, and bullying is smoke.

— *Benjamin Disraeli*

It is not the clear-sighted who rule the world. Great achievements are accomplished in a blessed, warm fog. — *Joseph Conrad*

The darkest places in hell are reserved for those who maintain their neutrality in times of moral crisis. — *Dante Alighieri*

There are risks and costs to a program of action. But they are far less than the long-range risks and costs of comfortable inaction.

— *John F. Kennedy*

No one could make a greater mistake than he who did nothing because he could do only a little. — *Edmund Burke*

First they came for the Communists but I was not a Communist so I did not speak out. Then they came for the Socialists and the Trade Unionists but I was not one of them, so I did not speak out. Then they came for the Jews but I was not Jewish so I did not speak out. And when they came for me, there was no one left to speak out for me.

— *Martin Niemoeller*

Let no man imagine that he has no influence. Whoever he may be, and wherever he may be placed, the man who thinks becomes a light and a power. — *Henry George*

There are moments in your life when you must act, even though you cannot carry your best friends with you. The "still small voice" within you must always be the final arbiter when there is a conflict of duty.

— *Mahatma Gandhi*

WAR, PEACE, AND POLITICS

The thing women have yet to learn is nobody gives you power. You just take it.

— ROSEANNE BARR

One of the best ways to persuade others is with your ears—by listening to them.
— *Dean Rusk*

Never explain—your friends do not need it and your enemies will not believe you anyway.
— *Elbert Hubbard*

The nation which forgets its defenders will be itself forgotten.
— *Calvin Coolidge*

When you strike at a king, you must kill him.
— *Ralph Waldo Emerson*

When I came back to Dublin I was court-martialed in my absence and sentenced to death in my absence, so I said they could shoot me in my absence.
— *Brendan Behan*

An infallible method of conciliating a tiger is to allow oneself to be devoured.
— *Konrad Adenauer*

Money doesn't talk, it swears.
— *Bob Dylan*

Power tends to corrupt, and absolute power corrupts absolutely.
— *Lord Acton*

Power corrupts. Absolute power is kind of neat.
— *John Lehman*

It is said that power corrupts, but actually it's more true that power attracts the corruptible. The sane are usually attracted by other things than power.
— *David Brin*

If absolute power corrupts absolutely, does absolute powerlessness make you pure?
— *Harry Shearer*

Money speaks sense in a language all nations understand.
— *Aphra Behn*

Neutrality helps the oppressor, never the victim. Silence encourages the tormentor, never the tormented.
— *Elie Wiesel*

The price good men pay for indifference to public affairs is to be ruled by evil men.
— *Plato*

What luck for rulers that men do not think.
— *Adolf Hitler*

Our patience will achieve more than our force.
— *Edmund Burke*

You can make a throne of bayonets, but you can't sit on it for long.
— *Boris Yeltsin*

An invasion of armies can be resisted, but not an idea whose time has come.
— *Victor Hugo*

I believe in benevolent dictatorship provided I am the dictator.
— *Richard Branson*

Of all the preposterous assumptions of humanity over humanity, nothing exceeds most of the criticisms made on the habits of the poor by the well-housed, well-warmed, and well-fed.
— *Herman Melville*

The genius of our ruling class is that it has kept a majority of the people from ever questioning the inequity of a system where most people drudge along, paying heavy taxes for which they get nothing in return.

— *Gore Vidal*

Civilization is unbearable, but it is less unbearable at the top.

— *Timothy Leary*

I went to Zimbabwe. . . . I know how white people feel in America now—relaxed! 'Cause when I heard the police car I knew they weren't coming after me!

— *Richard Pryor*

You can't hold a man down without staying down with him.

— *Booker T. Washington*

Society attacks early when the individual is helpless.

— *B. F. Skinner*

In critical moments even the very powerful have need of the weakest.

— *Aesop*

A friend in power is a friend lost.

— *Henry Adams*

A bone to the dog is not charity. Charity is the bone shared with the dog, when you are just as hungry as the dog.

— *Jack London*

Never doubt that a small group of thoughtful, committed citizens can change the world. Indeed, it is the only thing that ever has.

— *Margaret Mead*

The real problem is what to do with the problem-solvers after the problems are solved.

— *Gay Talese*

I am sometimes a fox and sometimes a lion. The whole secret of government lies in knowing when to be the one or the other.

— *Napoleon Bonaparte*

Dictators ride to and fro upon tigers which they dare not dismount. And the tigers are getting hungry.

— *Winston Churchill*

To punish me for my contempt for authority, fate made me an authority myself.

— *Albert Einstein*

You cannot strengthen the weak by weakening the strong.
You cannot help small men by tearing down big men.
You cannot help the poor by destroying the rich.
You cannot lift the wage earner by pulling down the wage payer.
You cannot keep out of trouble by spending more than your income.
You cannot further the brotherhood of man by inciting class hatreds.
You cannot establish security on borrowed money.
You cannot build character and courage by taking away a man's initiative and independence.
You cannot help men permanently by doing for them what they could and should do for themselves.

— WILLIAM J. H. BOETCKER

WAR, PEACE, AND POLITICS

One cannot govern with "buts."
— *Charles de Gaulle*

There are two ways of exerting one's strength: one is pushing down, the other is pulling up.
— *Booker T. Washington*

You can kill a man but you can't kill an idea.
— *Medgar Evers*

Distrust all in whom the impulse to punish is powerful!
— *Friedrich Nietzsche*

***

Law and Order

The trouble with law is lawyers.
— *Clarence Darrow*

If there is any truth to the old proverb that "one who is his own lawyer has a fool for a client," the Court now bestows a constitutional right on one to make a fool of himself.
— *Harry A. Blackmun*

The layman's constitutional view is that what he likes is constitutional and that which he doesn't like is unconstitutional.
— *Hugo Black*

The Constitution is not neutral. It was designed to take the government off the backs of people.
— *William O. Douglas*

You need only reflect that one of the best ways to get yourself a reputation as a dangerous citizen these days is to go about repeating the very phrases which our founding fathers used in the struggle for independence.
— *Charles Austin Beard*

Our Constitution was not written in the sands to be washed away by each wave of new judges blown in by each successive political wind.
— *Hugo Black*

The Constitution does not provide for first- and second-class citizens.
— *Wendell Willkie*

Big Brother in the form of an increasingly powerful government and in an increasingly powerful private sector will pile the records high with reasons why privacy should give way to national security, to law and order, to efficiency of operation, to scientific advancement and the like.
— *William O. Douglas*

In law, nothing is certain but the expense.
— *Samuel Butler*

A society that has more justice is a society that needs less charity.
— *Ralph Nader*

I know no method to secure the repeal of bad or obnoxious laws so effective as their stringent execution.
— *Ulysses S. Grant*

We have a criminal jury system which is superior to any in the world; and its efficiency is only marred by the difficulty of finding twelve men every day who don't know anything and can't read.
— *Mark Twain*

Judges Speak

When you throw on a robe and preside over a courtroom day in and day out, you're going to develop pretty good insight into the human condition. Here's what some of our top jurists had to say about society and life in general.

Timeless thoughts? You be the judge.

We can have democracy in this country, or we can have great wealth concentrated in the hands of a few, but we can't have both.

⤙ LOUIS D. BRANDEIS

The courtrooms of America all too often have Piper Cub advocates trying to handle the controls of Boeing 747 litigation.

⤙ WARREN E. BURGER

Everything I did in my life that was worthwhile, I caught hell for.

⤙ EARL WARREN

Having family responsibilities and concerns just has to make you a more understanding person.

⤙ SANDRA DAY O'CONNOR

In a big family the first child is kind of like the first pancake. If it's not perfect, that's okay, there are a lot more coming along.

⤙ ANTONIN SCALIA

When I was 40, my doctor advised me that a man in his 40s shouldn't play tennis. I heeded his advice carefully and could hardly wait until I reached 50 to start again.

⤙ HUGO BLACK

Lawyers spend a great deal of their time shoveling smoke.
≺ OLIVER WENDELL HOLMES, JR.

There are no menial jobs, only menial attitudes.
≺ WILLIAM J. BRENNAN, JR.

If Columbus had an advisory committee he
would probably still be at the dock.
≺ ARTHUR J. GOLDBERG

It is easy to be popular. It is not easy to be just.
≺ ROSE ELIZABETH BIRD

When we lose the right to be different,
we lose the privilege to be free.
≺ CHARLES EVANS HUGHES

Remember there's always a voice saying the right thing to
you somewhere if you'll only listen for it.
≺ THOMAS HUGHES

Swift justice demands more than just swiftness.
≺ POTTER STEWART

The judicial system is the most expensive machine ever invented
for finding out what happened and what to do about it.
≺ IRVING R. KAUFMAN

Man perfected by society is the best of all animals; he is the most terrible of all when he lives without law, and without justice.

— *Aristotle*

Any fool can make a rule, and any fool will mind it.

— *Henry David Thoreau*

A law is something which must have a moral basis, so that there is an inner compelling force for every citizen to obey.

— *Chaim Weizmann*

Regulations grow at the same rate as weeds.

— *Norman R. Augustine*

If you have ten thousand regulations you destroy all respect for the law.

— *Winston Churchill*

You cannot stop the spread of an idea by passing a law against it.   — *Harry S. Truman*

Laws are like sausages. It's better not to see them being made.   — *Otto von Bismarck*

The law must be stable, but it must not stand still.   — *Roscoe Pound*

It is a truism that almost any sect, cult, or religion will legislate its creed into law if it acquires the political power to do so.

— *Robert A. Heinlein*

Justice delayed, is justice denied.

— *William Gladstone*

When you go into court you are putting your fate into the hands of 12 people who weren't smart enough to get out of jury duty.

— *Norm Crosby*

A jury consists of 12 persons chosen to decide who has the better lawyer.

— *Robert Frost*

Common sense often makes good law.

— *William O. Douglas*

An eye for an eye makes the whole world blind.   — *Mahatma Gandhi*

Injustice anywhere is a threat to justice everywhere.   — *Martin Luther King, Jr.*

Capital punishment turns the state into a murderer. But imprisonment turns the state into a gay dungeon-master.   — *Jesse Jackson*

A man's respect for law and order exists in precise relationship to the size of his paycheck.   — *Adam Clayton Powell, Jr.*

Well, if crime fighters fight crime and fire fighters fight fire, what do freedom fighters fight? They never mention that part to us, do they?   — *George Carlin*

The penalty for laughing in a courtroom is six months in jail; if it were not for this penalty, the jury would never hear the evidence.   — *H. L. Mencken*

The degree of civilization in a society can be judged by entering its prisons.

— *Fyodor Dostoyevsky*

It is better that ten guilty escape than one innocent suffer.   — *William Blackstone*

The law isn't justice. It's a very imperfect mechanism. If you press exactly the right buttons and are also lucky, justice may show up in the answer. A mechanism is all the law was ever intended to be.

— *Raymond Chandler*

In my youth I stressed freedom, and in my old age I stress order. I have made the great discovery that liberty is a product of order.

— *Will Durant*

WAR, PEACE, AND POLITICS

The Human Condition

We are at the very beginning of time for the human race. It is not unreasonable that we grapple with problems. But there are tens of thousands of years in the future. Our responsibility is to do what we can, learn what we can, improve the solutions, and pass them on. — *Richard Feynman*

Any man who afflicts the human race with ideas must be prepared to see them misunderstood. — *H. L. Mencken*

I think we risk becoming the best-informed society that has ever died of ignorance. — *Ruben Blades*

We would like to live as we once lived, but history will not permit it. — *John F. Kennedy*

Nature has never read the Declaration of Independence. It continues to make us unequal. — *Will Durant*

History repeats itself. That's one of the things wrong with history. — *Clarence Darrow*

When we are planning for posterity, we ought to remember that virtue is not hereditary. — *Thomas Paine*

We are a people who do not want to keep much of the past in our heads. It is considered unhealthy in America to remember mistakes, neurotic to think about them, psychotic to dwell on them. — *Lillian Hellman*

The meek shall inherit the earth, but not the mineral rights. — *J. Paul Getty*

The test of every religious, political, or educational system is the man that it forms. — *Henri-Frédéric Amiel*

Any idiot can face a crisis— it's day-to-day living that wears you out.

— ANTON CHEKHOV

The past is the only dead thing that smells sweet. — *Edward Thomas*

History will never accept difficulties as an excuse. — *John F. Kennedy*

The future, according to some scientists, will be exactly like the past, only far more expensive. — *John Sladek*

If there were in the world today any large number of people who desired their own happiness more than they desired the unhappiness of others, we could have paradise in a few years. — *Bertrand Russell*

What we're saying today is that you're either part of the solution or you're part of the problem. — *Eldridge Cleaver*

If you think there's a solution, you're part of the problem. — *George Carlin*

Love thy neighbor as yourself, but choose your neighborhood. — *Louise Beal*

If you will protest courageously, and yet with dignity and Christian love, when the history books are written in future generations, the historians will have to pause and say, "There lived a great people—a black people—who injected new meaning and dignity into the veins of civilization." — *Martin Luther King, Jr.*

Individual commitment to a group effort—that is what makes a team work, a company work, a society work, a civilization work. — *Vince Lombardi*

America's greatest strength, and its greatest weakness, is our belief in second chances, our belief that we can always start over, that things can be made better. — *Anthony Walton*

No snowflake in an avalanche ever feels responsible. — *George Burns*

Pray for the dead and fight like hell for the living. — *Mother Jones*

If living conditions don't stop improving in this country, we're going to run out of humble beginnings for our great men. — *Russell P. Askue*

If fifty million people say a foolish thing, it is still a foolish thing. — *Anatole France*

There are plenty of problems in the world, many of them interconnected. But there is no problem which compares with this central, universal problem of saving the human race from extinction. — *John Foster Dulles*

I choose the poverty of our poor people. But I am grateful to receive [the Nobel Peace Prize] in the name of the hungry, the naked, the homeless, of the crippled, of the blind, of the lepers, of all those people who feel unwanted, unloved, uncared-for throughout society, people that have become a burden to the society and are shunned by everyone. — *Mother Teresa*

It is characteristic of all deep human problems that they are not to be approached without some humor and some bewilderment. — *Freeman Dyson*

The aim of a joke is not to degrade the human being, but to remind him that he is already degraded. — *George Orwell*

My country is the world and my religion is to do good. — *Thomas Paine*

Common sense is the knack of seeing things as they are, and doing things as they ought to be done. — *Harriet Beecher Stowe*

All this talk about equality.
The only thing people really have in common
is that they are all going to die.

— BOB DYLAN

WAR, PEACE, AND POLITICS

Because things are the way they are,
things will not stay the way they are.

— Bertolt Brecht

There are many ways of going forward, but
only one way of standing still.

— Franklin D. Roosevelt

Half the world is composed of people who
have something to say and can't and the
other half who have nothing to say and keep
on saying it.

— Robert Frost

Many a man's reputation would not know
his character if they met on the street.

— Elbert Hubbard

Courage is doing what you're afraid to do.
There can be no courage unless you're scared.

— Eddie Rickenbacker

Brave men are all vertebrates; they have their
softness on the surface and their toughness
in the middle.

— G. K. Chesterton

A really great man is known by three signs
... generosity in the design, humanity in the
execution, moderation in success.

— Otto von Bismarck

People are difficult to govern because they
have too much knowledge.

— Lao-tzu

I have observed that the world has suffered far
less from ignorance than from pretensions to
knowledge. It is not skeptics or explorers but
fanatics and ideologues who menace decency
and progress. No agnostic ever burned anyone at the stake or tortured a pagan, a heretic,
or an unbeliever.

— Daniel J. Boorstin

I learned that it is the weak who are cruel,
and that gentleness is to be expected only
from the strong.

— Leo Rosten

One of the indictments of civilizations is
that happiness and intelligence are so rarely
found in the same person.

— William Feather

In times like these, it helps to recall that
there have always been times like these.

— Paul Harvey

In every age "the good old days" were a
myth. No one ever thought they were good
at the time. For every age has consisted of
crises that seemed intolerable to the people
who lived through them.

— Brooks Atkinson

I would renounce, therefore, the attempt to
create heaven on earth, and focus instead on
reducing the hell.

— A. Alan Borovoy

It requires wisdom to understand wisdom:
the music is nothing if the audience is deaf.

— Walter Lippmann

A hundred years ago, the electric
telegraph made possible—indeed,
inevitable—the United States of
America. The communications satellite
will make equally inevitable a United
Nations of Earth; let us hope that the
transition period will not be equally bloody.

— Arthur C. Clarke

Those who don't know how to weep
with their whole heart, don't know how to
laugh either.

— Golda Meir

How I wish that somewhere there existed
an island for those who are wise and of
goodwill! In such a place even I would be
an ardent patriot.

— Albert Einstein

There are two kinds of men who never
amount to much: those who cannot do
what they are told and those who can
do nothing else.

— Cyrus H. Curtis

THE HUMAN CONDITION

Forgiveness is almost a selfish act because of its immense benefits to the one who forgives.
— *Lawana Blackwell*

Shyness has a strange element of narcissism, a belief that how we look, how we perform, is truly important to other people.
— *Andre Dubus*

There are two kinds of people in the world, those who believe there are two kinds of people in the world and those who don't.
— *Robert Benchley*

Stoop and you'll be stepped on; stand tall and you'll be shot at.   — *Carlos A. Urbizo*

There are two kinds of people, those who finish what they start and so on.
— *Robert Byrne*

There are two types of people—those who come into a room and say, "Well, here I am!" and those who come in and say, "Ah, there you are."
— *Frederick L. Collins*

***

The Battlefield

Never in the field of human conflict was so much owed by so many to so few.
— *Winston Churchill*

I never saw a pessimistic general win a battle.
— *Dwight D. Eisenhower*

No enterprise is more likely to succeed than one concealed from the enemy until it is ripe for execution.   — *Niccolò Machiavelli*

Never interrupt your enemy when he is making a mistake.   — *Napoleon Bonaparte*

If men make war in slavish obedience to rules, they will fail.   — *Ulysses S. Grant*

The enemy is anybody who's going to get you killed, no matter which side he's on.
— *Joseph Heller*

You can discover what your enemy fears most by observing the means he uses to frighten you.   — *Eric Hoffer*

Above all things, never be afraid. The enemy who forces you to retreat is himself afraid of you at that very moment.   — *André Maurois*

He who fears being conquered is sure of defeat.   — *Napoleon Bonaparte*

The only thing we have to fear is fear itself.
— *Franklin D. Roosevelt*

Courage—fear that has said its prayers.
— *Dorothy Bernard*

I have not yet begun to fight! — *John Paul Jones*

Damn the torpedoes! Full speed ahead!
— *David G. Farragut*

Danger—if you meet it promptly and without flinching—you will reduce the danger by half. Never run away from anything. Never!   — *Winston Churchill*

In every battle there comes a time when both sides consider themselves beaten, then he who continues the attack wins.

— *Ulysses S. Grant*

The best victory is when the opponent surrenders of its own accord before there are any actual hostilities. . . . It is best to win without fighting.

— *Sun-tzu*

A wise man fights to win, but he is twice a fool who has no plan for possible defeat.

— *Louis L'Amour*

It is better to die on your feet than to live on your knees.

— *Emiliano Zapata*

If a person is determined to fight to the death, then they may very well have that opportunity.

— *Donald Rumsfeld*

He who demands mercy and shows none burns the bridges over which he himself must later pass.

— *Thomas Adams*

Why does the Air Force need expensive new bombers? Have the people we've been bombing over the years been complaining?

— *George Wallace*

An army marches on its stomach.

— *Napoleon Bonaparte*

A soldier will fight long and hard for a bit of colored ribbon.

— *Napoleon Bonaparte*

Never, never, never believe any war will be smooth and easy, or that anyone who embarks on the strange voyage can measure the tides and hurricanes he will encounter. The statesman who yields to war fever must realize that once the signal is given, he is no longer the master of policy but the slave of unforeseeable and uncontrollable events.

— *Winston Churchill*

A good plan, violently executed now, is better than a perfect plan next week.

— *George S. Patton*

In preparing for battle I have always found that plans are useless, but planning is indispensable.

— *Dwight D. Eisenhower*

Battles are won by slaughter and maneuver. The greater the general, the more he contributes in maneuver, the less he demands in slaughter.

— *Winston Churchill*

A weapon is a device for making your enemy change his mind.

— *Lois McMaster Bujold*

Forewarned, forearmed; to be prepared is half the victory.

— *Miguel de Cervantes*

The way to win an atomic war is to make certain it never starts.

— *Omar N. Bradley*

Ours is a world of nuclear giants and ethical infants. We know more about war than we know about peace, more about killing than we know about living.

— *Omar N. Bradley*

In any war, the first casualty is common sense, and the second is free and open discussion.

— *James Reston*

In war, truth is the first casualty.

— *Aeschylus*

A man who says that no patriot should attack the war until it is over ... is saying no good son should warn his mother of a cliff until she has fallen. — *G. K. Chesterton*

Before a war military science seems a real science, like astronomy; but after a war it seems more like astrology. — *Rebecca West*

One is left with the horrible feeling now that war settles nothing; that to win a war is as disastrous as to lose one. — *Agatha Christie*

War may sometimes be a necessary evil. But no matter how necessary, it is always an evil, never a good. We will not learn how to live together in peace by killing each other's children. — *Jimmy Carter*

If there is a God, the phrase that must disgust him is—holy war. — *Steve Allen*

Wars teach us not to love our enemies, but to hate our allies. — *W. L. George*

War is much too serious a matter to be entrusted to the military. — *Georges Clemenceau*

It is well that war is so terrible, or we should grow too fond of it. — *Robert E. Lee*

If it's natural to kill, how come men have to go into training to learn how? — *Joan Baez*

Man is ready to die for an idea, provided that idea is not quite clear to him. — *Paul Eldridge*

History teaches that wars begin when governments believe the price of aggression is cheap. — *Ronald Reagan*

Sometime they'll give a war and nobody will come. — *Carl Sandburg*

Either war is obsolete or men are. — *R. Buckminster Fuller*

The only winner in the War of 1812 was Tchaikovsky. — *Solomon Short*

After each war there is a little less democracy to save. — *Brooks Atkinson*

You can no more win a war than you can win an earthquake. — *Jeannette Rankin*

Mankind must put an end to war or war will put an end to mankind. — *John F. Kennedy*

How could man rejoice in victory and delight in the slaughter of men? — *Lao-tzu*

The time not to become a father is 18 years before a war. — *E. B. White*

War would end if the dead could return. — *Stanley Baldwin*

The military don't start wars. Politicians start wars. — *William Westmoreland*

Don't be a fool and die for your country. Let the other sonofabitch die for his. — *George S. Patton*

War does not determine who is right— only who is left. — *Bertrand Russell*

All war is a symptom of man's failure as a thinking animal. — *John Steinbeck*

It's silly talking about how many years we will have to spend in the jungles of Vietnam when we could pave the whole country and put parking stripes on it and still be home by Christmas. — *Ronald Reagan*

War is God's way of teaching Americans geography. — *Ambrose Bierce*

> The most dangerous creation of any society
> is the man who has nothing to lose.
>
> — JAMES BALDWIN

The tragedy of modern war is that the young men die fighting each other— instead of their real enemies back home in the capitals. *— Edward Abbey*

The quickest way to end a war is to lose it. *— George Orwell*

War is a way of shattering to pieces, or pouring into the stratosphere, or sinking in the depths of the sea, materials which might otherwise be used to make the masses too comfortable, and hence, in the long run, too intelligent. *— George Orwell*

Every gun that is made, every warship launched, every rocket fired, signifies in the final sense a theft from those who hunger and are not fed, those who are cold and are not clothed. *— Dwight D. Eisenhower*

What difference does it make to the dead, the orphans and the homeless, whether the mad destruction is wrought under the name of totalitarianism or the holy name of liberty or democracy? *— Mahatma Gandhi*

When the rich wage war it's the poor who die. *— Jean-Paul Sartre*

Glory is like a circle in the water, Which never ceaseth to enlarge itself, Till by broad spreading it disperse to naught. *— William Shakespeare*

Glory is fleeting, but obscurity is forever. *— Napoleon Bonaparte*

I am convinced that the best service a retired general can perform is to turn in his tongue along with his suit and to mothball his opinions. *— Omar N. Bradley*

No doubt there are other important things in life besides conflict, but there are not many other things so inevitably interesting. The very saints interest us most when we think of them as engaged in a conflict with the Devil. *— Robert Lynd*

I thoroughly disapprove of duels. If a man should challenge me, I would take him kindly and forgivingly by the hand and lead him to a quiet place and kill him. *— Mark Twain*

The fascination of shooting as a sport depends almost wholly on whether you are at the right or wrong end of the gun. *— P. G. Wodehouse*

I have given two cousins to war and I stand ready to sacrifice my wife's brother. *— Artemus Ward*

If you shoot at mimes, should you use a silencer? *— Steven Wright*

We have met the enemy, and he is us. *— Walt Kelly*

I believe everybody in the world should have guns. Citizens should have bazookas and rocket launchers too. I believe that all citizens should have their weapons of choice. However, I also believe that only I should have the ammunition. Because frankly, I wouldn't trust the rest of the goobers with anything more dangerous than string. — *Scott Adams*

The very existence of flame-throwers proves that some time, somewhere, someone said to themselves, "You know, I want to set those people over there on fire, but I'm just not close enough to get the job done."

— *George Carlin*

***

Peace

The grim fact, however, is that we prepare for war like precocious giants and for peace like retarded pygmies. — *Lester B. Pearson*

Those who love peace must learn to organize as well as those who love war.

— *Martin Luther King, Jr.*

If everyone demanded peace instead of another television set, then there'd be peace.

— *John Lennon*

You can't separate peace from freedom because no one can be at peace unless he has his freedom. — *Malcolm X*

The object of government in peace and in war is not the glory of rulers or of races, but the happiness of the common man.

— *William Beveridge*

If you want peace, you must work for justice.

— *Pope Paul VI*

Peace is not made at the Council table or by treaties, but in the hearts of men.

— *Herbert Hoover*

The main goal of the future is to stop violence. The world is addicted to it.

— *Bill Cosby*

We decry violence all the time in this country, but look at our history. We were born in a violent revolution, and we've been in wars ever since. We're not a pacific people. — *James Lee Burke*

I am proud of the fact that I never invented weapons to kill. — *Thomas Alva Edison*

The world will never have lasting peace so long as men reserve for war the finest human qualities. Peace, no less than war, requires idealism and self-sacrifice and a righteous and dynamic faith.

— *John Foster Dulles*

Any intelligent fool can make things bigger, more complex, and more violent. It takes a touch of genius—and a lot of courage— to move in the opposite direction.

— *E. F. Schumacher*

WAR, PEACE, AND POLITICS

Peace is not a relationship of nations.
It is a condition of mind brought about by
a serenity of soul. Peace is not merely the
absence of war. It is also a state of mind.
Lasting peace can come only to
peaceful people.   — *Jawaharlal Nehru*

If you want to make peace, you don't talk to
your friends. You talk to your enemies.
                              — *Moshe Dayan*

I guess we'd be living in a boring,
perfect world if everybody wished
everybody else well.   — *Jennifer Aniston*

It's possible to disagree with someone about
the ethics of nonviolence without wanting
to kick his face in.   — *Christopher Hampton*

The right things to do are those that keep
our violence in abeyance; the wrong things
are those that bring it to the fore.
                          — *Robert J. Sawyer*

We will not have peace by afterthought.
                          — *Norman Cousins*

To live without killing is a thought which
could electrify the world, if men were only
capable of staying awake long enough to let
the idea soak in.   — *Henry Miller*

The direct use of force is such a poor
solution to any problem, it is generally
employed only by small children and
large nations.   — *David Friedman*

I have no secret methods. I know no
diplomacy save that of truth. I have no
weapon but nonviolence. I may be
unconsciously led astray for a while, but
not for all time.   — *Mahatma Gandhi*

Nonviolence is a flop. The only bigger flop
is violence.   — *Joan Baez*

I like to believe that people in the long run
are going to do more to promote peace than our
governments. Indeed, I think that people want peace
so much that one of these days governments had
better get out of the way and let them have it.

— DWIGHT D. EISENHOWER

Our **Amazing** World

A flower blooming at your feet, the night sky blossoming with stars, and everything in between—is nature just too awesome for words? No, not by a long shot for the authors whose opinions appear here.

Nature

Over the long haul of life on this planet, it is the ecologists, and not the bookkeepers of business, who are the ultimate accountants.

— *Stewart Udall*

Like music and art, love of nature is a common language that can transcend political or social boundaries.

— *Jimmy Carter*

I just wish the world was twice as big and half of it was still unexplored.

— *David Attenborough*

I love to think of nature as an unlimited broadcasting station, through which God speaks to us every hour, if we will only tune in.

— *George Washington Carver*

I believe in God, only I spell it Nature.

— *Frank Lloyd Wright*

In every walk with nature one receives far more than he seeks.

— *John Muir*

To the dull mind nature is leaden. To the illumined mind the whole world burns and sparkles with light.

— *Ralph Waldo Emerson*

Although human subtlety makes a variety of inventions by different means to the same end, it will never devise an invention more beautiful, more simple, or more direct than does nature, because in her inventions nothing is lacking, and nothing is superfluous.

— *Leonardo da Vinci*

For four-fifths of our history, our planet was populated by pond scum.

— *J. W. Schopf*

Some national parks have long waiting lists for camping reservations. When you have to wait a year to sleep next to a tree, something is wrong.

— *George Carlin*

Camping is nature's way of promoting the motel business.

— *Dave Barry*

I hate the outdoors. To me the outdoors is where the car is.

— *Will Durst*

This is the foundation of all. We are not to imagine or suppose, but to *discover*, what nature does or may be made to do.

— *Francis Bacon*

Human judges can show mercy. But against the laws of nature, there is no appeal.

— *Arthur C. Clarke*

Every time I have some moment on a seashore, or in the mountains, or sometimes in a quiet forest, I think this is why the environment has to be preserved.   — *Bill Bradley*

I go to nature to be soothed and healed, and to have my senses put in order.

— *John Burroughs*

They are ill discoverers that think there is no land, when they can see nothing but sea.

— *Francis Bacon*

Nature provides exceptions to every rule.

— *Margaret Fuller*

I am among those who think that science has great beauty. A scientist in his laboratory is not only a technician: he is also a child placed before natural phenomena which impress him like a fairy tale.   — *Marie Curie*

The world is round and the place which may seem like the end may also be only the beginning.

— *Ivy Baker Priest*

Climb the mountains and get their good tidings. Nature's peace will flow into you as sunshine flows into trees. The winds will blow their own freshness into you, and the storms their energy, while cares will drop away from you like the leaves of Autumn.

— *John Muir*

God could cause us considerable embarrassment by revealing all the secrets of nature to us. We should not know what to do for sheer apathy and boredom.

— *Johann von Goethe*

Air pollution is turning Mother Nature prematurely gray.

— *Irv Kupcinet*

To see a world in a grain of sand
And a heaven in a wild flower,
Hold infinity in the palm of your hand
And eternity in an hour.

— *William Blake*

The world's as ugly as sin, and almost as delightful.

— *Frederick Locker-Lampson*

Nature does not loathe virtue: it is unaware of its existence.

— *Françoise Mallet-Joris*

 Deserts are beautiful for about fifteen minutes, but they're always located out in the middle of nowhere. And they're teeming with deadly snakes.

— GARRISON KEILLOR

I would feel more optimistic about a bright future for man if he spent less time proving that he can outwit Nature and more time tasting her sweetness and respecting her seniority.

— *E. B. White*

Thank God men cannot as yet fly and lay waste the sky as well as the earth!

— *Henry David Thoreau*

The art of medicine consists in amusing the patient while nature cures the disease.

— *Voltaire*

We have probed the earth, excavated it, burned it, ripped things from it, buried things in it.... That does not fit my definition of a good tenant. If we were here on a month-to-month basis, we would have been evicted long ago.

— *Rose E. Bird*

A true conservationist is a man who knows that the world is not given by his fathers, but borrowed from his children.

— *John James Audubon*

May your trails be crooked, winding, lonesome, dangerous, leading to the most amazing view. May your mountains rise into and above the clouds.

— *Edward Abbey*

The fog comes
on little cat feet.
It sits looking
over harbor and city
on silent haunches
and then moves on.

— *Carl Sandburg*

Nature does not hurry, yet everything is accomplished.

— *Lao-tzu*

Nature never makes any blunders. When she makes a fool she means it.— *Archibald Alexander*

Eternity—waste of time.

— *Natalie Clifford Barney*

Rocks are records of events that took place at the time they formed. They are books. They have a different vocabulary, a different alphabet, but you learn how to read them.

— *John McPhee*

Everything is connected … no one thing can change by itself.

— *Paul Hawken*

The highest purpose is to have no purpose at all. This puts one in accord with nature, in her manner of operation.

— *John Cage*

First the doctor told me the good news: I was going to have a disease named after me.

— *Steve Martin*

***

Plants

The trees that are slow to grow bear the best fruit.

— *Molière*

I like trees because they seem more resigned to the way they have to live than other things do.

— *Willa Cather*

As the poet said, "Only God can make a tree"—probably because it's so hard to figure out how to get the bark on.

— *Woody Allen*

I think that I shall never see
A poem lovely as a tree.

— *Joyce Kilmer*

I think that I shall never see
A billboard lovely as a tree.
Indeed, unless the billboards fall,
I'll never see a tree at all.

— *Ogden Nash*

Any fine morning, a power saw can fell a tree that took a thousand years to grow.

— *Edwin Way Teale*

The creation of a thousand forests is in one acorn.

— *Ralph Waldo Emerson*

Solitary trees, if they grow at all, grow strong.

— *Winston Churchill*

The true meaning of life is to plant trees, under whose shade you do not expect to sit.

— *Nelson Henderson*

Hugging trees has a calming effect on me. I'm talking about enormous trees that will be there when we are all dead and gone. I've hugged trees in every part of this little island.

— *Gerry Adams*

Cabbage: A familiar kitchen-garden vegetable about as large and wise as a man's head.

— *Ambrose Bierce*

A gardener who cultivates his own garden with his own hands, unites in his own person the three different characters, of landlord, farmer, and laborer. His produce, therefore, should pay him the rent of the first, the profit of the second, and the wages of the third.

— *Adam Smith*

OUR AMAZING WORLD

The jungle is dark but full of diamonds.
— *Arthur Miller*

There is no gardening without humility. Nature is constantly sending even its oldest scholars to the bottom of the class for some egregious blunder. — *Alfred Austin*

A garden is half-made when it is well planned. The best gardener is the one who does the most gardening by the winter fire.
— *Liberty Hyde Bailey*

Gardens and flowers have a way of bringing people together, drawing them from their homes. — *Clare Ansberry*

One of the healthiest ways to gamble is with a spade and a package of garden seeds.
— *Dan Bennett*

A good farmer is nothing more nor less than a handyman with a sense of humus.
— *E. B. White*

I have a rock garden. Last week three of them died. — *Richard Diran*

The Amen of nature is always a flower.
— *Oliver Wendell Holmes*

I hope that while so many people are out smelling the flowers, someone is taking the time to plant some. — *Herbert Rappaport*

Flowers are the sweetest things God ever made and forgot to put a soul into.
— *Henry Ward Beecher*

The earth laughs in flowers. — *e. e. cummings*

A single rose can be my garden ... a single friend, my world. — *Leo Buscaglia*

If the English language made any sense, *lackadaisical* would have something to do with a shortage of flowers. — *Doug Larson*

Our national flower is the concrete cloverleaf. — *Lewis Mumford*

What is a weed? A plant whose virtues have never been discovered.
— *Ralph Waldo Emerson*

Crabgrass can grow on bowling balls in airless rooms, and there is no known way to kill it that does not involve nuclear weapons.
— *Dave Barry*

A weed is a plant that has mastered every survival skill except for learning how to grow in rows. — *Doug Larson*

Even if I knew that tomorrow the world would go to pieces, I would still plant my apple tree. — *Martin Luther King, Jr.*

Gardens are not made by sitting in the shade.
— RUDYARD KIPLING

Benjamin Franklin

Many Hats, Many Quotes

How much wisdom can you pack into one life? To answer that question, look no further than the career of Benjamin Franklin, one of the Founding Fathers of the United States.

You probably already have an image of the portly, 18th-century gent with a receding hairline scribbling his name on the Declaration of Independence and commenting, "We must all hang together, or assuredly we shall all hang separately." Not content with his accomplishments as a statesman, Franklin was also a renowned scientist, inventor, philosopher, publisher, economist, and musician.

How fitting that a man so fond of words would start his working life as a printer. Having served as an apprentice to his brother, Franklin was a talented, full-fledged printer by age 17. By age 22 he had opened his own print shop in Philadelphia. He became an innovative publisher, best known for his newspaper *The Pennsylvania Gazette* and his yearly *Poor Richard's Almanack,* the source of many of his most famous sayings.

Here's a sampling of ol' Ben's wit and wisdom.

*

If you would not be forgotten,
As soon as you are dead and rotten,
Either write things worthy reading,
Or do things worth the writing.

*

Well done is better than well said.

*

An investment in knowledge always pays the best interest.

*

Be civil to all; sociable to many; familiar with few; friend to one; enemy to none.

*

He that falls in love with himself will have no rivals.

*

Three may keep a secret, if two of them are dead.

*

Having been poor is no shame, but being ashamed of it is.

*

I am in the prime of senility.

*

But in this world nothing can be said to be certain, except death and taxes.

*

To lengthen thy life, lessen thy meals.

*

If your head is wax, don't walk in the sun.

Animals

Biologically speaking, if something bites you it's more likely to be female.

— *Desmond Morris*

The trouble with America is that there are far too many wide-open spaces surrounded by teeth.

— *Charles Luckman*

All the good ideas I ever had came to me while I was milking a cow.

— *Grant Wood*

Look at those cows and remember that the greatest scientists in the world have never discovered how to make grass into milk.

— *Michael Pupin*

Nothing is made in vain, but the fly came near it.

— *Mark Twain*

A boy can learn a lot from a dog: obedience, loyalty, and the importance of turning around three times before lying down.

— *Robert Benchley*

A dog is the only thing on earth that loves you more than he loves himself.

— *Josh Billings*

I can tell you that I'd rather be kissed by my dogs than by some people I've known.

— *Bob Barker*

Dogs have no money. Isn't that amazing? They're broke their entire lives. But they get through. You know why dogs have no money? No pockets.

— *Jerry Seinfeld*

Cats are smarter than dogs. You can't get eight cats to pull a sled through snow.

— *Jeff Valdez*

Cats are intended to teach us that not everything in nature has a function.

— *Garrison Keillor*

Authors like cats because they are such quiet, lovable, wise creatures, and cats like authors for the same reasons.

— *Robertson Davies*

The problem with cats is that they get the same exact look whether they see a moth or an ax murderer.

— *Paula Poundstone*

Ever consider what pets must think of us?
I mean, here we come back from a grocery store
with the most amazing haul—chicken, pork, half a cow.
They must think we're the greatest hunters on earth!

— ANNE TYLER

Dachshunds are ideal dogs for small children, as they are already stretched and pulled to such a length that the child cannot do much harm one way or the other.
— *Robert Benchley*

Dogs laugh, but they laugh with their tails.
— *Max Eastman*

Money can buy you a fine dog, but only love can make him wag his tail.
— *Kinky Friedman*

Our perfect companions never have fewer than four feet.
— *Colette*

If a dog jumps in your lap, it is because he is fond of you; but if a cat does the same thing, it is because your lap is warmer.
— *Alfred North Whitehead*

The dog is the god of frolic.
— *Henry Ward Beecher*

Don't accept your dog's admiration as conclusive evidence that you are wonderful.
— *Ann Landers*

If you are a dog and your owner suggests that you wear a sweater, suggest that he wear a tail.
— *Fran Lebowitz*

A door is what a dog is perpetually on the wrong side of.
— *Ogden Nash*

Did you ever walk into a room and forget why you walked in? I think that's how dogs spend their lives.
— *Sue Murphy*

The cat could very well be man's best friend but would never stoop to admitting it.
— *Doug Larson*

Eagles may soar, but weasels don't get sucked into jet engines.
— *John Benfield*

If called by a panther
Don't anther.
— *Ogden Nash*

There are 350 varieties of shark, not counting loan and pool.
— *L. M. Boyd*

Which came first, the intestine or the tapeworm?
— *William S. Burroughs*

A camel makes an elephant feel like a jet plane.
— *Jackie Kennedy Onassis*

A horse is dangerous at both ends and uncomfortable in the middle.
— *Ian Fleming*

A wounded deer leaps the highest.
— *Emily Dickinson*

If you want to save a species, simply decide to eat it. Then it will be managed— like chickens, like turkeys, like deer, like Canadian geese.
— *Ted Nugent*

I believe implicitly that every young man in the world is fascinated with either sharks or dinosaurs.
— *Peter Benchley*

There is nothing in which the birds differ more from man than the way in which they can build and yet leave a landscape as it was before.
— *Robert Lynd*

God gives every bird its food, but He does not throw it into its nest.
— *J. G. Holland*

Birds sing after a storm; why shouldn't people feel as free to delight in whatever sunlight remains to them?
— *Rose Kennedy*

Always behave like a duck—keep calm and unruffled on the surface but paddle like the devil underneath.
— *Jacob Braude*

The perils of duck hunting are great— especially for the duck.
— *Walter Cronkite*

Cats regard people as warm-blooded furniture.

— JACQUELYN MITCHARD

You can know the name of a bird in all the languages of the world, but when you're finished, you'll know absolutely nothing whatever about the bird. ... So let's look at the bird and see what it's doing—that's what counts. I learned very early the difference between knowing the name of something and knowing something.   — *Richard Feynman*

I realized that if I had to choose, I would rather have birds than airplanes.
          — *Charles Lindbergh*

The very idea of a bird is a symbol and a suggestion to the poet. A bird seems to be at the top of the scale, so vehement and intense his life. ... The beautiful vagabonds, endowed with every grace, masters of all climes, and knowing no bounds—how many human aspirations are realized in their free, holiday-lives—and how many suggestions to the poet in their flight and song!   — *John Burroughs*

I hope you love birds too. It is economical. It saves going to heaven.   — *Emily Dickinson*

You can put wings on a pig, but you don't make it an eagle.   — *Bill Clinton*

God loved the birds and invented trees. Man loved the birds and invented cages.
          — *Jacques Deval*

A hen is only an egg's way of making another egg.   — *Samuel Butler*

Both the cockroach and the bird would get along very well without us, although the cockroach would miss us most.
          — *Joseph Wood Krutch*

Aerodynamically, the bumblebee shouldn't be able to fly, but the bumblebee doesn't know it so it goes on flying anyway.
          — *Mary Kay Ash*

Behold the turtle. He makes progress only when he sticks his neck out.
          — *James Bryant Conant*

I like pigs. Dogs look up to us. Cats look down on us. Pigs treat us as equals.
          — *Winston Churchill*

It is even harder for the average ape to believe that he has descended from man.
          — *H. L. Mencken*

Some people are uncomfortable with the idea that humans belong to the same class of animals as cats and cows and raccoons. They're like the people who become successful and then don't want to be reminded of the old neighborhood.
          — *Phil Donahue*

Do not free a camel of the burden of his hump; you may be freeing him from being a camel.   — *G. K. Chesterton*

The Seasons

If we had no winter, the spring would not be so pleasant: if we did not sometimes taste of adversity, prosperity would not be so welcome.   — *Josh Billings*

Spring is nature's way of saying, "Let's party!"   — *Robin Williams*

In the spring, at the end of the day, you should smell like dirt.   — *Margaret Atwood*

Ah, summer, what power you have to make us suffer and like it.   — *Russell Baker*

People don't notice whether it's winter or summer when they're happy.   — *Anton Chekhov*

Tears of joy are like the summer rain drops pierced by sunbeams.   — *Hosea Ballou*

Fall is my favorite season in Los Angeles, watching the birds change color and fall from the trees.   — *David Letterman*

It was one of those perfect English autumnal days which occur more frequently in memory than in life.   — *P. D. James*

Autumn is a second spring when every leaf is a flower.   — *Albert Camus*

A woodland in full color is awesome as a forest fire, in magnitude at least, but a single tree is like a dancing tongue of flame to warm the heart.   — *Hal Borland*

This is a place where you can hear fall coming for miles.   — *Charles Kuralt*

God gave us memory so that we might have roses in December.   — *James M. Barrie*

Winter is on my head, but eternal spring is in my heart.   — *Victor Hugo*

There are only two seasons— winter and baseball.   — *Bill Veeck*

The only way I'd worry about the weather is if it snows on our side of the field and not theirs.   — *Tommy Lasorda*

A lot of people like snow. I find it to be an unnecessary freezing of water.   — *Carl Reiner*

Don't knock the weather. If it didn't change once in a while, nine out of ten people couldn't start a conversation.   — *Kin Hubbard*

Money is the opposite of the weather. Nobody talks about it, but everybody does something about it.   — *Rebecca Johnson*

Live each season as it passes; breathe the air, drink the drink, taste the fruit, and resign yourself to the influences of each.

— *Henry David Thoreau*

Martin Luther King Jr.

Man with a Dream

He was born to preach.

The son and grandson of Baptist ministers, Martin Luther King, Jr., mixed his theological studies with an exploration of Mahatma Gandhi's nonviolent techniques for bringing social change. In 1955, Rosa Parks refused to cooperate with the segregation policy on the buses in Montgomery, Alabama. Black residents boycotted the transportation system and elected King the president of the new Montgomery Improvement Association. The success of that campaign launched King to the forefront of the civil rights movement in the United States. He went on to earn the Nobel Peace Prize and was arrested 30 times for his civil rights activities.

King was a charismatic speaker who awakened the public conscience and gave new hope to African Americans and poor people everywhere. Whenever there was injustice to address, King was there. From 1957 to 1968, he traveled more than 6 million miles and delivered more than 2,500 speeches. King delivered his famous "I Have a Dream" speech on the steps of the Lincoln Memorial in Washington, D.C., in 1963.

In 1968, King gave his final speech—"I Have Been to the Mountaintop"—to striking sanitation workers in Memphis, Tennessee. He was assassinated the next day.

*I have a dream that my four children will one day live in a nation
where they will not be judged by the color of their skin,
but by the content of their character.*

*I submit that an individual who breaks a law that conscience tells him is unjust,
and who willingly accepts the penalty of imprisonment in order to arouse
the conscience of the community over its injustice, is in reality expressing
the highest respect for the law.*

Never forget that everything Hitler did in Germany was legal.

*Before the Pilgrims landed at Plymouth, we were here. Before the pen of Jefferson
etched across the pages of history the majestic words of the Declaration of
Independence, we were here. If the inexpressible cruelties of slavery could not stop us,
the opposition we now face will surely fail.*

*The question is not whether we will be extremists
but what kind of extremists we will be.*

*We have moved into an era where we are called upon to raise certain basic questions
about the whole society. We are still called upon to give aid to the beggar who finds
himself in misery and agony on life's highway. But one day, we must ask the question
of whether an edifice which produces beggars must not be restructured and refurbished.*

*Well, I don't know what will happen now. We've got some difficult days ahead.
But it really doesn't matter with me now, because I've been to the mountaintop and
I don't mind. Like anybody, I would like to live a long life. Longevity has its place.
But I'm not concerned about that now. I just want to do God's will,
and He's allowed me to go up to the mountain. And I've looked over and I've seen
the Promised Land. I may not get there with you, but I want you to know tonight,
that we as a people will get to the Promised Land. And I'm happy tonight;
I'm not worried about anything. I'm not fearing any man.
Mine eyes have seen the glory of the coming of the Lord.*

279

Being Alive

I arise in the morning torn between a desire to improve the world and a desire to enjoy the world. This makes it hard to plan the day.
— *E. B. White*

I think; therefore I am. — *René Descartes*

I get mail; therefore I am. — *Scott Adams*

Life. Consider the alternative.
— *Marshall McLuhan*

Brain: An apparatus with which we think we think. — *Ambrose Bierce*

The first question I ask myself when something doesn't seem to be beautiful is why do I think it's not beautiful. And very shortly you discover that there is no reason.
— *John Cage*

All the things one has forgotten scream for help in dreams. — *Elias Canetti*

We ought to think that we are one of the leaves of a tree, and the tree is all humanity. We cannot live without the others, without the tree. — *Pablo Casals*

The world is very different now. For man holds in his mortal hands the power to abolish all forms of human poverty, and all forms of human life. — *John F. Kennedy*

From birth, man carries the weight of gravity on his shoulders. He is bolted to earth. But man has only to sink beneath the surface and he is free. — *Jacques Yves Cousteau*

I think perhaps the most important problem is that we are trying to understand the fundamental workings of the universe via a language devised for telling one another when the best fruit is. — *Terry Prachett*

Man is the only creature that refuses to be what he is. — *Albert Camus*

We're a planet of nearly six billion ninnies living in a civilization that was designed by a few thousand amazingly smart deviants.
— *Scott Adams*

I would feel more optimistic about a bright future for man if he spent less time proving that he can outwit Nature and more time tasting her sweetness and respecting her seniority. — *E. B. White*

Man is the only animal that laughs and weeps, for he is the only animal that is struck with the difference between what things are and what they ought to be.
— *William Hazlitt*

All modern men are descended from a worm-like creature, but it shows more on some people. — *Will Cuppy*

It is of interest to note that while some dolphins are reported to have learned English, up to fifty words used in correct context, no human being has been reported to have learned dolphinese.
— *Carl Sagan*

Man is a complex being: He makes deserts bloom—and lakes die. — *Gil Stern*

The body is a sacred garment.
— *Martha Graham*

If any thing is sacred the human body is sacred. — *Walt Whitman*

OUR AMAZING WORLD

I recently had my annual physical examination, which I get once every seven years, and when the nurse weighed me, I was shocked to discover how much stronger the Earth's gravitational pull has become since 1990. — *Dave Barry*

Why isn't there a special name for the tops of your feet? — *Lily Tomlin*

One thing about baldness: It's neat. — *Don Herold*

Disease is the retribution of outraged Nature. — *Hosea Ballou*

To me every hour of the day and night is an unspeakably perfect miracle. — *Walter Chrysler*

The only thing that makes life possible is permanent, intolerable uncertainty; not knowing what comes next. — *Ursula K. Le Guin*

A brother is a friend given by Nature. — *Gabriel Marie Legouvé*

My soul can find no staircase to Heaven unless it be through Earth's loveliness. — *Michelangelo*

When all is said and done, the weather and love are the two elements about which one can never be sure.

— ALICE HOFFMAN

They say atomic radiation can hurt your reproductive organs. My answer is, so can a hockey stick. But we don't stop building them. — *Johnny Carson*

The city is not a concrete jungle, it is a human zoo. — *Desmond Morris*

We all have the extraordinary coded within us, waiting to be released. — *Jean Houston*

Sooner or later every one of us breathes an atom that has been breathed before by anyone you can think of who has lived before us—Michelangelo or George Washington or Moses. — *Jacob Bronowski*

Reality is that which, when you stop believing in it, doesn't go away. — *Philip K. Dick*

The more you find out about the world, the more opportunities there are to laugh at it. — *Bill Nye*

We live on the leash of our senses. — *Diane Ackerman*

Maybe this world is another planet's hell. — *Aldous Huxley*

Eternity's a terrible thought. I mean, where's it all going to end? — *Tom Stoppard*

To perceive is to suffer.

— ARISTOTLE

I believe in humanity. We are an incredible species. We're still just a child creature, we're still being nasty to each other. And all children go through those phases. We're growing up, we're moving into adolescence now. When we grow up—man, we're going to be something! — *Gene Roddenberry*

The most beautiful thing we can experience is the mysterious. It is the source of all true art and science. — *Albert Einstein*

Men love to wonder, and that is the seed of our science. — *Ralph Waldo Emerson*

Nature is trying very hard to make us succeed, but nature does not depend on us. We are not the only experiment. — *R. Buckminster Fuller*

Man is an animal which, alone among the animals, refuses to be satisfied by the fulfillment of animal desires. — *Alexander Graham Bell*

Nature makes only dumb animals. We owe the fools to society. — *Honoré de Balzac*

Man is the only animal that can remain on friendly terms with the victims he intends to eat until he eats them. — *Samuel Butler*

The goal of all inanimate objects is to resist man and ultimately defeat him. — *Russell Baker*

Man is distinguished from all other creatures by the faculty of laughter. — *Joseph Addison*

I want all my senses engaged. Let me absorb the world's variety and uniqueness. — *Maya Angelou*

I still get wildly enthusiastic about little things. ... I play with leaves. I skip down the street and run against the wind. — *Leo Buscaglia*

Security is mostly a superstition. It does not exist in nature. ... Life is either a daring adventure or nothing. — *Helen Keller*

Something unknown is doing we don't know what. — *Arthur Eddington*

We don't know a millionth of one percent about anything. — *Thomas Alva Edison*

You will die but the carbon will not; its career does not end with you. It will return to the soil, and there a plant may take it up again in time, sending it once more on a cycle of plant and animal life. — *Jacob Bronowski*

The best and most beautiful things in the world cannot be seen or even touched. They must be felt within the heart. — *Helen Keller*

Water

When beholding the tranquil beauty and brilliancy of the ocean's skin, one forgets the tiger heart that pants beneath it; and would not willingly remember that this velvet paw but conceals a remorseless fang.

— *Herman Melville*

Irrigation of the land with seawater desalinated by fusion power is ancient. It's called "rain."

— *Michael McClary*

For all at last returns to the sea—to Oceanus, the ocean river, like the everflowing stream of time, the beginning and the end.

— *Rachel Carson*

The reason I love the sea I cannot explain— it's physical. When you dive you begin to feel like an angel. It's a liberation of your weight.

— *Jacques Yves Cousteau*

Either you decide to stay in the shallow end of the pool or you go out in the ocean.

— *Christopher Reeve*

The sea has never been friendly to man. At most it has been the accomplice of human restlessness.

— *Joseph Conrad*

A lot of people attack the sea. I make love to it.

— *Jacques Yves Cousteau*

When I was a boy the Dead Sea was only sick.

— *George Burns*

Let the rain kiss you. Let the rain beat upon your head with silver liquid drops. Let the rain sing you a lullaby.

— *Langston Hughes*

Water and air, the two essential fluids on which all life depends, have become global garbage cans.

— *Jacques Yves Cousteau*

Wherever we've traveled in this great land of ours, we've found that people everywhere are about 90 percent water.

— *David Letterman*

***

Energy

Electricity is really just organized lightning.

— *George Carlin*

The reason lightning doesn't strike twice in the same place is that the same place isn't there the second time.

— *Willie Tyler*

Electricity is actually made up of extremely tiny particles called electrons, that you cannot see with the naked eye unless you have been drinking.

— *Dave Barry*

It is impossible to travel faster than the speed of light, and certainly not desirable, as one's hat keeps blowing off.

— *Woody Allen*

If I had to choose a religion, the sun as the universal giver of life would be my god.

— *Napoleon Bonaparte*

There is a muscular energy in sunlight
corresponding to the spiritual energy
of wind.   — *Annie Dillard*

Morning comes whether you set the alarm
or not.   — *Ursula K. Le Guin*

I am always most religious upon a
sunshiny day.   — *Lord Byron*

A day without sunshine is like,
you know, night.   — *Steve Martin*

I envy people who can just look at a
sunset. I wonder how you can shoot it.
There is nothing more grotesque to me
than a vacation.   — *Dustin Hoffman*

I like the evening in India, the one magic
moment when the sun balances on the rim of
the world, and the hush descends, and ten
thousand civil servants drift homeward on a
river of bicycles, brooding on the Lord
Krishna and the cost of living.

— *James Cameron*

Our ancestors worshipped the Sun, and
they were not that foolish. It makes sense to
revere the Sun and the stars, for we are
their children.   — *Carl Sagan*

The grand show is eternal. It is always sunrise somewhere; the dew is never dried all at
once; a shower is forever falling; vapor is ever
rising. Eternal sunrise, eternal dawn and
gloaming, on sea and continents and islands,
each in its turn, as the round earth rolls.

— *John Muir*

Nothing is more beautiful than the
loveliness of the woods before sunrise.

— *George Washington Carver*

Science will never be able to reduce the value
of a sunset to arithmetic. Nor can it reduce
friendship or statesmanship to a formula.

— *Louis Orr*

Truth is like the sun. You can shut it out for
a time, but it ain't goin' away.   — *Elvis Presley*

***

$\mathcal{B}$eyond Earth

God does not play dice with the universe.
— *Albert Einstein*

Now there is one outstandingly important
fact regarding Spaceship Earth, and that is
that no instruction book came with it.
— *R. Buckminster Fuller*

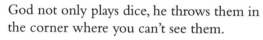

God not only plays dice, he throws them in
the corner where you can't see them.
— *Stephen Hawking*

Give me a lever long enough and a fulcrum
on which to place it, and I shall move the
world.   — *Archimedes*

The last sound on the worthless earth will
be two human beings trying to launch a
homemade spaceship and already quarreling
about where they are going next.

— *William Faulkner*

There are no passengers on Spaceship Earth.
We are all crew. — *Marshall McLuhan*

We had the sky up there, and we used to
lay on our backs and look up at them,
and discuss whether they was made or
just happened. — *Mark Twain*

I don't know what you could say about a
day in which you have seen four beautiful
sunsets. — *John Glenn*

Man is slightly nearer to the atom than to
the star. ... From his central position man can
survey the grandest works of Nature with
the astronomer, or the minutest works with
the physicist. — *Arthur Eddington*

As long as the world is turning and spinning,
we're gonna be dizzy and we're gonna make
mistakes. — *Mel Brooks*

The scientific theory I like best is that the
rings of Saturn are composed entirely of lost
airline luggage. — *Mark Russell*

It may be that the universe is just one of
those things that happens from time to time.
— *Edward Tryon*

If Mr. Einstein doesn't like the natural laws
of the universe, let him go back to where he
came from. — *Robert Benchley*

I look for what needs to be done. After all,
that's how the universe designs itself.
— *R. Buckminster Fuller*

Our sun is one of 100 billion stars in our
galaxy. Our galaxy is one of billions of
galaxies populating the universe. It would
be the height of presumption to think
that we are the only living things in that
enormous immensity. — *Wernher von Braun*

A vacuum is a hell of a lot better than some
of the stuff that nature replaces it with.
— *Tennessee Williams*

There is no such thing as an empty space
or an empty time. There is always something to see, something to hear. In fact, try
as we may to make a silence, we cannot.
— *John Cage*

Space isn't remote at all. It's only an hour's
drive away if your car could go straight
upwards. — *Fred Hoyle*

Not only is the universe stranger than we
imagine, it is stranger than we can imagine.
— *Arthur Eddington*

No pessimist ever discovered the secret of
the stars or sailed an uncharted land, or
opened a new doorway for the human spirit.
— *Helen Keller*

It's very hard to take yourself too
seriously when you look at the world
from outer space. — *Thomas K. Mattingly II*

It is not easy to see how the more extreme
forms of nationalism can long survive
when men have seen the Earth in its true
perspective as a single small globe against
the stars. — *Arthur C. Clarke*

It suddenly struck me that that tiny pea,
pretty and blue, was the Earth. I put up my
thumb and shut one eye, and my thumb
blotted out the planet Earth. I didn't feel like
a giant. I felt very, very small.
— *Neil Armstrong*

Don't tell me that man doesn't belong
out there. Man belongs wherever he wants
to go—and he'll do plenty well when he
gets there. — *Wernher von Braun*

The more clearly we can focus our attention on the wonders and realities of the universe about us, the less taste we shall have for destruction. *— Rachel Carson*

When it is dark enough, you can see the stars. *— Ralph Waldo Emerson*

The universe is full of magical things, patiently waiting for our wits to grow sharper. *— Eden Phillpotts*

We are an impossibility in an impossible universe. *— Ray Bradbury*

We are just an advanced breed of monkeys on a minor planet of a very average star. But we can understand the Universe. That makes us something very special. *— Stephen Hawking*

Space is big. You just won't believe how vastly, hugely, mind-bogglingly big it is. I mean, you may think it's a long way down the road to the drug store, but that's just peanuts to space. *— Douglas Adams*

I'm astounded by people who want to "know" the universe when it's hard enough to find your way around Chinatown. *— Woody Allen*

The belief that there are other life forms in the universe is a matter of faith. There is not a single shred of evidence for any other life forms, and in forty years of searching, none has been discovered. There is absolutely no evidentiary reason to maintain this belief. *— Michael Crichton*

Interestingly, according to modern astronomers, space is finite. This is a very comforting thought—particularly for people who cannot remember where they left things. *— Woody Allen*

If you wish to make an apple pie truly from scratch you must first invent the universe. *— Carl Sagan*

Sometimes I think we're alone in the universe, and sometimes I think we're not. Either way, the idea is quite staggering. *— Arthur C. Clarke*

Everything you've learned in school as "obvious" becomes less and less obvious as you begin to study the universe. For example, there are no solids in the universe. There's not even a suggestion of a solid. There are no absolute continuums. There are no surfaces. There are no straight lines. *— R. Buckminster Fuller*

The Universe has as many different centers as there are living beings in it. *— Aleksandr Solzhenitsyn*

When they discover the center of the universe, a lot of people will be disappointed to discover they are not it. *— Bernard Bailey*

One, a robot may not injure a human being, or through inaction, allow a human being to come to harm; Two, a robot must obey the orders given it by human beings except where such orders would conflict with the First Law; Three, a robot must protect its own existence as long as such protection does not conflict with the First or Second Laws. *— Isaac Asimov, the Laws of Robotics*

Somewhere, something incredible is waiting to be known. *— Carl Sagan*

There is a coherent plan in the universe, though I don't know what it's a plan for. *— Fred Hoyle*

Sometimes I think the surest sign
that intelligent life exists elsewhere in the universe
is that none of it has tried to contact us.

— BILL WATTERSON

The Witty and the Wise

Profiles of 18 people renowned for their insightfulness, cleverness, and wonderful way with words and their most memorable quotes.

Other Features

From great insults to unforgettable song lyrics, these eight quotable collections go far beyond the ordinary.

Author Index

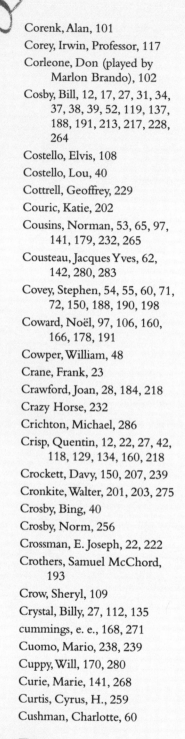